Haunting
Biology

EXPERIMENTAL FUTURES
Technological Lives, Scientific Arts, Anthropological Voices
A series edited by Michael M. J. Fischer and Joseph Dumit

Haunting Biology

Science and
Indigeneity
in Australia

Emma
Kowal

Duke University Press   *Durham and London*   2023

Project Editor: Liz Smith
Designed by Courtney Leigh Richardson
Typeset in Portrait and Comma Base by Westchester Publishing Services

Library of Congress Cataloging-in-Publication Data
Names: Kowal, Emma, author.
Title: Haunting biology : science and indigeneity in Australia / Emma Kowal.
Other titles: Experimental futures.
Description: Durham : Duke University Press, 2023. | Series: Experimental futures |
Includes bibliographical references and index.
Identifiers: LCCN 2023003957 (print)
LCCN 2023003958 (ebook)
ISBN 9781478025375 (paperback)
ISBN 9781478020592 (hardcover)
ISBN 9781478027539 (ebook)
Subjects: LCSH: Aboriginal Australians—Research—History. | Human biology—
Research—Social aspects—Australia. | Human genetics—Research—Social aspects—
Australia. | Anthropology—Research—Australia. | Ethnohistory—Australia. |
Scientific racism—Australia—History. | BISAC: SOCIAL SCIENCE /
Anthropology / Cultural & Social | SOCIAL SCIENCE / Indigenous Studies
Classification: LCC GN345.2 .K68 2023 (print) | LCC GN345.2 (ebook) | DDC
305.899/150072—dc23/eng/20230518
LC record available at https://lccn.loc.gov/2023003957
LC ebook record available at https://lccn.loc.gov/2023003958

Cover art: *Burning Ghosts,* 1979. © Judy Watson. Courtesy the artist, Tolarno Galleries, and James Cook University, Special Collections.

To Ramona and Dave, with gratitude

Contents

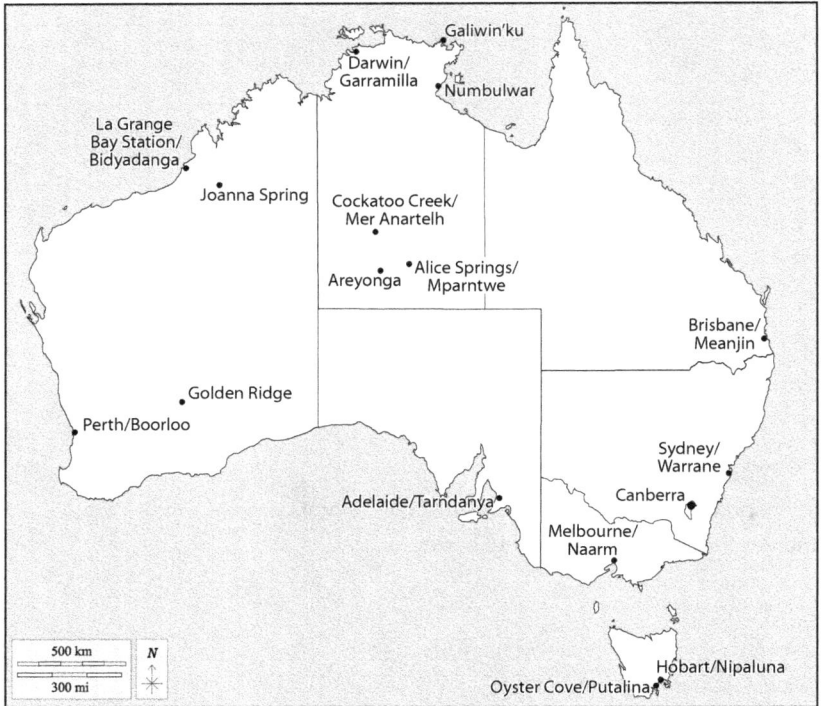

MAP 1. Map of Australia with locations relevant to the text.

WARNING: This book contains images of Aboriginal and Torres Strait Islander people who have passed away.

A Note on Terminology

The terms used to refer to the Indigenous peoples of Australia have changed over time and vary depending on who is using them. In the historical periods discussed in this book, terms including "native," "aborigine," "full-blood," and "half-caste" were often used. Adjectives such as "primitive" were also common. All of these terms are no longer acceptable for general use but can be found in this book as part of historical quotes or in quotation marks when discussing their historical contexts. Today, common general terms for Indigenous peoples of Australia are "Aboriginal and Torres Strait Islanders" (the Torres Strait Islands lie between the Australian mainland and Papua New Guinea) and "Indigenous Australians." In recent years, the terms "First Nations" and "First Peoples" have become more popular and may replace "Aboriginal and Torres Strait Islanders" and "Indigenous Australians" as preferred terms in the future. I tend to use "Indigenous Australians" throughout the book as a currently acceptable term, while acknowledging it may become outdated and it would not have been the term historical actors would have used. In some chapters that focus specifically on the historical theories of the "race" of Indigenous mainlanders (i.e., not Torres Strait Islanders), I refer to "Aboriginal" rather than "Indigenous" people. The term "traditional owners" is used when referring to Indigenous people who are recognized as the custodians of a specific area. In some historical passages of the book that discuss the science of racial origins, "Australian" refers to Indigenous Australians, but otherwise it refers to the Australian nation-state. The varied use of the troubled concept of "race" is a major subject of the book, and the term is used frequently, often but not always with quotation marks. Even where quotation marks are omitted for stylistic reasons, readers should maintain a highly critical stance to the term.

I capitalize "Indigenous" and "Aboriginal" in this book, in line with a practice that is well established in Australia (since the 1970s). As Indigenous people in other countries are increasingly capitalizing "Indigenous," I capitalize the word throughout. I use the currently accepted terms to refer to Indigenous groups from other countries such as Native Americans in the United States, Maori in Aotearoa/New Zealand, and Aboriginal or First Nations people in Canada. The term "non-indigenous" refers to Australians who are not Indigenous. "White Australians" refers to Australians of Anglo-Celtic background (the majority of settlers) and can also include descendants of southern and eastern European migrants who arrived in great numbers after World War II. "Settler" is a more recent signifier used by progressive non-indigenous Australians as an alternative to "non-indigenous," as it foregrounds settler colonialism. Where I use "we" in the book, it usually refers to settler Australians, although at times it denotes my "generation"—people born in or adjacent to the 1970s.

While there are no photographs of human remains in this book, I wrestled over whether to include historical images of living Indigenous people. Images of relatives that have since passed away can be distressing for their Aboriginal and Torres Strait Islander descendants. At the same time, historical images help the reader to understand the material. Encouraged by readers and reviewers, I have made the decision to include some images, together with the warning that Aboriginal and Torres Strait Islander readers should proceed with caution.

Acknowledgments

The process of writing this book was bookended by two life disasters: a divorce and the pandemic. Navigating the many demands of solo parenting, juggling multiple projects, increasing leadership responsibilities at work, and two years of home schooling has squeezed my writing life into precious lacunae between meetings and domestic tasks. Thank you to Ken Wissoker, who never gave up on me despite the delays. His belief in me allowed me to look beyond all the obstacles and suspend my disbelief that they could be overcome.

Many colleagues have helped me along the way. Joanna Radin invited me in 2015 to be a visiting professor in history of science and medicine at Yale University, where this book was conceived, and where Projit Mukharji suggested I think about ghosts. The generative collaboration Joanna and I have shared was crucial to this book's conception. Warwick Anderson has been a mentor, colleague, and friend for well over two decades. I owe many things to him, including the audacity to reach across disciplines. He provided the opportunity to present part of the manuscript to the Postcolonial Tensions: Science, History and Indigenous Knowledges workshop at Harvard University. I benefited greatly from presenting at several other places: the Department of Science and Technology Studies at Cornell University (thanks to Suman Seth), the anthropology department at the University of Connecticut (thanks to Deborah Bolnick), the History and Sociology of Science Department at the University of Pennsylvania (thanks to Projit Mukharji), the Department of Anthropology at New York University (thanks to Fred Myers), the science and technology studies (STS) cross-faculty program at MIT (thanks to Stefan Helmreich), and seminars throughout Australia including at the Australian National University, the University of Melbourne, the University of Sydney, Deakin University, and the Dyason lecture of the Australasian Association for

Historical, Philosophical and Sociological Studies of Science. Chapter 6 has its origins in the How Collections End workshop at the University of Cambridge's Department of the History and Philosophy of Science that I co-convened with Jenny Bangham and Boris Jardine. Our resulting special issue of the journal *BJHS Themes*, "How Collections End" (2019), contains an earlier version of that chapter.

My colleagues at the Alfred Deakin Institute at Deakin University have provided all kinds of support—intellectual, emotional, practical, and more. Thanks especially to its director, Fethi Mansouri, and fellow deputy director Shahram Akbarzadeh, who have taught me so much as we work to carve out hospitable places for humanities and social science research. Thanks to cherished Alfred Deakin Institute colleagues Tim Neale, Victoria Stead, Thao Phan, Carina Truyts, Andrea Witcomb, Anita Harris, Eben Kirksey, Billy Griffiths, Melinda Hinkson, Jon Altman, Tanya King, David Giles, Yamini Narayanan, Holly High, Jason Gibson, Alex Roginski, Jaya Keaney, Joe Latham, Will Smith, Chris Mayes, Tiffany Shellam, Rose Butler, Sarah Hayes, and Miguel Vatter. Outside of the Alfred Deakin Institute, the Deakin Science and Society Network, the Australasian STS Graduate Network, the Trans-AsiaSTS Network, and the Society for Social Studies of Science (4S) have all been wonderful venues to support STS scholarship and to be inspired by junior and senior colleagues. I wrote the book concurrently with work on other projects that helped my slow thinking through this book's questions. These include two Australian Research Council Discovery Projects: one on genetic testing and Indigeneity in collaboration with Cressida Fforde and Elizabeth Watt, and one on epigenetics and Indigeneity in collaboration with Megan Warin, Maurizio Meloni, Jaya Keaney, and Henrietta Byrne. The book itself is an outcome of my Australian Research Council Future Fellowship (FT160100093).

Questions about Indigeneity that ground this book were percolated over two decades in conversation with many Australian anthropology colleagues including David Trigger, John Morton, Ghassan Hage, Nicolas Peterson, Marcia Langton, Gillian Cowlishaw, Elizabeth Povinelli, Martha Macintyre, John Morton, Philip Batty, Tess Lea, Eve Vincent, Jennifer Deger, Maggie Brady, Tim Rowse, David Martin, Julie Finlayson, Elizabeth Ganter, Diane Smith, Will Sanders, Patrick Sullivan, Pam McGrath, Yasmine Musharbash, Stephen Muecke, Lisa Stefanoff, Melinda Hinkson, Jon Altman, Peter Sutton, Francesca Merlan, Diane Austin-Broos, Jeremy Beckett, Philip Batty, Françoise Dussart, and Fred Myers. While my home discipline is anthropology, the primary conversation in my head as I wrote this book was with scholars of race, science, and power from diverse disciplines and perspectives. These include Warwick

Anderson, Kim TallBear, Alondra Nelson, Dorothy Roberts, Evelynn Hammonds, Keith Wailoo, Helen Verran, Susan Lindee, Susan Reverby, Ricardo Ventura Santos, Amade M'charek, Donna Haraway, Sandra Harding, Troy Duster, Max Liboiron, Anne Pollock, Charis Thompson, Jenny Reardon, Joan Fujimura, Joanna Radin, Bronwen Douglas, Cathy Waldby, Projit Mukharji, Ruha Benjamin, Banu Subramaniam, Suman Seth, Michelle Murphy, Gabriela Soto Laveaga, Gabrielle Hecht, Vivette Garcia Deister, Rosanna Dent, Katharina Schramm, Duana Fullwiley, Jonathan Kahn, Gisli Palsson, Soraya de Chadarevian, Tom Özden-Schilling, Ann Kakaliouras, Jennifer Hamilton, Rick Smith, Catherine Bliss, David Skinner, Catherine Nash, Kapil Raj, Itty Abraham, Peter Wade, Steven Epstein, Richard Rottenberg, Amy Hinterberger, Yulia Egorova, Jenny Bangham, Noah Tamarkin, Laura Foster, Nadine Ehlers, Ricardo Roque, Sebastián Gil-Riaño, Jonathan Marks, Michael Robinson, Sandra Soo-Jin Lee, Amit Prasad, Gyan Prakash, Elise Burton, Marianne Sommer, Veronika Lipphardt, Hannah Landecker, and Susanne Bauer. I am grateful to Mike Fischer for including this book in the Experimental Futures series, a series that includes so many of my academic heroes.

Thanks to all those who tolerated questions from a researcher about various obscure subjects, especially John Morton, Tony Birch, Philip Batty, and Lindy Allen for talking to me about Baldwin Spencer's double. Martha Macintyre, Lynette Russell, and Elizabeth Povinelli have provided invaluable support at critical times and have always cheered me on. Three anonymous Duke University Press reviewers generously engaged with the argument and made it better. "Book buddy" Anne Pollock provided encouragement to press home with the final stage of revisions. Thanks to my friends who are always up for a walk-and-talk; you know who you are. Thanks, finally, to my mother and stepfather, Ramona Koval and Dave Mayes, whose unwavering support has made so many things possible, and to my beloved girls, Maya and Eden.

Introduction

The camp was pitch-black and below freezing as three scientists rose from their beds and gathered up their equipment: gas cylinder, masks, rubber tubes, paper. The rest of the expedition party—nine other scientists and a guide, a cinematographer, a pastor, and an Aboriginal interpreter—lay snoring in their swags, the camels tethered nearby. Shivering in the desert night, they made their way by the light of kerosene lanterns through acacia forest to the "native" camp. There they encountered a row of nine young Anmatjerre men lying naked in shallow depressions dug into the sand, their heads beneath a low windbreak made of grasses and branches. Small fires, some still smoldering, lay at their feet and in between them. Although the men appeared to be sleeping, the scientists knew they were being carefully watched.

The three scientists, led by New Zealand–born physiologist C. Stanton Hicks, had traveled from Adelaide, the capital of South Australia, to Cockatoo Creek in Australia's central desert for this rendezvous with the Anmatjerre men. Together with their anthropology, archaeology, medical, and dental science colleagues from the University of Adelaide and the South Australian Museum, they formed the 1931 cohort of the annual Board for Anthropological Research expeditions. The objective of Hicks and his assistants was to record the Anmatjerre men's basal metabolic rate (BMR), a measure of how much oxygen the body needs for its basic internal functions. By the 1930s BMR had been measured in diverse world populations and found to differ between different "racial" groups (and by sex). Hicks had taken on the task of calculating the "Aboriginal" BMR to add to global knowledge.

Their early morning start was necessary because BMR had to be measured in bed, just as someone woke from a night's sleep. For accurate measurements, the nostrils had to be tightly clipped so that no air would escape. All breathing had to be done through a mask fit snugly around the mouth. Measurements were continuously taken for fifteen minutes and, after a short break, repeated twice more. Although the scientists struggled to securely attach the mouthpiece and noseclips, which were designed for European subjects, they successfully took multiple measurements on three subjects who, Hicks recalled, "suffered . . . indignities at our hands without one single departure from the strict requirements of our precise measurement of their oxygen intake!" (1974, 33). After further experiments with men (and only men) of other desert tribes on subsequent Board for Anthropological Research expeditions, by the mid-1930s Hicks concluded that Aboriginal people had the same BMR as Europeans. Like all good scientists, however, he was attuned to the questions raised by his results. The ability of his subjects to maintain a "normal" metabolic rate while lying naked in below-freezing conditions led to a research program that attracted the attention of postwar US defense scientists. A large team made multiple visits in the 1950s to investigate the possibility that the desert sleepers could enter a state of torpor—temporary hibernation—previously thought to occur only in certain birds and mammals.

Not long ago, I became aware that this potential biological superpower was still being actively investigated, not in the men of the central desert but in US Navy SEALS, an elite group of soldiers. A biomimicry expert contacted me, claiming to work for a secret company conducting classified research for an unnamed government. While his identity was unverifiable, and our communication only virtual, there was more to his story than I anticipated. Apparently driven to contact me by his guilty conscience, he was concerned that unique biological properties evolved by Indigenous people of central Australia were to be exploited by the US Department of Defense for the purposes of developing covert biological warfare and the future colonization of Mars. The far-reaching connections and implications of Hicks's early morning encounters with the Anmatjerre may seem surprising. But in global histories of scientific research on Indigenous biological difference, spectacular afterlives are the rule rather than the exception. Hicks's experiments in Aboriginal physiology, a story I tell in chapter 5, were one of a plethora of scientific studies on Indigenous people across the nineteenth and twentieth centuries. In the earliest years of British colonization after the initial invasion in 1788, European scientific leaders scrambled to access newly available Aboriginal skeletal remains taken from burial sites by doctors, amateur naturalists, and government officials (MacDonald 2010; Turnbull 2017). Leading comparative anatomists such as German physician and anthropologist Johann Friedrich Blumenbach were sent

Australian skulls to add to their international collections, developing theories of racial variation from their analyses of cranial form. The American physician and scientist Samuel George Morton systematized skull measurements by filling them with shot pellets to measure their "internal capacity," producing tables of biological data that mirrored the racial hierarchies of the time (A. Fabian 2010; Stepan 1982; Stocking 1968). Australians often appeared at the bottom of the list, above only the "Tasmanians," the inhabitants of the large island directly south of mainland Australia, who were considered a separate race altogether.

The growing influence of evolutionists Charles Darwin, Alfred Russel Wallace, and Thomas H. Huxley in the last decades of the nineteenth century further increased the perceived value of Aboriginal remains. Emerging theories of human evolution viewed Indigenous Australians as the living remnants of "stone-age man," and their remains were thought to contain the "missing link" between humans and nonhuman apes. In the mid-nineteenth century, the leading scientific elites in several Australian colonies established museums and sought to fill their collections with "native" skeletons and cultural objects.

As the twentieth century dawned, a new kind of collecting emerged. Research in Australia was key to this shift: the 1898 Cambridge Anthropological Expedition to Torres Straits, led by ethnologist Alfred C. Haddon (discussed in chapter 3), is often credited with the first use of the term "fieldwork." Rather than relying solely on the reports of colonial correspondents, ethnologists and physicians began collecting their own data from living subjects. These practitioners of the burgeoning field of anthropology performed ever more systematized anthropometric measurements of faces, limbs, hair, and skin (W. Anderson 2002).

Soon, the emerging experimental and field sciences of physiology and human biology joined the Aboriginal research enterprise. Research conducted during World War I in the port of Salonika on blood group differences between "races" had found that group A blood was predominantly found in Europeans, and group B in Asians. From the 1920s, University of Adelaide pathologist J. B. Cleland led blood group research, demonstrating the absence of group B blood in Indigenous Australians (W. Anderson 2002; D. Thomas 2004). This finding, repeated among thousands of subjects, was regarded as confirming an origin theory that had circulated since the late nineteenth century (discussed in detail in chapter 4): Aboriginal people were archaic Caucasians, "primitive" cousins of present-day Europeans. Hicks's physiological studies in Cockatoo Creek similarly found that the BMR of "native" Australians was the same as that of Europeans, confirming his view that "the aborigines are, in fact, archaic Europeans" (1974, 38).

By midcentury, advances in serology and portable freezing technologies brought other disciplines into the mix. Human biologists such as R. L. Kirk (discussed in chapter 2) collected blood samples from Indigenous people across Australia and transported them to his laboratory (first in Perth, then, from 1967, in Canberra) for analysis of the protein variants contained within them. Kirk (2001) mapped possible relationships between Australians and their Asia-Pacific neighbors by comparing the frequency of different variants of newly understood blood components: haptoglobins, transferrins, and lipoproteins (see also Mukharji 2020). As archaeologists used new carbon dating techniques to gauge a time depth of Aboriginal occupation of at least forty thousand years, the archaic Caucasian hypothesis was replaced by debate over whether humans had arrived in one migration or two, or even three, and by what route (Kirk and Thorne 1976).[1] For human biologists, the tens of thousands of years of evolution in relative isolation on the Australian continent promised, and delivered, many serological discoveries. Most famously, Kirk supplied Baruch Blumberg with serum from Aboriginal people in central Australia, from which Blumberg isolated the "Australia antigen." This mysterious entity was found to be hepatitis B, a discovery that netted a Nobel Prize (Blumberg 1976; Bootcov 2024).

Drawing on both famous and obscure episodes in the history of scientific research on Indigenous bodies and populations, this book tells a larger story of how and why biological knowledge about Indigenous Australians was produced. Through these stories I address questions that have relevance for scientific and health research in all diverse societies: *How are we to understand Indigenous biological difference in the twenty-first century?* Is it a racist ruse, a stubborn residue of racial pseudoscience? Is it something that exists but that should not be allowed to have social or political relevance? Or is it a potentially empowering force that can be unlocked by newly accurate science? Or by being under Indigenous control?

To answer these questions, *Haunting Biology* traces the rise and fall of different lines of biological and medical inquiry over the twentieth century and up to the present. Each new discipline that sought to produce biological knowledge about Indigenous people claimed new theories or methods that were superior to previous modes of knowledge production. Along the way, thousands of bones, hair samples, blood samples, pathology slides, placental samples, and much more were acquired, collated, and stored in museums and laboratories across Australia and the countries of the Global North. The following chapters illustrate how the material persistence of samples over decades and centuries folds together the fates of different scientific methodologies. Blood, bones, hair, comparative anatomy, human biology, physiology, and anthropological genetics all haunt each other across time and space, together with the many racial theories they produced and sustained. In the stories ahead, we will meet a variety of ghostly presences: a dead anatomist, a fetishized piece of hair hidden away in a war trunk, an elusive "white" Indigenous person, a secret physiological superpower, and a statue of an iconic collector that refuses to be still.

AS A WORK OF historical anthropology—in conversation with the history of science, science and technology studies, and Indigenous studies—this book looks to the past with an eye on the present. Contemporary Australian views of the sciences of Indigenous biological difference are highly influenced by critiques made since the 1970s. Both the history of the twentieth-century sciences and the history of Indigenous critique of these sciences are central to the questions I explore in the following chapters. Biological knowledge about Indigenous Australians was always already loaded with meaning. Nineteenth-century studies lent scientific kudos to long-standing racial hierarchies that justified British colonialism and denied the very humanity (let alone human rights) of Australian "natives." From the late 1960s, Indigenous activists and their non-indigenous supporters campaigned in earnest for an end to discrimination against Indigenous people. The cause was dramatically endorsed by the vast majority of Australians in a 1967 referendum that amended the Constitution to allow the Commonwealth (the national government) to pass legislation regarding Indigenous people, a privilege formerly reserved for the states. This change underpinned the many positive interventions of the progressive Labor government led by Gough Whitlam in the 1970s, including steps toward Aboriginal land rights (Chesterman and Galligan 1997).[2]

In this quest for Indigenous people to be treated as equals, earlier scientific research was newly considered exploitative and demeaning and soon became an object of sharp critique. The Australian Institute of Aboriginal Studies, an institution discussed in chapter 2, was the site in 1974 of the first Indigenous critique of the disciplinary authority of archaeology and anthropology, with critiques of other disciplines soon to follow (Briscoe 1978; Langford 1983; Langton 1981; Liddle and Shaw [ca. 1983]; McNiven and Russell 2008; Widders 1974). Indigenous health research, itself a new field in the 1970s, persisted but became closely regulated by the 1990s (National Health and Medical Research Council 1991). In Australia the disciplines that studied Indigenous biology without a clear health rationale, particularly the genetic sciences, largely became taboo.

Research funding in these areas dried up, and graduate students found non-Australian or nonhuman subjects to study.

In these tumultuous times of the mid-1970s, I entered the picture. I was born in Melbourne to two children of Holocaust survivors. Their parents had arrived in the 1950s as Jewish refugees from rural Poland, a country where 90 percent of the Jewish population were murdered by the Nazis. Three of my grandparents were the sole survivors from their families; one of them was the only Jew from his village to survive. The main attractions of Australia were its distance from war-ravaged Europe and its willingness to admit them. At university in the 1990s, I became aware of the war against Indigenous people that continued to ravage my family's adopted country, a country I learned was stolen from its original inhabitants. Informed by my familial knowledge of genocide and its aftermath, my career in medicine, public health, and finally anthropology has focused on both addressing Indigenous disadvantage and analyzing the bitter ironies of this task.[3]

When I began working in Indigenous health as a young doctor over twenty years ago, I and most of my colleagues considered the idea that Indigenous people might be genetically susceptible to some diseases to be categorically racist. Almost no research was being conducted on Indigenous Australian genetics. The critiques of Indigenous biological sciences that began in the 1970s had been further sharpened by the Human Genome Diversity Project in the 1990s. This project (a companion to the better-known Human Genome Project) sought to sample and characterize genetic diversity among Indigenous peoples worldwide (M'charek 2005). Run by population geneticists who referred to Indigenous groups as "Isolates of Historical Interest," it was soon met with global resistance from Indigenous groups who dubbed it the "vampire project," as discussed in chapter 2 (Reardon 2005). Indigenous Australian leaders compared genetic research to the racial science of the nineteenth and early twentieth centuries that had served to justify Indigenous dispossession and relentless state control. Indigenous people exercised their hard-won agency over the conduct of research and declined to participate (*Green Left Weekly* 1994).

My dissertation research focused on the ways that non-indigenous people construct the idea of Indigenous cultural difference in Indigenous health research (Kowal 2006, 2008, 2015). As I completed the fieldwork for that project in the mid-2000s, the question of biological difference began to interest me. Even as Indigenous and progressive opinion had firmly rejected research into Indigenous biological difference, genetic research on other populations had made great strides, fueled by enormous public (and some private) investments in the Human Genome Project. In the years after the first draft of the human genome sequence was completed in 2000, it became clear that the influence of genetics and genomics on all aspects of human life would only increase.[4] I realized that the interdisciplinary field of science and technology studies (STS) had many scholars working on historical and contemporary questions of race, science, and colonialism.[5] It seemed to me that the rise of genomics would inevitably collide with the stigma of biological difference within Indigenous research. I believed that analyzing this collision could lead to important insights on twenty-first-century intersections of race, science, and justice.

Over the course of my research on the implications of genetics for Indigenous people, the field has changed dramatically. In the past decade, the taboo on studies of Indigenous biological difference appears to have been lifted. Genomics has become a relatively common tool in studies of Indigenous health, ancient DNA studies of deep Indigenous history have proliferated, and growing numbers of Indigenous people are using direct-to-consumer genomic ancestry testing to inform their family history and identity (Kowal 2012b; Watt and Kowal 2019a, 2019b; Watt, Kowal, and Cummings 2020). Rather than a passive observer, I have been an active participant in these shifts. My background in Indigenous health care and research, combined with my activist disposition, led me to support national conversations among Indigenous leaders on how genetic research should be governed (Kowal and Anderson 2012; Kowal, Rouhani, and Anderson 2011). Genomics was coming to Indigenous Australia, and it was important to me that Indigenous people had the opportunity to control how this unfolded. This led me to play a key role in the development of the National Centre for Indigenous Genomics, the world's first Indigenous-governed genome facility and part of the story I tell in chapter 2.

I come to this topic, then, as an anthropologist of science and Indigeneity, and as a participant in Indigenous-governed genomics: simultaneously an anthropologist and part of my anthropological object. My involvement in the transition from the late twentieth-century rejection to the twenty-first-century relative embrace of genomics in Indigenous research has made me appreciate the importance of careful histories of twentieth-century biology, an area of growing interest in the history of science. An appreciation of how the current scientific understanding of human difference relies on or recapitulates earlier paradigms, including those that had devastating effects for certain populations, is important to temper current enthusiasm about the potential benefits of the science of human differences to improve health and well-being through stratification and precision medicine.[6] No one who makes knowledge about Indigenous people in the present is immune to these legacies.

It is equally crucial *not* to essentialize contemporary science as simply a continuation of the nineteenth-century beliefs in distinct and hierarchical races that underpinned harmful policies based on eugenics or assimilation. Scholars such as Troy Duster (1990) and Dorothy Roberts (2011) have made powerful arguments about the continuities between eugenics and genome science.[7] However, it is also important to trace the changing scientific conceptions of "race" across the twentieth century and avoid conflating or collapsing different disciplines, tools, and theories (one example with regard to conceptions of race in Australia is the differing aims of "absorption" and "assimilation" discussed in chapter 4). My aim is not to indict twentieth- or twenty-first-century biology for being "just like" nineteenth-century racial science but rather to understand the rise and fall of different disciplines—including comparative anatomy, human biology, population genetics, and evolutionary biology—within a longer story of making biological knowledge about Indigenous Australians. This will allow a better answer to the question of whether a just genome science is possible, or whether the tools of genomics will inevitably reinforce lines of historical oppression.

My use of the terms "Indigenous biological difference" and "biological knowledge" in this book is deliberately broad and reflects my methodological commitment to resisting claims of historical discontinuity (e.g., "what we do now is completely different from our predecessors") and, equally, resisting claims of homogeneity (e.g., "precision medicine is no different from eugenics"). To illustrate my approach, let's consider two attempts to produce biological knowledge about Indigenous people. When W. L. H. Duckworth (1894), a Cambridge physical anthropologist, took forty-four separate measurements of twenty-eight Aboriginal skulls, including cranial capacity, "estimated by using No. 8 shot, which was arranged by shaking the skull and occasional use of a wooden rammer" (287), he was looking for evidence of fixed racial characteristics.[8] The second example takes place over seventy years later and two continents away. In the wake of the 1967 referendum that demonstrated national support for Indigenous rights, medical researcher David G. Jose and colleagues from the Queensland Institute of Medical Research conducted a health survey of around six hundred children living on twelve Queensland missions. Analysis of their blood, physical examinations, and mission records demonstrated high rates of child mortality and preventable diseases, including rheumatic fever (Jose, Self, and Stallman 1969). The damning results were partially censored by the Queensland state government (Kidd 1997).

At first glance, these two examples represent very different kinds of biological knowledge. One demonstrates the inevitably inferior features of the

Aboriginal "race" using nineteenth-century racial science, while another high-lights the woeful shortcomings of state-sanctioned missions in providing for their Aboriginal wards and recommends improvements in "housing, diet and education" (Jose, Self, and Stallman 1969, 86). However, Jose's research had more continuities with Duckworth's than meets the eye. Two years after blood samples were collected, Jose sent a small portion of each sample to R. L. Kirk at the Australian National University to further his research on the genetic structure of the Cape York Aboriginal population. Kirk (1973) published results of blood group, serum proteins, and enzyme variation across the region, calculating the genetic distance between various groups to provide clues to their origins. Jose did not see any contradiction between his own research on the acquired diseases of Aboriginal people and Kirk's genetic research on Aboriginal origins—both were inherently valuable.

From the perspective of the present, it is tempting to support Jose's research and disparage Kirk's, and certainly Duckworth's. The creation of biological knowledge that views differences as socially or environmentally determined may seem far less harmful—indeed, beneficial—compared to biological knowledge of characteristics that are considered inherited and fixed. This book refuses the comfort of this division. To be sure, the range of historical and contemporary actors that populate these chapters mean different things when they measure or interpret a biological difference between Indigenous and non-indigenous people. Some see evidence of a fixed racial type—or the merging of two or more fixed racial types—and others see the transitory impact of the environment on a person or group of people. Most waver between these extremes of "hard" and "soft" heredity, perceiving shorter or longer timescales of adaptation and varying modes of inheritance.[9]

My refusal to distinguish between "good" and "bad" biological knowledge aims neither to dismiss all biological knowledge as racist nor to excuse any of its negative effects on Indigenous people. Instead, I argue that biological data as different as diabetes incidence and hair form both contain haunting possibilities and resonances.[10] From chapter 2 to chapter 6 of this book, I examine twentieth-century episodes in the production of biological knowledge about Indigenous people and find persistent ghostly presences.

The increasing engagement of Indigenous Australians in genomics across the past decade has troubled the relative certainty I experienced twenty years ago that there were no essential biological differences between Indigenous and non-indigenous people, there were only inequalities resulting from disadvantage and oppression. For some, that certainty continues: the sciences of biological difference are pseudoscience, as we are all the same under the skin. For others, both Indigenous and non-indigenous, the status of biological differences between human groups is ever more confusing. Jenny Reardon's analysis of the perpetual return of the "crisis" of biological race is cogent here. She argues that the post–World War II consensus—epitomized in the UNESCO statements of 1950 and 1951 (UNESCO 1952)—of "biology as a distinct realm of knowledge production that exists apart from any societal taint" (Dunklee, Reardon, and Wentworth 2006) produced a division of labor between social scientists and biologists (see Latour 1993). The consensus promised that as long as biologists ensured their work was "not political," biology as usual could proceed. Social scientists could be reassured that biology was (for now) no longer racist and keep their attention on properly "social" concerns.

The consequence of this division has been periodic crises of racialized biology (a fairly recent episode, for example, was triggered by leading geneticist David Reich's defense of meaningful genetic differences between racial groups; Kahn et al. 2018; Reich 2018). Reardon and colleagues argue that the surprise experienced by both scientists and social scientists when these crises recur is a "consequence of a system that delineates the social and the political from the biological: sociologists and humanists can only encounter race's return within biology when they fail to see it all along; biologists can only experience a shock of politicization when the ongoing political dimensions of their work are out of view" (Dunklee, Reardon, and Wentworth 2006). Writing well over a decade ago, Reardon and colleagues hoped that scholars might finally transcend the division between social and biological inquiry to interrupt the cycle of periodic crisis.

The story that opens the next chapter shows this has not yet been achieved, although this book is another hopeful attempt at interruption. The chapter explains my approach to haunting and why it matters to Indigenous worlds that have always been thick with ghosts but have encountered genomics only recently. I start with a spectacular example of the politicization of Indigenous biological difference in the genomic era. The lead-up to the 2019 parliamentary elections for New South Wales, Australia's most populous state, demonstrated how the status of biological difference has enormous implications, potentially affecting the very identities of Indigenous Australians.

"DNA Testing Plan for Aboriginal People"

The state election was just two weeks away, and political parties vied for media attention.[1] For one week in March 2019, all eyes were on Mark Latham, a candidate for the upper house of the New South Wales Parliament for the minor political party One Nation. For those unfamiliar with Australia, states are one of three levels of government: local, state, and federal. The six states (New South Wales, Victoria, Queensland, Western Australia, South Australia, and Tasmania) and two internal territories (Northern Territory and the Australian Capital Territory, which contains Canberra) elect governments led by a premier (for states) or chief minister (for territories). The Australian nation, led by the Commonwealth government, was formed in 1901 by the federation of the six states and is led by a prime minister. States, territories, and the federal government each have two houses of Parliament, and voting has been compulsory since 1924.

Mark Latham had experience in both federal and state politics and had been promiscuous across the political spectrum. Earlier in his career, he was a prominent progressive, rising to lead the federal Australian Labor Party in opposition in 2003. Two years later, having lost a federal election, he resigned from his position and embarked on a second career as a popular social commentator. He was known for spouting increasingly controversial views on women and migrants and became a darling of conservative media. In 2018 he announced he had joined One Nation, a far-right party known for anti-immigration and protectionist policies and, more recently, explicit white nationalism.[2]

Latham dominated the media spotlight that week in March with a radical policy announcement. One Nation's policy on Indigenous affairs would focus on stopping "welfare rorters" (welfare cheats) who the party believed were wrongfully claiming benefits aimed at supporting Indigenous people. Their policy document spelled out their argument: "Australians are sick and tired of seeing people with blonde hair and blue eyes declaring themselves to be Indigenous, when clearly they have no recognizable Aboriginal background and are doing it solely to qualify for extra money. We will tighten the eligibility rules for Aboriginal identity to require DNA evidence of at least 25 per cent Indigenous—the equivalent of one fully Aboriginal grandparent" (quoted in Han 2019).

The backlash in the media and on social media was swift and decisive.[3] A few far-right voices agreed with Latham, but the vast majority pointed out the major flaws in the policy: false identification was not a problem, and even if it was, the proposed solution would not work. The policy was blatantly racist. Another commonly cited reason, and one of particular interest here, was that Aboriginality cannot be defined by DNA. As expressed in various commentaries, this inability has two main aspects. The first relates to the specific definition of Indigenous status used in Australia. Contemporary recognition of Indigenous people in Australia is not dependent on degrees of ancestry. Since the 1980s the working definition of Indigeneity has had three parts. The first is self-identification as Indigenous. The second is Indigenous ancestry. There is no specific minimum of ancestors: one known Indigenous ancestor is enough. The final part of the definition is acceptance by an "Indigenous community," without a specific definition of an Indigenous community. In practice, a range of community groups, from local councils to health services to Stolen Generations organizations, issue "Certificates of Aboriginality" or membership cards that act to administratively authenticate Indigenous identity (Australian Bureau of Statistics 1999).

This definition is not a bureaucratic quirk but the outcome of decades of activism by Indigenous people and non-indigenous allies to overturn harmful state policies that dictated Indigenous people's lives according to their blood quantum as judged by government officials (Chesterman and Galligan 1997). Summarizing a plethora of scholarship in history, Indigenous studies, and postcolonial studies, Indigenous scholar Bronwyn Carlson told the media, "The grading of Aboriginality for the purposes of denying someone the right to 'be Aboriginal' is a colonial tool" (quoted in Latimore 2019). Contemporary Indigenous scholars are clear that Indigenous identity is not equivalent to a particular skin, eye, or hair color, or any other bodily form (Carlson 2016).

The second aspect of genetics' failure to define Indigeneity was scientific rather than cultural or bureaucratic. A leading commentator of the scientific critique was Associate Professor Misty Jenkins, a woman from the Gunditjmara nation of western Victoria and a leading Indigenous scientist. After growing up in the large town of Ballarat, studying science at the University of Melbourne in the late 1990s (where we first became friends through the Indigenous solidarity student group I helped to start), and then obtaining a PhD with Nobel Prize winner Peter Doherty in immunology, she spent time in Oxford and Cambridge before returning to Melbourne. She was eventually appointed as a lab head at the Water and Eliza Hall Institute, Australia's premier research institute in medical sciences. The Jenkins Lab has developed killer T cells, a leading light of precision medicine, for use in brain cancer. T lymphocytes (a kind of white blood cell) removed from the bodies of people suffering from cancer are bioengineered to kill the patient's specific cancer and reinjected, an approach called "chimeric antigen receptor T cell" (CAR-T cell) therapy. Alongside her prolific scientific career, she is a leading advocate and representative in Indigenous scientific and medical research. Her many roles have included founding board member and deputy chair of the National Centre for Indigenous Genomics.

Jenkins was perfectly placed to respond to the Mark Latham controversy, and the media duly found her. Her quoted response was quite different from Bronwyn Carlson's, focusing not on the moral or historical overtones of using DNA but on the practical obstacles: "When DNA is examined to determine ancestry, the DNA is compared to a 'reference' genome. An Australian Aboriginal genome does not exist and therefore to even propose that a test is possible is scientifically inaccurate" (quoted in Latimore 2019). One Nation's policy was nonsensical, in this reading, not (only) because it was offensive or inaccurate, but because it could not (yet) be done.[4]

A closer analysis of these critiques of One Nation's policy is useful for parsing out the questions that animate this book. Three overlapping but distinct views emerge from media articles and voluminous associated comments made by members of the public. The first view sees the very concept of Indigenous DNA as a misnomer. The idea that we are all the same under the skin takes its cue, in part, from the post–World War II scientific backlash against racial science, and more directly from genetic evidence—widely circulated in the social sciences literature since the 1970s—that biological differences between "races" are insignificant compared to the variation *within* recognized populations (Lewontin 1972, 1974). This approach was reinforced by former US president Bill Clinton, who, when the draft of the Human Genome Project was completed, famously proclaimed the overwhelming sameness of the human species: "I believe one of the great truths to emerge from this triumphant expedition inside the human genome is that in genetic terms, all human beings, regardless of race, are more than 99.9 percent the same" (quoted in CNN 2000). Proponents of this view would see any attempt to specify Indigenous genetic material as fundamentally misguided.

A second argument discernible in the critiques of Mark Latham's policy announcement relies less on a scientific debunking of Indigenous biological difference and more on countering the social misuse of any differences that may exist. This view concedes that something like "Indigenous DNA" might exist, but it should not be used for any socially meaningful purposes such as group membership. This is close to the view expressed in the UNESCO statements on race in the wake of World War II that recognized meaningful biological difference between groups but cautioned they did not predict intelligence and should not be used to classify or govern (UNESCO 1952).

A third view is contained in Jenkins's comment quoted above. Here Indigenous DNA is something that *could* be measured, providing the correct scientific tools are available. This objection to Indigenous DNA is neither epistemological nor political nor social but technical. This view leaves open the possibility that once an Aboriginal reference genome is assembled and Indigenous genomic information can be accurately measured, it could be used for a variety of purposes. Jenkins and other Indigenous scholars who voiced this opinion would, to be sure, expect that Indigenous people and communities—and not governments—would be in control of how any knowledge of Indigenous biological difference might be used. (For example, a possible community-sanctioned use for Indigenous genetic knowledge is family reconnection for Indigenous people who have lost links to their biological family due to past state policies of child removal.)

Parsing these responses to Latham's proposal reveals three distinct contemporary orientations to Indigenous biological difference: as a myth, as a biological reality that can't or shouldn't be used for social purposes, and as a reality only possible if the science improves and if Indigenous control is put in place. These orientations overlap in some ways and contradict each other in others. Importantly, they are implicit rather than explicit in the various commentaries—for the most part, the status of Indigenous biological difference remains a question beneath the surface and between the lines. The ubiquitous but hidden question behind these commentaries is also the central question that animates this book: *How are we to understand Indigenous biological difference in the twenty-first century?* Is it racist pseudoscience all over again? Is it a minimalist biological reality that should not be granted social or political relevance? Or is an antiracist biology of human difference possible once better data are available and once Indigenous people control the science?

The chapters that follow resist a straightforward answer to these questions. This should not be taken as an indication that answering these questions is not important. The stakes are enormously high for Indigenous people, as One Nation's misguided policy illustrates. I have spent some years bringing these questions into public view in order to generate constructive conversations about them, most of all among Indigenous people themselves.

However, for this inquiry into the haunting and haunted nature of Indigenous biological difference, my intention in posing these questions is not to offer clear answers. The intuitions behind this book are that (a) for many people, these questions are unanswerable and (b) the inscrutability of these questions is a source of haunting. From the 1970s until recently, for most social science and humanities scholars the answer to the question of Indigenous biological difference was the first possibility I proposed above: the persistence of racist pseudoscience. The possibility of Indigenous biological difference was easily categorized as wrong, defended only by those with racist intent. It was clear to progressive Australians what to think of it (as false) and what to think about right-wing people who asserted that meaningful biological differences between Indigenous people and others did in fact exist (as racist). These beliefs are behind the first ghost of the haunted biology of this book: the ghost of racial science. The following pages contain many examples of nineteenth- and twentieth-century science that made claims of biological difference that were used to harm Indigenous people. Those making biological knowledge about Indigenous people in the present are haunted by the fear of resembling their forebears.

The uncertainty of the current moment—illustrated by the range of rebuttals to Latham's ridiculous proposal—has spawned a second ghost. Now that the *possibility* of meaningful Indigenous biological difference has been rehabilitated (and by highly respected Indigenous scientists, no less), for many, the epistemological and moral certainty that held since the 1970s is lost. The second ghost that haunts the Indigenous science of the present is the possibility that some Indigenous Australians *do* have biologically meaningful differences attributable to their Indigenous ancestry.

This possibility may seem entirely prosaic to many readers, especially those who are not Australian. However, given the damage that scientific racism has inflicted on Indigenous people, health researchers in recent decades have gone to much effort to argue that the poor health of Indigenous people is decidedly *not* due to "faulty biology" but instead due to colonialization, the denial of sovereignty, ongoing racism (reflected in high rates of poverty and incarceration), and intergenerational trauma. Admitting the possibility of inherent biological difference is thus highly politically charged.

Indigenous biological difference is discursively explosive. Invoking it is playing with fire. It has a haunting and shocking history. Harnessing it for good may be possible and could lead to health benefits. This historical and anthropological inquiry into episodes of past research—all with reverberations in the present—is my attempt to identify the ghosts that line the path to an Indigenous-controlled genomics, a field I explain further in the next section. It is the responsibility of those engaged in the range of activities that flow from research on Indigenous biological difference—including genomic medicine, evolutionary biology, and genetic genealogy—to acquaint themselves with these haunting possibilities.

The Ghosts of Indigenous Genomics

The adoption of racialized genomics by a right-wing Australian political party is absurd and demands strong opposition. It is more difficult to pass judgment on situations where Indigenous researchers and communities choose to draw on genomic technologies for their own purposes. Such situations make the questions I ask in this book all the more complicated and make the answers more important. As my inquiry into the history of scientific research and its ghostly afterlives was motivated by the unfolding of Indigenous genomics in the twenty-first century, I will spend some time explaining the recent uses of genomics in Indigenous Australia and then consider what it might mean to think of them as haunted.

There are two main areas where a relative embrace of what we might call "Indigenous genomics" has taken place. In the sphere of health, Indigenous scholars in the United States, Canada, and New Zealand have called for the inclusion of Indigenous people in genomics research (Claw et al. 2018; Garrison et al. 2019; Hudson, Russell, et al. 2016). In Australia, the National Centre for Indigenous Genomics was developed as an Indigenous-governed genome facility that aims to conduct research controlled by Indigenous people and for their benefit (Kowal, Easteal, and Gooda 2016). Indigenous researchers in Queensland have led the development of guidelines for Indigenous genomic research in that state (QIMR Berghofer Medical Research Institute 2019). Genomics Aotearoa, the national genomics platform of New Zealand, is focused on Maori genomics under Maori governance (Genomics Aotearoa, n.d.). The narrative of all these projects is similar: Indigenous people have been harmed by past genetic research projects, such as the Human Genome Diversity Project, but this should not cause them to miss out on the potential benefits of twenty-first-century genomics. Genomics research needs to include them by conducting research that follows their guidelines and includes them as active partners and ideally researchers (Bardill 2018; Bliss 2012). In South Dakota, Indigenous geneticists Assistant Professor Keolu Fox, Assistant Professor Matt Anderson, Assistant Professor Krystal Tsosie, and Joseph Yracheta have gone a few steps further. In partnership with the Cheyenne River Sioux Tribe and located within their reservation, and independent of any university, these Indigenous scientists developed the Native BioData Consortium, the first biobank run wholly by Indigenous scientists (Tsosie et al. 2021).

Another way that genetics and genomics have been used to try to benefit Indigenous and minority peoples is through what Alondra Nelson describes as "reconciliation" projects "aimed at ameliorating the injurious repercussions of the past" (2012, 20). Examples are ancestry testing services for African Americans that can result in financial support for the African communities that the test ties them to (Nelson 2008), attempts to use genetic and epigenetic findings to obtain reparations for slavery (J. Hamilton 2012), and the use of forensic genetics in Argentina and South Africa to identify the remains of the "disappeared" exhumed from mass graves (Aronson 2012). A further version of such projects is attempts by Indigenous minorities to use genomics to assert their traditional ownership of land over the claims of others (Kent 2013).

The repatriation of human remains removed from Indigenous communities is a newer addition to these genomic reconciliation projects. This application of genomics came to global attention in 2015 when a group led by Eske Willerslev, a geneticist we will meet in chapter 3, analyzed DNA from the most contested skeletal remains in US history, known to non-Native scientists as Kennewick Man and to Native Americans as the Ancient One. Craniological examination of the skeleton in the 1990s had classified it as a member of a human group thought to have preceded the Native Americans, and therefore not an ancestor of present-day Native Americans and not suitable for repatriation. Twenty years of bitter legal battles between scientists and tribes ensued. The fate of the remains was transformed by the evidence that they were closely genetically related to contemporary Native Americans. The earlier craniological findings were overturned, and Kennewick Man/the Ancient One was repatriated and reburied the following year (Burke et al. 2008; Colwell 2017; Kakaliouras 2019; Rasmussen, Sikora, et al. 2015). In Australia, archaeologists and geneticists are working with Indigenous communities to develop genetic tools that could facilitate the repatriation of thousands of unprovenanced human remains held for decades or centuries in museums (Collard et al. 2019; Wright et al. 2018).

If not for examples like these, it would be easier to dismiss the whole notion of racialized biological difference as a nineteenth- and twentieth-century phenomenon best left behind. This was certainly my point of view—absorbed by reading works in Aboriginal history, Indigenous studies, critical race theory, and cultural anthropology—when I began to be interested in these questions some fifteen years ago. I was persuaded by the arguments of Kim TallBear, J. Kehaulani Kauanui, and others that Western scientific ideas of biological inheritance were a colonial imposition on Indigenous peoples and incompatible with their own concepts of kinship and sociality (Australian Law Reform Commission 2003; Bardill 2018; Howard 1990; Kauanui 2008; Kolopenuk 2014; Strathern 1992; TallBear 2013).[5]

Some scholars accordingly hold the view that all attempts by Indigenous people and minority groups to draw on genomics are destined to fail because of the cultural incompatibility of genomics and Indigenous ways of knowing and being, and because of the colonial and neocolonial forces that inevitably structure relations between Indigenous and scientific interests (Dodson 2000; Harry, Howard, and Shelton 2000). The view that genomics is inherently colonial is in tension with the agency of those Indigenous groups who increasingly use genomics for the varied purposes outlined above (Garrison et al. 2019; Kent 2013).

This recent uptake of technologies of biological difference is foremost in my mind as I consider the haunting legacies of twentieth-century scientific research on Indigenous people in the remaining chapters of this book. The Indigenous people leading and supporting these recent projects are worlds apart from the white men of science I write about, men who used these tools for purposes they believed were for the good of "mankind" (a category that either excluded Indigenous people or included them in very limited ways). In using the same tools (and sometimes their actual samples) for measuring and interpreting biological differences, however, contemporary Indigenous people and their allies are haunted by these white men of science, unable to completely escape their shared histories.

The very existence of the National Centre for Indigenous Genomics, for example, could be seen as an Achilles' heel of critiques of One Nation's outrageous plan to use DNA ancestry testing to revive state control over who can claim to be Indigenous. If there is such a thing as Indigenous genomics, a proponent of the plan might say, then it can be used to distinguish between "real" and "fake" Indigenous people. It can be more difficult to argue against a particular use of Indigenous genomics if you concede that biological difference is real. This hypothetical illustrates that even Indigenous-led genomics is conducted in the shadow of the past crimes and misdemeanors of racial science.

This book considers such relationships among the past, present, and future through the trope of haunting. In the title, *Haunting Biology*, "haunting" works in two grammatical registers, as an adjective and a verb. Adjectivally, the possibility of Indigenous biological differences and the scientific efforts to demonstrate them are haunting in many senses: lingering, recurring, intangible, melancholy, evocative, troubling, and discomforting. The reader may encounter any or all these qualities in the chapters that follow.

The second valence of the title, "haunting" as a verb, is one of the aims of the book: to haunt contemporary research into Indigenous biological differences, and human biological research in general. Woven through the text is an argument that all contemporary researchers need to be cognizant of their recent and more distant predecessors. Dismissing them as misguided, politically immature, or racist may be based on a fair judgment of their work from the perspective of contemporary science and ethics but may miss the historical lessons they offer. I wish to trouble a notion of "good science" that can entirely overcome the less-than-perfect pasts of every discipline (Thompson 2013). Accepting that the past of a science haunts its present is, in my view, the only way to proceed.

Producing a book with the word "haunting" in the title is inherently ambitious given the breadth and quality of scholarship this industrious concept has spawned. To begin with, any academic exploration of haunting must wrestle with philosopher Jacques Derrida's (1994) concept of "hauntology," a portmanteau of "haunting" and "ontology" (the study of ways of being). Writing *Specters of Marx* in 1993 after the fall of the Berlin Wall, Derrida argued that the futures predicted by Karl Marx haunted Europe long after the demise of the man himself and the political movement he inspired. Hauntology has had many afterlives in critical theory and popular culture, but the main insight I draw on is that ways of being in the present are haunted by "absent presences."[6] These absent presences are elements of the past—and the futures foretold in those pasts—that act in the present. They are present in both the sense of time (disobeying linear temporality to bring past and future to bear on the present) and the sense of ontology (exerting their presence despite their absence).

Another touchstone in the theorization of haunting is sociologist Avery Gordon's *Ghostly Matters* (2008). She explores haunting not primarily as a condition of all life and meaning making, as it is for Derrida, but as a specific effect of gendered and racialized violence. She draws on the Freudian idea that we repress those things that we cannot admit into our consciousness lest they shatter the cohesion we—as individuals, as nations—need to function. Repression must be continually renewed: haunting occurs when a glitch in the mechanism of repression allows the ghost to appear in the present.[7] The presence of the ghost demands a response, or, in Gordon's idiom, a "something to be done" (202).

Growing up in a settler colony like Australia provides the perfect conditions for developing an attunement to ghosts (Gelder 1994; Pinkney 2005; Read 2003; W. Wolfe 2007).[8] The smooth running of the settler colony requires the continued repression of histories of violent dispossessions across the continent and their ongoing legacies. In recent decades settler and Indigenous scholars have challenged "the great Australian silence" that anthropologist W. E. H. Stanner famously diagnosed in his 1968 Boyer lecture, writing powerful accounts of the historical and contemporary treatment of Indigenous Australians (Broome 2002; K. Gilbert 1973; Haebich 2000; Noonuccal 1970; Read 1982; Reynolds 1987, 2000; Rowley 1972; L. Ryan 1977; Bernard Smith 1980; Stanner [1968] 1979).[9] One thread of this scholarship has paid particular attention to the workings of memory—at individual, family, and collective levels—in maintaining or disrupting the colonial forgetting that repression relies on (Attwood 2005; Gooder and Jacobs 2000; C. Healy 1997, 2008; McKenna 2002).

A key work for me here is Ken Gelder and Jane Jacobs's *Uncanny Austra-lia* (1998). Writing in the 1990s, they relate the workings of ghostliness to the reconciliation movement. This was a state-supported effort, begun by Paul Keating's progressive Labor federal government and managed by the Council for Aboriginal Reconciliation (1991–2000), to educate all Australians about the facts of colonial history and build a shared understanding of the country's past and common future. The reconciliation movement can be thought of as an attempt to domesticate the ghosts of colonialism. Those on the conservative side of politics, who were in power by the time the decade of reconciliation was completed, were—unsurprisingly—not supportive of this effort. To the conservative government, the dangers of acknowledging ghosts outweighed the possible benefits of taming them.

For Gelder and Jacobs, the repression of the violent colonial past and the ongoing denial of Indigenous sovereignty make contemporary Australia a constitutively uncanny place, at once homely and unhomely, settled and un-settled, familiar and strange.[10] They structure their book around the possible responses to the ghosts who will inevitably make an appearance. They take their lead from philosopher Julia Kristeva's oft-cited musing on how best to deal with ghosts: "To worry or smile, such is the choice when we are assailed by the strange; our decision depends on how familiar we are with our own ghosts" (1991, 191). Ghosts can offer gifts and helpful advice, cause unwelcome disrup-tion, or seek revenge. Becoming more familiar with our own ghosts can help us know whether to run toward or away from them when they materialize.

Many stories told in this book are concerned with the haunting proper-ties of objects. These include biological specimens of various kinds, such as a hair sample stored for eighty-eight years in a museum and then a laboratory (chapter 3), but also, in chapter 6, a problematic statue made for a postcolonial museum exhibit. I explore these strange objects through the idea of folding, drawing on Amade M'charek's (2014) evocative use of Michel Serres's (1995) concept of topology to describe DNA as a folded object. Serres argues that humans do not experience time and space as linear but rather in a topologi-cal fashion. For him, topology is "the science of nearness and rifts," explained through the analogy of the handkerchief (60). An ironed handkerchief has a metrical geometry, analogous to linear time and space. Once crumpled into a pocket, the relationships between different parts of the handkerchief are dra-matically changed. Parts that were distant become proximate, and parts that were next to each other may find their former connections interrupted. In my account folded objects are a mechanism of haunting. A bone, a blood sample, a lock of hair, and a DNA sequence are folded objects in that they collapse time and space, bringing colonial history, scientific exchange routes, biocapital, genomic sovereignty, postcolonial reconciliation projects, and deep time into close proximity. With all this temporal and spatial traffic, it is no wonder that topological relations can become haunted.

While these Western theorists offer much to think with for non-indigenous, settler Australians, Indigenous cultures have far more experience with ghosts. Later in this chapter and the next, we will meet an Indigenous filmmaker and an Indigenous poet who have plenty to say about ghosts. Interestingly, however, ghosts are absent from Indigenous academic scholarship. The focus of Indigenous scholars has tended toward issues of more practical import, including legal scholarship on Indigenous rights, the history of Indigenous activism, scholarship on contemporary Indigenous identity, and analysis of the ways Indigenous peoples and knowledges have been (mis)represented by the West (for example, Behrendt 2003; Carlson 2016; Langton 1993; Marshall 2017; Maynard 2007; Nakata 2007; Russell 2001b). This leaves me in the uncanny position of turning to non-indigenous ethnographers, both dead and alive, for scholarly accounts of Indigenous ghosts.

In the classical ethnographies of many Australian "tribes" (Berndt and Berndt 1964; Elkin 1946, 1974; Spencer and Gillen [1899] 1968; Strehlow 1971; Warner 1937; Worms 1998) and more recent studies of Aboriginal healing (Cawte 1993; Reid 1983), both the spirits of the dead and the spirits of ancestral beings are a frequent presence. They can be helpful, offering useful advice or warnings, or harmful, even inflicting mortal injury. A. P. Elkin's classic monograph *Aboriginal Men of High Degree* (1946) focuses on the skills and personalities of traditional healers known as "medicine men" or "clever men" (his exclusive focus was on men) across Australia. The worlds he depicts are thick with ghosts. Medicine men can summon the spirit world to diagnose and cure sorcery through exorcism, appear and disappear at will, read minds, create illusions to confuse enemies, and much else. He stresses that although their skills are highly respected, they are not extraordinary: everyone communicates with spirits, but medicine men possess advanced techniques for interpreting their messages and intervening in the spirit world.

Ian Keen (2006) describes a variety of spirits in Yolngu society in northeastern Arnhem Land in the north of Australia. Spirits are central to human substance, as conception requires that the father find a spirit in the waters of his ancestral homelands and convey it to the mother. After death, the spirit of the deceased person is often in contact with the living in a benign or malevolent way. Keen presents a three-part typology of ghosts. The first two categories are ghosts of people who were known in life: "*Birrimbirr* denotes the benign aspect of spirits of the dead that are believed to travel to the person's patri-group waters after the person's death, and/or to one or more distant lands of the dead. *Mokuy* or *mokuy birrimbirr* are malicious ghosts of the dead which haunt a camp immediately after a death and later inhabit forests and vine jungle clumps, lingering near trees, and making people sick or insane" (520).

The third category are the spirits of ancestral beings (*Wangarr*) who created the world and who make themselves known through events large or small, in-cluding animal behavior, weather patterns, and human illness (causing or cur-ing it): "Country is imbued with spirits of the dead who communicate with the living. One is obliged to invoke the ancestors when hunting, ask for their aid, and under certain circumstances to make gifts to ancestors in the land and waters" (521).

Ghosts and spirits are thus an everyday presence in many Indigenous communities, reflecting the porousness of the categories of humans, nonhu-mans, Country, ancestral creator beings, the living, and the dead. From this perspective, there is nothing that needs to be *done* about ghosts.

In colonial times, ghosts have become highly syncretic (Clarke 2007; Fisher 2019; Marett 2000; Benjamin Smith 2008). From the time of colonization, the first Europeans encountered by a particular Indigenous group were often taken to be ghostly spirits of returned ancestors. To this day, many of the words used by Indigenous groups across the country to refer to white people mean "ghost," such as *djanga* in southern Western Australia or *gubba* in New South Wales (Clarke 2007). The most recent anthropological work on ghosts tends to focus on the malevolent kind. In the introduction to the important collection *Monster Anthropology in Australasia and Beyond* (2014), Yasmine Mu-sharbash argues that "monsters" is a "monstrously rewarding" umbrella term for phenomena that are usually considered separately by anthropologists: spir-its, ghosts, witches, and devils (16). Interestingly, she uses the verb "haunt" to describe all the actions of this wide variety of creatures.

Contemporary ghosts and monsters often reflect postcolonial concerns. One example is Burnt Woman, a ghost that haunts a former mission on Banjalang country in the state of New South Wales and preys on young men, especially intoxicated ones. Mahnaz Alimardanian (2014) argues that Burnt Woman is an amalgam of two previously distinct ghosts: an angelic figure who tempts young men (*gawunggan*) and an evil witch (*darargan*). This composite ghost can be understood as a reaction to the chaos that colonialism has wreaked on Banjalang life, including an increase in the relative power of women. Men are terrified of encountering Burnt Woman, while women tend to find the whole thing amusing.

Benjamin Smith's (2008) analysis of ghosts in Coen, a town in northern Queensland, stands out in the recent literature as explicitly hauntological. Ghosts are a constant presence. The recently deceased require management to "settle them" lest they commit malevolent acts on surviving kin. Once settled in their traditional lands, or more recently in town cemeteries, ghosts become spirits that linger in place but do not cause harm so long as they are treated with respect (such as greeting them when hunting or when driving past the cemetery). However, in recent years some Indigenous people have deliberately deferred mortuary rites to keep the ghosts of their dead relatives around. These families experience their ghosts as helpful domestic presences, protecting the living. Smith argues that to "keep the dead with us" and not "chase 'em away" is a move that usefully destabilizes the division among past, present, and future, allowing a temporal coexistence that helps to comprehend a confusing colonial present (96).

Providing a means to better comprehend a confusing colonial present seems a good description for many of the ghostly theories I have discussed in this chapter. Gordon, Gelder, and Jacobs all struggle to understand a harmful form of politics (for Gelder and Jacobs, settler colonialism; for Gordon, dictatorship and slavery). Ghosts function here to interrupt the usual way of proceeding and raise questions about what is being forgotten, erased, or disavowed. This resonates with philosopher Isabelle Stengers's proposal for a "cosmopolitics," an approach to politics that begins when something intervenes to "slow down reasoning and create an opportunity to arouse a slightly different awareness of the problems and situations mobilizing us" (2005, 994). Anthropologist Marisol de la Cadena explores this as a space of "pluriversal politics" that becomes available when more-than-human actors make their presence felt in the political sphere. She focuses on "earth-beings," sentient beings (such as mountains) with desire, needs, and the ability to act. For Indigenous people in the Andes, earth-beings are political actors: Western thought classifies them as religious, spiritual, or cultural *beliefs* and thus banishes them from the political sphere. Earth-beings and ghosts alike offer an opportunity to "slow down reasoning . . . and rather than asserting, adopt an intellectual attitude that proposes and thus creates possibilities for new interpretations" (2010, 336). Paying attention to earth-beings, witches, and all kinds of ghosts becomes not (just) a scintillating experience but a cosmopolitical strategy.

This survey of just some perspectives on haunting raises many questions. What is to be done about the presence of ghosts? Is haunting something that can or should be minimized or overcome, or is it a permanent condition? How can we distinguish between helpful and harmful ghosts?

Such questions can be focused on the two kinds of ghosts I have proposed are specific to Indigenous genomics: the ghosts of past racial science and the haunting possibility of Indigenous biological difference. Are the ghosts of past efforts to define Indigenous biological difference a helpful presence? Or should we aim to exorcise them? Can an Indigenous-led genomics escape these ghosts? And are there better and worse ways to be haunted?

The chapters that follow wrestle with these questions. For now, my modest proposals are (1) that there are ways to live and to make knowledge that are more, or less, vulnerable to haunting; and (2) that a certain attunement to haunting can help avoid repeating the worst mistakes of the past and make it more likely that the promises of twenty-first-century genomics will be fulfilled.

Digging Up My Ancestors

It is one thing to prepare for the ghosts who might appear to those who make biological knowledge about Indigenous people. It is another thing entirely to intentionally seek out haunting possibilities.

For contemporary anthropologists in Australia, the history of biological research on Indigenous people is something to be left well alone. This is reflected in Geoffrey Gray's history of Australian anthropology. He describes the maturation of the discipline in the first half of the twentieth century from a "concern with biology and physical anthropology (a remnant of nineteenth and early twentieth-century racial science)" to "social and cultural anthropology which focused on living peoples" (2007, 29). According to Gray, the Adelaide-based program of biological research that housed C. Stanton Hicks's physiological studies—referred to in his book as the "Adelaide scientists"—"represented a style of anthropology not readily compatible" (61) with the increasingly dominant social brand of anthropology.[11] The stories told in the chapters that follow would equally be considered incompatible with Australian anthropology's current vision of itself.

To be sure, sociocultural anthropology has much to be embarrassed about, not least our manifold complicity with colonialism (Asad 1973; Clifford and Marcus 1986; N. Thomas 1994; P. Wolfe 1999). But the biological aspects of anthropological research are considered at least a few degrees worse (Lindee and Santos 2012). An Australian iteration of this can be seen in the embrace of classical anthropological knowledge by prominent anthropologist Gillian Cowlishaw, a scholar widely known for her wonderful, excoriating books that critique older anthropological approaches (Cowlishaw 1988, 1999, 2004). In a late-career shift, she argues for the value of an "older anthropology" that sought to document the traditional culture of Aboriginal "tribes." She most prominently defends the genealogical method of Alfred C. Haddon (the subject of chapter 3), which began to unlock the secrets of kinship on his landmark 1898 Cambridge Anthropological Expedition to Torres Straits. Once a trenchant critic of her disciplinary forebears, Cowlishaw (2015) now argues it is wrong to condemn these texts for their outdated language when they offer invaluable lessons on topics such as "the genius of small-scale social organization, linguistic complexity and Indigenous ontologies."

Among others, she highlights the contribution of Norman B. Tindale, an anthropologist at the South Australian Museum until 1968 and the leader of many expeditions of the Board for Anthropological Research. Describing him as "infamous for his painstaking measurements of Aboriginal bodies," she points out that Tindale's extensive research demonstrating the ancestral territories of Aboriginal groups across the continent was important in establishing land rights. Crucially for my argument, Cowlishaw (2015) advocates for Tindale's social anthropology while condemning his "infamous" biological measurements. Kinship charts and descriptions of ceremonies are morally salvageable—as expressed in the title of her article, they must be seen as "friend" rather than "foe" if Aboriginal people are to be truly recognized—but biological knowledge is beyond the pale.

In refusing to clearly separate the "good" cultural and "bad" biological research of the past, this book risks incurring the wrath of some scholars. Even though only some of the scientists I explore in these chapters identified as anthropologists—others were comparative anatomists, human biologists, and physiologists—I see them all as disciplinary ancestors. My interest in exploring the nature and significance of "Indigenous biological difference" makes me an unusual anthropologist, and I do not expect all my anthropological colleagues to claim these disciplinary forebears. As my recent biological ancestors (my grandparents' generation) were all victims or survivors of the worst excesses of racial science, I arguably have the moral option of distancing myself from the twentieth-century dead white men who populate this book. But I choose not to. In my view, a serious engagement with those who made knowledge about Indigenous people in the past—recognizing the commitments we have in common as well as those that wildly differ—is necessary to provide useful accounts of how the history of biological difference matters in the present, and whether it can or should matter differently.

Hauntological Methodology

How to study ghosts? First, they must be recognized, and then responded to. To think through the different ways this might be done, I return once more to the haunted field that inspired these questions: twenty-first-century Indigenous genomics. As I have discussed in this chapter, there are two poles discernible in social science and humanities commentaries on the recent hopeful embrace of human biological research by some Indigenous people. Some scholars of race and indigeneity are wary of such efforts, which they argue inevitably reinforce genetic determinism of identity, disease, or both. They are suspicious of the motives of minority or Indigenous leaders (be they tribal elders, Indigenous scientists, or Indigenous politicians) who may be leading their constituents down the path to genomic dystopias of racism and dispossession and pandering to Big Pharma in the process (Kahn 2013; TallBear 2013). What I call "strategic biological essentialism"—Indigenous and minority groups biologizing or rebiologizing themselves by embracing genetic technologies that essentialize their differences—tends to be seen by these scholars as a dangerous move (Warin, Kowal, and Meloni 2020).[12]

Another line of scholarship sees bioethics and community participation as creating historical discontinuity with racial science. Those aligned with this view might believe that as long as we design ethical approaches that keep Nazi science, the Yanomami (an Indigenous group in Brazil I discuss in the next chapter), and Henrietta Lacks in mind, and make sure Indigenous people are meaningfully participating in science, we will be saved from repeating the past.[13] These scholars support Indigenous-led genome projects that seek to ensure their communities are not excluded from the benefits of genomic science, including precision medicine and the repatriation of unprovenanced human remains (Claw et al. 2018; Garrison et al. 2019; Hudson, Russell, et al. 2016; Kowal 2012b).

We can characterize these two poles in terms of their ghostliness. One set of responses seeks not to disturb the ghosts of the past: better to leave racialized biological difference well alone. Scholars writing from the opposite view consider that the ghosts of the past can and should be tamed—and, if possible, exorcised—for the promise of future benefits. Both approaches—leaving ghosts undisturbed and banishing them—have their merits, and at different times I have authored publications that take up each position. In this book, however, I explore an alternative way of interacting with the ghosts of racial science: living with them.

There are potential rewards for "keep[ing] the dead with us" and not "chas[ing] 'em away," as Smith (2008, 96) describes the relationship of the people of Coen with their ghosts. This is in part a task of response, in Donna Haraway's sense. Our ability to respond—our response-ability—to the myriad human and nonhuman entities we encounter is also our ability to recognize the threads that make up the values, objects, and practices we live with and to decide whether to untie the knots and attempt to retie them in more livable ways (Haraway 2008). There is no rulebook for what constitutes "better" ways of tying the knots of physiology, racial science, DNA sequencing, colonial violence, Indigenous self-determination, regimes of state recognition, scientific prestige, and much else that produce the material-semiotic figurations of Indigenous biological difference. This lack of any guarantee is a key part of what Haraway calls "staying with the trouble." Living in troubled times requires us to resist seeing the present as "a vanishing pivot point between awful or Edenic pasts and apocalyptic or salvific futures" and instead remain close to the present, "entwined in myriad unfinished configurations of places, times, matters, meaning" (Haraway 2016, 1). It is in this soup of figurations and beings of all kinds that cosmopolitical potentials emerge.

Staying close to the "myriad unfinished configurations" of the present seems aligned with the extraordinary work of Aboriginal filmmaker Warwick Thornton. Thornton (b. 1970) grew up in Alice Springs (Mparntwe in the local Arrernte language), a town of 25,000 people in the middle of the Australian desert. Twenty percent of the Alice Springs population is Indigenous, but the town is the service center for an additional 35,000 Indigenous people who are the residents of the remote communities of central Australia. The economy consists of government services, tourism, and the US spy base at Pine Gap. It is a place of stark contradictions, with cosmopolitan cafés and art dealers alongside camps of homeless Aboriginal people living in the creek bed, all in the shadow of the majestic MacDonnell ranges (Tjoritja in Arrernte) (Ottosson 2014). Many of Thornton's films are about Alice Springs and surrounding communities, most famously his debut, Palme d'Or–winning film *Samson and Delilah* (Thornton 2009).

Thornton's second feature film, *The Darkside*, explores the notion of embracing ghosts. A scene from the film opens the next chapter, but I will explain the genesis of the film here. The project began in 2012, when Thornton placed advertisements in print and social media calling for true Indigenous ghost stories, "the scarier the better." He was quickly inundated with over 150 stories, but their tone surprised him. "When I embarked on this journey to the other side, I imagined finding a whole bunch of scary as hell ghost stories," he explains, "but what I ended up finding was a beautiful collection of poignant stories about family and connection." The stories that flooded in were "not about being afraid, but embracing ghosts" (Transmission Films 2013). This approach to ghosts befits Thornton's upbringing in Alice Springs, a place he describes in supernatural terms: "It's full of angels and it's full of demons" (Thornton 2010). His world was, and is, saturated with ghosts: "Every time you walk in the bush past a tree or a rock, you just know that it's watching you, and it has a soul and it's one of your ancestors." He hoped the film "helps us to realize they are still around" (quoted in Redwood 2014, 87).

Coexisting with ghosts—even embracing them—is an ambivalent enterprise. It does not imply a wholehearted endorsement of their position, and an absent presence does not entirely determine the present it haunts. In exploring the idea of living with the ghosts of biological research, I don't mean to depict the contemporary sciences of Indigenous biological difference as zombie sciences, reanimated from the past and destined to inflict further racial injuries on Indigenous people. Equally, I don't *endorse* the precepts of biological hierarchy that animated earlier scientific eras—embracing as in *agreement*—but embracing in the sense of *holding close* the ghosts that are "still around" (cited in Redwood 2014, 87). Acknowledging our ghosts is often uncomfortable, but this is a productive discomfort that is necessary to make useful knowledge in a settler colony.

Outline of Chapters

In the stories I tell in this remainder of book, I adopt a broad interpretation of ghostliness. The narrative is bookended by two hauntings: Aboriginal writer Romaine Moreton's terrifying encounter with the ghost of comparative anatomist William Colin Mackenzie (chapter 2), and the ghostly presence of Baldwin Spencer's likeness in the Melbourne Museum (chapter 6). Moreton's confrontation leads to a reckoning with the grisly history of accumulating human remains from Aboriginal and Torres Strait Islander people in the name of science. I trace the story of the bones that still haunt the National Museum of Australia, and the frozen blood samples whose fate was surprisingly interconnected to the bones, both in the 1960s and today. While not strictly spectral, the ghost of Spencer described in chapter 6 is disembodied—made of plastic and paint—and mobile, even if a living human is required to push the trolley. Watching over the secret and sacred Aboriginal objects he collected in a dark room, he is seen by Aboriginal knowledge holders and non-indigenous curators alike as both creepy and strangely appropriate.

In between these two chapters, the ghosts inhabiting the text signal epistemological uncertainty in subtler ways. In chapter 3 the ghostly presence is a century-old length of hair clipped off at a remote railway station in Western Australia for the purposes of scientific study. In 2011 it became the poster child for the "first Aboriginal genome" to be sequenced, a research project endorsed by a group of Aboriginal people through a process that raises important questions about postcolonial genomics. Although the hair sample was materially sacrificed to science—chemically treated and pulverized to extract its scant and invaluable DNA—the sample's images haunt the media coverage, signaling the absence of the person the hair was once connected to.

The ghost of chapter 4 is the specter of colonial violence that haunts the Australian state. Settlers are inevitably positioned by history as violent perpetrators, a psychic position that many resist, repress, or displace. One strategy used to repress originary colonial violence and make the psychic life of the settler livable is to see Indigenous people as *really* white. This whiteness itself has been ghostly: enigmatic and fleeting. This chapter traces the "archaic Caucasian" theory, a dominant scientific belief from the nineteenth to the mid-twentieth century that Indigenous Australians and Europeans were part of the same racial family. The brutal story of colonization could thus be retold as a family reunion of distant cousins. Isolated cases of white (in fact, albino) Aboriginal people haunted the public imagination and supported—both scientifically and politically—efforts to biologically absorb and socially assimilate Indigenous people into the majority-European population, most infamously through the mass child removal now known as the Stolen Generations. The past few decades have seen these efforts fail to achieve their aim of disappearing Indigenous identity from Australia. Instead, tens of thousands of Australians who would be judged by the architects of assimilation as wholly white have newly embraced their Indigenous heritage and identity, sometimes aided by DNA testing. The ghostly presence of whiteness has shape-shifted into the persistence of Indigeneity in an increasingly diverse Indigenous polity. The failure of Indigenous people to follow the eliminatory script and conveniently disappear reflects and produces an intricate play of identification and disavowal.

In chapter 5 the source of haunting is twofold. The first is the mysterious interlocutor I briefly described in the introduction who claimed to be a bio-mimicry researcher developing the human capability for temporary hibernation. He contacted me to express his concern that a unique biological capacity possessed by Aboriginal people of the central desert was being exploited by international defense interests. The twin ghostly presences in this chapter are, first, the man I knew only as DT and, second, the remarkable ability of Aboriginal men to reduce their basal metabolism that physiologist Hicks believed he observed one morning in 1931 (as described in the opening passage of this book). In spectacular fashion, the potential physiological superpower contained within the bodies and genomes of Indigenous desert men is the subject of wild speculation and a possible cover-up.

In the final chapter, the ghostly object is a museum prop designed to critique Baldwin Spencer, the ur-collector of late nineteenth- and early twentieth-century Australia. The objects he collected were the basis of Museums Victoria's original collection and include thousands of secret-sacred objects from northern and central Aboriginal communities. In a postcolonial turn in museology, a likeness was created of Spencer from paint and plastic in 2000 and placed in a glass case. After a decade or so, a decolonial turn in Indigenous curation saw Spencer's double banished to the museum store rooms, where he had a surprising second life. My account of the career of this troubling object offers a haunting critique of decolonial approaches to science that see the past as something that can be left behind. In the conclusion I return to the question of how best to study ghosts and why it is ever more pressing to learn to live with the haunting presences around us.

Blood, Bones, and the Ghosts of the Ancestors

One night in the winter of 2009, the ghost of a dead anatomist visited an Aboriginal poet and sliced through her body with a scalpel.

At the time of the phantom assault, Romaine Moreton, a filmmaker and academic, had begun a three-month Indigenous research fellowship at the National Film and Sound Archive (NFSA) in Canberra, Australia's capital city. The NFSA has housed the national audiovisual collection since its establishment in the mid-1980s. Among the two-million-plus objects it holds, 25,000 make up the Indigenous collection, including rare ethnographic films documenting secret and sacred ceremonies (National Film and Sound Archive, n.d.). The archive is housed in a grand building constructed in 1930, an early example of Stripped Classical, with embellishments depicting Australian marsupials.[1] "Australian Institute of Anatomy" is inscribed above the soaring stone

FIGURE 2.1. Conference delegates in front of the Australian Institute of Anatomy, Canberra, 1933. *Source:* National Archives of Australia (http://guides.naa.gov.au /records-about-act/gallery/image015.aspx).

columns framing the entrance (figure 2.1). The institute was built to house the collection of Sir William Colin Mackenzie, an Australian orthopedic surgeon and comparative anatomist who appeared in Romaine Moreton's bedroom seven decades after his death.

The story of her haunting came to light in a 2013 movie by acclaimed Aboriginal director Warwick Thornton. *The Darkside* is composed of twelve "true" Indigenous ghost stories collected as audio interviews and evocatively retold on-screen with prominent Australian actors. Aboriginal people told of hearing dead relatives crying in the night, and of seeing a protective spirit that led them to rescue a young boy. White people told of nocturnal encounters with the silent ghosts of a massacred Indigenous tribe, and of glimpsing a mission girl in a 1960s dress deep in uninhabited wilderness.

Romaine Moreton's story is the only one in the film where the ghost is white. Her story is told differently from the others: instead of an actor narrating it on-screen, we hear Moreton's voice overlaying black-and-white images of the institute basement and film clips from Board for Anthropological Research expeditions of the 1930s.[2] In the archival footage, white male scientists

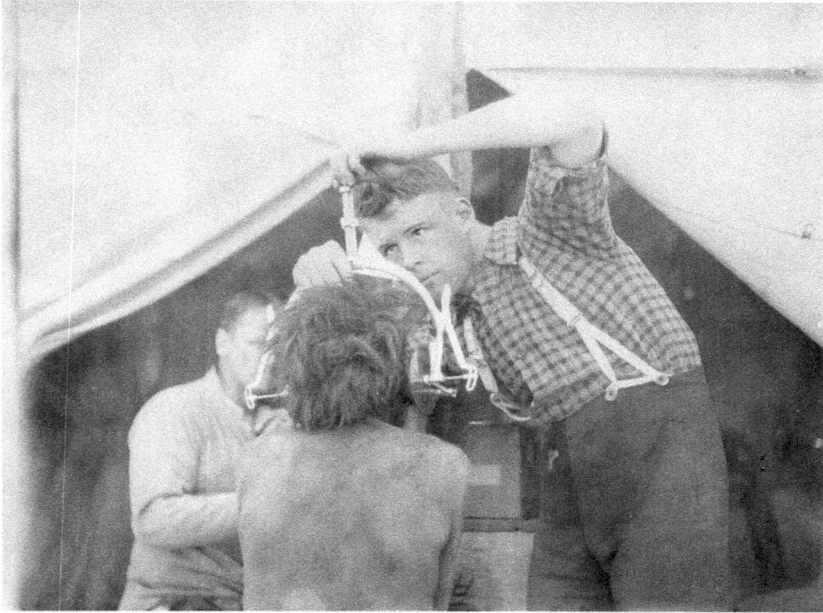

FIGURE 2.2. James Hugo Gray (1909–41), medical student and physical anthropologist to the expedition, measuring the head of an unknown Aboriginal man on a Board for Anthropological Research expedition, Cockatoo Creek, 1931. *Source:* South Australian Museum.

busily measure heads and adjust naked bodies for the best photographic angle (figure 2.2).

Moreton's narration tells of her time at the NFSA. Her plans to investigate the implications of Indigenous cultural and intellectual property for ethnographic film began to change when she discovered the building's former life and learned of the human skeletons that formed a key part of Mackenzie's collection. Most were Aboriginal bones stolen from grave sites in southeastern Australia in the 1930s and 1940s. As she discovered, many were unrepatriated, stranded in the National Museum of Australia's storage facility, ten kilometers to the north. Their uncertain provenance continues to preclude their return to their communities of origin.

Mackenzie became a focus of her thoughts as someone "who I realized would have been involved in and oversaw the anatomical dissection of Aboriginal people as specimens, as scientific specimens." As she moved through the building, she felt she was being "watched . . . studied, almost" by Mackenzie's "energy" and by mounted bronze casts of the heads of George Britton

FIGURE 2.3. Bronze face cast of Charles Darwin at the National Film and Sound Archive, Canberra, 2016. Photo by the author.

Halford, Charles Darwin, and Jean-Baptiste Lamarck that protruded from the walls (figure 2.3).[3]

At night, she slept next door to the institute, in Mackenzie's former private residence. She acutely felt his presence in the house and was "terrified to go to sleep" each night. After four weeks of increasing emotional intensity, he appeared:

> I was dozing in and out of sleep. I saw this man walking towards me. And he just got closer and closer, totally in silhouette, and he walked into my room. And in his right hand he was carrying a scalpel. And he raised his hand and he sliced the scalpel through my body. And I remember the pain of feeling the scalpel passing through my body. And I woke up. It was such a violent swing of the scalpel that made me wake up. I jolted awake. From that moment on, my research that I was originally there to do changed. I was now more and more interested in what happened to the remains of our people.

Being jarred awake by Mackenzie's scalpel drove Moreton's research down a different path, away from matters of property and toward "the rights of the dead undead, the still living spirits of our people who are yet to be treated right." By her account, the ghost compelled her to pay attention to the absent presence of spirits contained within displaced Indigenous body parts (Kowal, Radin, and Reardon 2013). This chapter considers Moreton's haunting not as a freak event but as an allegory of scientific research in a settler colony. In the wake of colonial devastation, to make biological knowledge about Indigenous people is to live with ghosts.

Below I first explore how aspects of twentieth-century scientific collection and the bodily fragments it left behind might be thought of as variously haunted. I then relate an interwoven story of the collection, storage, and use of bones and blood, beginning with William Colin Mackenzie, the inveterate collector of Australian fauna (a category that included Indigenous remains), then turning from his Institute of Anatomy to another key Canberra institute, the Australian Institute of Aboriginal Studies (AIAS), founded in 1961 and encapsulating a midcentury epistemology of collection. The Human Biology Advisory Committee was one of four committees of the AIAS, and many of the scientists discussed in this book were among its members. While initially this committee was something of a sequel to Mackenzie's earlier mode of collecting, things changed dramatically from the late 1960s, when the institute began to involve a new generation of Aboriginal leaders who shifted its guiding principle of *scientific knowledge* toward *Aboriginal benefit*. Grappling with this new political terrain, the Human Biology Advisory Committee took a progressive stance on bones. It was instrumental in reforming the Institute of Anatomy's most racially offensive exhibits and played a crucial role in the repatriation of Truganini, an Aboriginal Tasmanian woman internationally famous for being the "last of her race" to die, in 1876, and returned a century later to the Tasmanian Aboriginal community for reburial.

These stories highlight the contrasting fates of bones and blood. While battles over human remains held within and outside Australia have raged on through the decades, blood samples collected from Indigenous communities lie quietly in frozen storage. Many of these blood samples are now part of a third Canberra institute that I was closely involved with establishing, the National Centre for Indigenous Genomics (NCIG). These samples are being resurrected to found twenty-first-century approaches to Indigenous-led genomics and could also hold the key to repatriating the bones Mackenzie collected. But will the ghosts of Indigenous biological difference be finally buried along with the bones, or will they live on in the freezer?

MY USE OF "HAUNTING" here extends the discussion in the previous chapter of Jacques Derrida's (1994) hauntology and Avery Gordon's *Ghostly Matters* (2008). Hauntology encapsulates Derrida's critique of dominant modes of Western temporality and ontology. These are disrupted by the ghost, who is neither present nor absent, neither alive nor dead, and whose appearance is both a return from the past and an event in the present. Gordon uses haunting in a more historical mode to explore the ongoing effects of past injustices. Haunting expresses the action of the past in the present, a traumatic apparition that demands a response.[4] The persistence of blood, bones, and other Indigenous bodily substances displaced for scientific purposes provides fertile ground for ghosts.

Another focal theory in this chapter is geographer and sociologist Kevin Hetherington's analysis of haunting and disposal. Hetherington draws on sociologist Robert Hertz's (1960) analysis of two-stage burial, observed in many cultures, to theorize how disposal reproduces social relations through the management of absence.[5] For a first burial, a corpse is taken to a temporary shelter, buried in a grave, or cremated to dispose of the fleshy body. After some time, a literal or representational second burial involves placing bones in a final resting place, consecrating a grave, or scattering ashes in a meaningful place. The second burial allows the social ending of the person through ritual. In the time between the first and second burial, the soul prepares for its final departure, and surviving relatives and friends come to terms with the absence of the person.

Hetherington (2004, 169) argues that notions of first and second burial can also apply to inanimate objects, illustrated by Japanese traditions of conducting mortuary rites and building shrines for worn-out sewing needles or expired computer motherboards. Sites of first burial in this case can be household trash cans or a drawer into which objects are discarded but from which they are still retrievable until a later stage (for example, when the trash is put out for collection or when the drawer is cleaned out). In the time between first and second burial, the owner can contemplate the *value* of the item and come to terms with its impending absence.

When the process of disposal is disrupted, persons and objects become ghostly. To quote Hetherington, when "the act of second burial has failed, been hurried, or has not been carried out to its full effect," the "unfinished or unmanaged disposal is the ghost and its agency is expressed in the idea of haunting" (170). What should be absent is found to be present and haunts us.

What might this analysis mean for human biological materials collected by scientists to produce knowledge about Indigenous people? It is reasonably straightforward to apply this framework to human remains stolen from burial sites in the name of science. Collected bones were and are Indigenous people's relatives and ancestors.[6] By definition, their collection and storage are an interruption of first or second burial, and it is no surprise that they may haunt.

This story, as it unfolds across the twentieth and twenty-first centuries, concerns the collection of blood as well as bones. The science of serology emerged from blood group research in the early twentieth century (Bangham 2014; Schneider 1995, 1996). By midcentury the analysis of blood proteins had shifted the focus of many physical anthropologists from bones to blood, paving the way for disciplines including human biology, biological anthropology, and population genetics (W. Anderson 2002; Lindee and Santos 2012; Radin 2014b; Silverman 2000; Smocovitis 2012). However, as I will relate, in Australia the golden age of these blood-based disciplines that began in the 1950s was suspended by the wave of Indigenous political activism that broke in the early 1970s. This brought biological research on Indigenous people into disrepute, and these disciplines virtually disappeared from Australia in the following decade.

While it is clear that stolen bones may haunt, estimating the ghostliness of blood and other substances collected from the living for scientific study is less straightforward. Body parts removed from living bodies are often considered waste within Western legal frameworks, particularly those that regenerate or are shed, such as blood, urine, hair, or saliva.[7] Neither bodies nor their parts can be owned, but bodily substances removed from bodies for clinical or research purposes are owned by the institution overseeing their collection (see Rabinow 1996; Waldby and Mitchell 2006). Thus, blood samples and other body parts inhabit a liminal ontological space but are arguably more like inanimate objects than animate subjects within dominant Western culture.

The question of how diverse Indigenous people and peoples conceptualize the body and its parts further complicates a messy Western legal and moral landscape. While Indigenous people's varying ontologies of bones and significant cultural objects are reasonably well documented, largely as a side effect of the repatriation movement (Fforde 2004; Fine-Dare 2002; Kakaliouras 2012), beliefs about blood samples are less clear. One obstacle to understanding Indigenous beliefs about blood samples is their level of abstraction. Bones removed from the ground and placed in a museum change their location but not their form; circulating blood removed from the body with a syringe and stored in a glass or plastic vial is a different matter.

Indigenous Australian views on blood vary across the continent and across time, but the classical anthropological literature offers some clues to general trends. Within the cosmology of groups across northern and central Australia, blood is inseparable from land, personhood, and spirit. The complex and fluid relationships between these entities are enacted and acted on through the incorporation and shedding of blood. Blood is a source of abiding power with the ability to influence actions and emotions, to weaken and to heal the body, and to transform and commute energy through the body, the landscape, and the spiritual world. The use of blood in a range of traditional ceremonies demonstrates the importance of blood to the cosmological structure of traditional belief systems. These include circumcision and initiation ceremonies, usually performed on pubertal boys; "increase" ceremonies, which maintain the supply of edible plants and animals; and totemic rituals, in which blood is used symbolically and literally to transfer energy. Healing techniques and sorcery manipulate illnesses using blood, and menstrual blood is seen as both powerful and dangerous to lives, land, and spirits (Kowal, Greenwood, and McWhirter 2015).

Translating these beliefs to blood samples taken for clinical or research purposes is not straightforward. Jeannie Devitt and Anthony McMasters's (1998a, 1998b) research on the experiences of kidney dialysis patients in Central Australia in the 1990s provides some guidance. They noted that many Aboriginal patients continued to rely on customary belief as a framework for understanding the process of dialysis, which filtered their blood through a machine for many hours each week. Body and spirit were bound together physically and metaphysically, with blood a key mechanism of this melding. At the same time, the study illustrated how traditional understandings of blood were changed by the introduction of blood transfusions, dialysis, medication, and surgery. Devitt and McMasters argued that the traditional belief that the loss of blood can weaken a person or make them vulnerable to sorcery did not apply to biomedical blood donation. Anthony Rex Peile similarly noted in the 1970s that providing a blood specimen in a clinic was often objected to by Indigenous patients until they realized that only a small quantity would be taken (Wiminydji and Peile 1978). These sources suggest that removal of blood in biomedical contexts is likely to be tolerated.

Outside Australia, Indigenous peoples have expressed concerns about the retention and storage of blood samples for research purposes (Beaton et al. 2015; Hudson, Southey, et al. 2016; Mello and Wolf 2010; Sahota 2014; Tauali'i et al. 2014). In some cases, this has led to Indigenous groups seeking the return of blood samples, including the Nuu-chah-nulth of the Canadian West Coast (Wiwchar 2004), the Havasupai of Arizona (Mello and Wolf 2010), and the Yanomami of Brazil and Venezuela (Couzin-Frankel 2010b).

The case of the Yanomami is perhaps the most famous of these examples (figure 2.4). Blood samples collected in Brazil in the 1960s and 1970s were stored at various laboratories in the United States. When allegations of unethical practices by the researchers involved arose some decades later, the Yanomami demanded the return of the samples on cultural grounds (Borofsky 2005; Couzin-Frankel 2010b; Tierney 2001). The Yanomami and their advocates argued that according to their cultural belief system, the retention of frozen blood samples prevented their deceased donors from successfully departing the world. It was therefore necessary for shamans and elders to ritually destroy the samples to ensure the separation between the worlds of the living and the dead (nadjamarin22 2007; Survival for Tribal Peoples 2010).

For at least some of the Yanomami, blood samples were persons. Whether Indigenous people, individually or collectively, consider blood samples to be subjects, objects, or something in between has implications for interpreting their disposal in Hetherington's terms. For a sample-as-subject, the delay between the first and second burial would be a time for the soul to come to terms with its relocation and the bereaved to come to terms with the loss of the subject. For a sample-as-object, it would be a time for the owner to mull over the value of the object and weigh the loss of disposal. Either way, a failed second burial may lead to haunting.

FIGURE 2.4. Davi Kopenawa and other Yanomami burying blood samples in a funerary ceremony, 2015. *Source:* Estevão Benfica Senra and Instituto Socioambiental.

WILLIAM COLIN MACKENZIE WAS a gifted doctor and anatomist born in country Victoria to Scottish immigrants in 1877 (figure 2.5). Excelling at school, he gained a scholarship to Melbourne's exclusive Scotch College before studying medicine (MacCallum [1986] 2006). He came of age amid devastating polio epidemics and fears that Australia's unique fauna was on a path to extinction. As a major polio outbreak hit Australia in 1903, Mackenzie left for Europe, where he trained in advanced orthopedic methods. On his return, he applied his new knowledge to polio victims while developing his parallel interest in the anatomy of Australian marsupials and monotremes (the most famous being the platypus). His innovative synthesis of muscle therapy in polio was inspired by his dissection of koala shoulders (Mackenzie 1910; see also Robin 2003).[8]

Over the years, an increasing proportion of his St. Kilda Road surgery was given over to his expanding specimen collection. By the early 1920s, serious interest from collectors in the United States prompted the Australian government to establish the Australian Institute of Anatomy with Mackenzie as its first director.[9] The minister for home and territories welcomed Mackenzie's donation of his collection to the state as an act of "practical patriotism . . . at a time when our native fauna is rapidly becoming extinct" (quoted in Robin

FIGURE 2.5. William Colin Mackenzie, ca. 1930s. *Source:* National Museum of Australia.

2003, 253).[10] When the new building was finally completed under Mackenzie's close supervision in 1930 (see figure 2.1), it loomed large in a city that existed primarily in architectural plans, waiting for better economic times.

In the first few decades of the institute's life, it was one of only two Canberra institutions open to the public, the other being the Australian War Memorial. When the institute first opened, it would have been an imposing presence in the landscape. By that time, the collection it housed included human specimens, principally Aboriginal, among the marsupials and monotremes.[11] Most were acquired under Mackenzie's supervision in the 1930s and 1940s by George Murray Black, an engineer, farmer, and collector (Daley 2014; T. Griffiths 1996, 81).[12] Black was an expert in finding graves and digging them up, amassing 1,600 skeletons. The skeletons, along with thousands of ethnographic objects, were stored in the institute's two basements, with a selection displayed in the museum galleries.

Collectors expect their collections to outlive them and fear for their fate (Couzin-Frankel 2010a; see also W. Anderson 2000, 2008, 2015; Radin 2014a). Mackenzie's collecting was cut short by illness only seven years after the institute opened. He retreated to Melbourne and died of a cerebral hemorrhage the following year. In the years after he left, the Department of Health dissolved the director position at the institute and colonized the building, transforming storage rooms into offices and cramming the collection into an ever more crowded basement. While Mackenzie could not control the fate of the institute, he was able to maintain a presence. Before departing this world, he asked that his ashes be stored behind a memorial plaque in the main hall of the institute. His request was fulfilled. Although he was nearly removed when the institute was dissolved and the building handed to the National Film and Sound Archive in 1984, he still remains there (Dorning 1972; Truswell, Darnton-Hill, and Wood 2007). The plaque is displayed in the foyer, directly below Darwin's bronze head (figure 2.6). Mackenzie's epitaph, borrowed from the tomb of seventeenth-century polymath Christopher Wren, only underscores a desire to endure beyond the grave. *Si monumentum requiris circumspice*: If you seek his monument, look around you.

Mackenzie's immediate legacy was the hugely popular exhibits of the Institute of Anatomy, an obligatory passage point for the capital's growing cohort of schoolchildren.[13] The institute's best-known exhibits were the giant heart of our most famous racehorse (Phar Lap) and the skull of our most famous bushranger (Ned Kelly). Although Mackenzie never published research on the human remains stored in his institute, Aboriginal themes were prominent in the public exhibits. Alongside displays on Aboriginal food collection, hunting,

FIGURE 2.6. Memorial plaque for William Colin Mackenzie in the foyer of the National Film and Sound Archive, Canberra, 2016. Photo by the author.

and shelters, one concerned the evolution of human races. A set of four skulls were labeled, from left to right: "male gorilla," "female gorilla," "Australian Aborigine," and "Modern European Englishman." A handwritten interpretive note was included: "It is not suggested that the Modern European is a direct descendent of the gorilla and Australian Aborigine but these skulls are used to emphasize the lines along which the refinements of the modern skull evolved" (quoted in E. Moran 1972). Those who bothered to punctuate their visual sweep of the institute's many bones and organs to peer at the glass case of four skulls likely interpreted the exhibit as reflecting scientific truth, whether a point of interest or a site of passive ideological osmosis. This skeletal display of racial and species hierarchies became a site where the political and cultural shifts of the 1970s played out.

The first public record of concern about this exhibit (or any exhibit at the institute) is from 1972, when "an overseas visitor" staying in Sydney penned a letter to the *Canberra Times* complaining that "the way an exhibit of skulls and diagrams was arranged in order to demonstrate white racial superiority was nothing short of disgraceful in what purports to be a scientific establishment" (E. Moran 1972).[14] Three years after this first public critique, the exhibit came to the attention of the Human Biology Advisory Committee of the AIAS, a critical institution in the development and consolidation of the varying disciplines that made up the new field of Aboriginal studies.

The AIAS originated in the late 1950s when Bill Wentworth, a charismatic conservative politician, made public pleas for funding to record and preserve the languages and cultures of "Aboriginal tribes." While Wentworth was keenly interested in Aboriginal welfare (and later was the first minister for Aboriginal affairs), he envisaged the AIAS as a purely academic endeavor. He shared the cultural evolutionist view that the rapidly disappearing social organization and customs of Aboriginal people offered a unique window onto Europe's past (Lambert 2011, 30–38).

Rebadged as a new discipline—Aboriginal studies—and supported by generous funding, the AIAS research agenda nonetheless followed the classic four fields of anthropological inquiry: linguistics, cultural anthropology, prehistory (later rebadged as archaeology), and physical anthropology, also known as human biology. Of the four founding committees of the AIAS, the Human Biology Advisory Committee is of particular relevance to this story (Lambert 2011). First formed in 1962, the original members were N. W. G. "Black Mac" Macintosh, professor of anatomy at the University of Sydney; University of Adelaide professors of anatomy, genetics, and dentistry A. A. Abbie (discussed in chapter 4), J. H. Bennett (protégé of the great twentieth-century geneticist R. A. Fisher), and Thomas Draper Campbell, respectively; Roy Simmons from Commonwealth Serum Laboratories (also discussed in chapter 4); and R. L. Kirk, geneticist at the John Curtin School of Medical Research at the Australian National University. Abbie was the inaugural convener.

The committee was formed at a time when the "new synthesis" of physical anthropology that emerged in the wake of World War II was being embraced by the most prominent human biologists internationally (Kirk 1985; Washburn 1951). Discarding the discrete racial categories of an older notion of human difference, discredited above all by Nazi science, leading human biologists sought to unlock the secrets of microevolution and the history of human migration across the globe. As I discuss in chapter 4, the rise of serology, represented on the committee by Kirk, Simmons, and Bennett, was a major shift in the sciences of human origins. In comparison with the methods of physical anthropology, many saw the development of blood group testing in the early twentieth century as a far more scientific and objective measure of biological differences between population groups (analogous to the impact of ancient DNA science in the early twenty-first century, as I relate below), although the complexity of blood groups soon tempered this enthusiasm (Marks 1996).

Midcentury advances in mobile refrigeration and laboratory methods brought exciting possibilities to serology.[15] The ability to freeze cells so that they could be thawed intact was developed in 1949, when it was discovered that adding glycerol prevented irreparable cell damage (Landecker 2005, 2007; Parry 2004; Radin 2017). By the 1960s mechanical laboratory freezers and techniques for mobile cold storage using dry ice facilitated the accumulation of blood samples from remote places. Researchers traveled the world collecting samples that were transported to the laboratory for analysis and storage.

In human biology an important boost to this global effort came with the International Biological Program (IBP) (Radin 2017). The IBP was an international effort to take stock of the biosphere. Its Human Adaptability (HA) section was one of seven and the only one concerned with humans. Running from 1964 to 1974, the IBP-HA coordinated the efforts of human biologists to collect hundreds of thousands, if not millions, of blood samples from people in dozens of countries. The IBP-HA sought to place the study of humans in the context of the biosphere, enabling global science to ensure "the future of man in his environment" (Worthington 1975, 52). This was seen as an urgent task in the face of great changes heralded by industrialism and the transformation of "traditional" lifestyles of Indigenous peoples. The IBP-HA organizers felt their studies had "enduring value" through providing "important base-line and reference data" with which to measure the effects of cultural, social, demographic, and technological change (Collins and Weiner 1977, 21). Obtaining these baseline data required the creation of a massive global archive of human biological variation. As of 1974, eight hundred field visits had taken place under the auspices of the IBP, with over 1.25 million individuals measured and/ or sampled (1977, 14).

Of special interest to the human biologists involved with this comparative project were "simple societies still living under difficult 'natural' conditions." Groups now known as Indigenous "would provide object lessons of the actual adaptability achievable by man when relying largely on his biological endowment" (Collins and Weiner 1977, 3). Europeans, by contrast, were considered to have altered their surroundings to the point that their bodies were out of sync.

Australia contributed eight projects to the IBP-HA, of which two concerned Indigenous Australians. Their tens of thousands of years of isolation promised, and delivered, many novel protein types. The rarest blood group in existence—the complete absence of Rhesus antigens—was discovered in a woman from northern Western Australia, and the Australian antigen, now known to be a surface antigen of hepatitis B, was first identified in the blood of a man from central Australia (Vos et al. 1961; Blumberg 1976; Bootcov 2024). Scientists believed there was a critical time interval in which to gather such invaluable knowledge before Indigenous groups ceased to live as hunter-gatherers. Store-bought food and other European innovations would change the physiology of such "simple societies" forever, leaving open only a small window of scientific opportunity to collect vital biological and genetic information (Collins and Weiner 1977, 4). Those involved with the salvage projects of the IBP-HA sought to preserve this biological knowledge, and the actual bodily material from which it was derived, before it was too late.

The main Australian contributor to the IBP was Englishman R. L. "Bob" Kirk. He had been born in the Midlands, the youngest of three boys in a lower-middle-class family. He was educated at local boarding schools, mixing with communist-leaning friends, before studying chemistry at university. His politics led him to register as a conscientious objector in 1939, even though he was already exempt from service as a science undergraduate. This decision led to an invitation from the brilliant and radical biologist Lancelot Hogben to complete graduate studies in zoology at Birmingham University. In Birmingham Kirk met his future wife, Mildred, who was completing honors in zoology (Kirk, n.d.).

After a stint teaching in a small college in New York State, where he and Mildred were troubled by the prejudice they witnessed against African Americans, Kirk was recruited to the University of Western Australia in the early 1950s. Originally focused on nonhuman evolution, principally flies and snails, his interest in human biology began in the years after he settled in Perth. He soon realized the Aboriginal population residing in the enormous state of Western Australia offered a unique opportunity for the study of "primitive" man, and he began to organize collective trips to the north of the state (figure 2.7). Initially in collaboration with Perth hospital serologist Gerard Vos, Kirk began to analyze the novel proteins and blood types in remote Indigenous people using the new method of starch gel electrophoresis (Kirk 1966; Vos and Kirk 1962; Vos, Kirk, and Steinberg 1963). His sample collection accompanied him to the Australian National University in Canberra in 1967, where he moved after a two-year stint in Geneva with the World Health Organization (figure 2.8). He rapidly expanded his collection over the next decade as his large network of medical staff and research collaborators sought to promote his cutting-edge research by sending him blood. Kirk was perfectly positioned to contribute to the IBP, coordinating the collection of samples from Indigenous communities across Western Australia, the Northern Territory, and Queensland. Quiet and reserved, he was widely respected in serology and genetics internationally

FIGURE 2.7. Robert Kirk and an unknown man at Pineapple Bore, between Fitzroy Crossing and Hall's Creek, Western Australia, 1961. *Source:* Australian National University.

but overlooked for promotion by his own university. He was recruited to the Human Biology Advisory Committee of the AIAS and later became its chair.

The Human Biology Advisory Committee got off to a slow start, mainly funding small projects of its own members. Although Kirk received £183 in 1963 to collect blood samples in the Kimberley region and analyze the distribution of serum protein groups, A. A. Abbie (1965), inaugural chair of the committee, lamented that little had been spent up to that point because human biology was a small field compared to social anthropology, and many scientists already held external funding for their projects when the committee was established. Abbie could report on more activity in 1965, including his own physical anthropology survey of 1,200 Aboriginal people "from South Australia to Arnhem Land," which yielded "important material on skinfold thickness and on spectrophotometric findings [measurements of skin color]." There was also a comparative anatomy study of Ainu and Aboriginal people by a Japanese physical anthropologist Bin Yamaguchi, senior curator of the Department of Anthropology at the National Science Museum of Japan (now known as the National Museum of Nature and Science). He was primarily known for his research into the two supposed ancestral populations of modern Japanese, the "Indigenous" Jomon and the Yayoi immigrants who arrived from China and

FIGURE 2.8. Robert Kirk and Margorie Coggan examine serum protein differences used in tracing population affinities in the Pacific, Australian National University, Canberra, 1977. Photographer: Mike Finn. *Source:* Australian National University.

Korea around two thousand years ago. In Australia, Yamaguchi toured Australian bone collections, including the Institute of Anatomy, and collected hair samples in Kalgoorlie (close to the site of an earlier hair collection, discussed in the next chapter) (Yamaguchi 1967).[16]

Bryan Gandevia, a respiratory physician from the University of New South Wales, was also funded to measure lung capacity and survey respiratory diseases in the Central Australian community of Papunya (Gandevia 1967).[17] A further study was by psychiatrist John Cawte on ethnopsychiatry, language, behavior, and personality in another Central Australian community, Yuendemu. Cawte's lifelong interest in Aboriginal culture began during his childhood in rural South Australia, when he would visit Aboriginal camps of Pitjantjatjara people and fish with them. His research in Yuendemu inaugurated a remarkable research career in Aboriginal mental health and traditional healing practices in a range of communities, most of all the Warramirri clan of the Yolngu people, based in Galiwin'ku in northeast Arnhem Land (Cawte 1974, 1993, 1996).[18]

The final Human Biology project Abbie could report on was led by Cecil Cook, a doctor and health bureaucrat best known as chief medical officer and Chief Protector of Aborigines in the Northern Territory from 1927 (when he was only twenty-nine) until World War II. He coined the phrase "breeding out the colour" and is infamous today as a key architect of what became known as the Stolen Generations (Austin 1990). Retired and pushing seventy when the AIAS funded him in 1965, he completed a review of Aboriginal medical records, "which contain valuable data on physical characteristics, physiology, pathology and post-mortem findings" (Australian Institute of Aboriginal Studies 1965, 2–3; Cook 1970).

In this snapshot of the Human Biology Advisory Committee research program in the mid-1960s, we see a mix of old and new paradigms and players. Abbie's research was based on early twentieth-century racial paradigms (despite his use of newer physical anthropological tools to measure body composition and skin color), as was the comparison of Ainu and Aboriginal bones using Mackenzie's specimens. Gandevia's lung study was more contemporary, encompassing respiratory physiology and bacteriology, but Aboriginal research was only of fleeting interest to him. By contrast, Cawte dedicated his career to Indigenous people, advocating for traditional healing and an appreciation of Indigenous cosmologies. The final scientist of this inadvertent cohort, Cecil Cook, was strongly associated with older racial paradigms, but his AIAS research was an early example of epidemiology that aimed to improve the health of Aboriginal people rather than diagnose their racial origins. Despite this mixed bag of methodologies, it's unlikely Abbie would have predicted a major shift in the wings, one that would see an end to his style of physical anthropology and pose a major challenge to the legacies of Mackenzie's collecting.

ONLY A FEW YEARS after the AIAS was formed, the political landscape dramatically changed. Beginning in the late 1960s, the new generation of Indigenous people began to populate AIAS committees, a phenomenon that greatly accelerated when archaeologist Peter Ucko was appointed as principal of the AIAS in 1972.[19] The influence of this group of Aboriginal activists relates to the growing Indigenous critique of Western research, discussed in the previous chapter. Some of its major theorists developed their critiques while on AIAS committees (Lambert 2011, 90).

Of the many Indigenous leaders who came through the AIAS, Professor Marcia Langton is the most prominent in public life today. Langton had a transient upbringing with her mother in rural Queensland, including a period in an orphanage, before becoming more settled in her high school years and attending the University of Queensland in 1969. She left her studies to travel in Asia for some years, returning to various activist roles in Sydney before attending the Australian National University, where she completed honors in anthropology in 1984. It was during her time as a student in Canberra that she was invited to be the social issues adviser of the AIAS Social Anthropology Advisory Committee. She used her position to argue for better recognition for what we would now call Indigenous co-researchers, who were then labeled the "informants" of white anthropologists. The result was a change in official AIAS language from "informants" to "helpers" and eventually to "collaborators" and "consultants" (Lambert 2011, 199). This change was indicative of wider shifts at the institute, as I discuss below.

After completing her honors degree, Langton worked on land rights claims in Queensland and the Northern Territory while maintaining her AIAS commitments. She came to wider public attention through her work on the Royal Commission into Aboriginal Deaths in Custody in the 1980s and through her key role in negotiating the terms of the Native Title Act (1993), a piece of legislation that gave many Indigenous groups around the country access to a limited but significant form of land rights (Bartlett 2020).[20] Langton became the first female council chair of the institute, newly named the Australian Institute of Aboriginal and Torres Strait Islander Studies (AIATSIS), in 1992. She later moved into academia and since 2000 has been the foundation chair of Australian Indigenous studies at the University of Melbourne. Although she has attracted controversy at times, particularly for her views regarding the potential benefits of resource extraction for Indigenous people (Neale and Vincent 2016), she remains the leading Indigenous academic in Australia.

Langton was part of a group of Indigenous activists, including Gloria Brennan, Colin Bourke, Michael Mace, Steven Albert, and Michael Williams, whose voluntary AIAS work in the 1970s and 1980s effectively shifted the principle orienting the institute's research from *scientific knowledge* to *Aboriginal benefit*. The incremental but definite changes in AIAS priorities had uneven effects on the four fields on which the institute was founded. Linguistics and social anthropology survived the recalibration reasonably well. While the power relations between Indigenous knowledge holders and white "experts" were irrevocably changed, the utility of those disciplines themselves was clear to many Indigenous people who were, at that time, keen to have their languages and cultural knowledges preserved and recognized. It was a different story for the human biology and prehistory committees. As Peter Ucko frankly put it, "By 1974 [physical] anthropologists and archaeologists in universities had begun to run for cover" (1983, 15). The rise of the twin movements of Aboriginal heritage and repatriation made archaeological research sites and materials increasingly difficult to access (Lewin 1984). Archaeologists had to develop skills in consultation and ongoing negotiation with Indigenous traditional owners who, in some cases, had conflicting views about the interpretation of sites and objects (B. Griffiths 2018; C. Smith and Burke 2007).

Human biology met yet another fate. After committing in a 1973 meeting to "establishing co-operative ventures with the Aborigines" in human biology research, attempts to elicit research ideas from the newly formed AIAS Aboriginal Advisory Committee (and a visit by committee member Alan Thorne to the Roper River community) led the committee to add "Aboriginal health" to its research remit in 1975.[21] Two years later, at the initiative of Brisbane-based activist Sam Watson, who attended committee meetings as an Aboriginal representative, a question about benefit was added to the Human Biology Advisory Committee funding application: "Are there any advantages to Aboriginal people which will accrue from your research project, and if so please specify."[22] Slowly but surely, the broader shift of the AIAS from *scientific knowledge* to *Aboriginal benefit* moved the human biology agenda toward health research. In 1978 the name of the committee was changed to the Human Biology *and Health* Advisory Committee, "in view of the changed nature of the committee away from matters concerned with osteology."[23] In 1984 the name changed again to the Health and Human Biology Advisory Committee, elevating health above human biology and cementing the transformation.[24] The bulk of the human biology research agenda that served the AIAS for its first twenty years was simply no longer relevant.

In the mid-1970s, however, when the next scene took place, the fate of human biology was not yet clear. In 1974 a young paleoanthropologist named Alan Thorne took over from Kirk as chair of the committee. Thorne, a former student of University of Sydney professor of anatomy N. W. G. Macintosh, was the first to reconstruct remains of Australia's two best-known ancient skeletons, Mungo Lady and Mungo Man, and was a major proponent of multiregional theories of human evolution. He was enthusiastic about working cooperatively with Aboriginal people and led the committee's shifts toward Indigenous consultation.[25]

The Institute of Anatomy's exhibits provided an opportunity for the committee to showcase its changing perspective when it was approached in 1975 by "both White academics and members of the Aboriginal community regarding the current displays of both sacred and osteological material."[26] This referred to none other than the four-skull exhibit, as well as other questionable items. The committee dispatched Alan Thorne and fellow committee member

David Horton to investigate.[27] They duly recommended the four-skull exhibit be removed and other explanatory text be changed. The institute was sluggish in its response, prompting Peter Ucko to write a strongly worded letter to the minister for health outlining the racist exhibits that were "some thirty years out of date": "The errors and poor logic of these items surely pale before their basic racist implications."[28] By September 1976 Thorne could report to the committee that "the display of material in the field of human biology has been altered and is now more satisfactory."[29]

The committee was primed for this episode by its involvement the previous year in one of the first repatriations of human remains to an Indigenous group. Truganini (also spelled Trugernanner) was born around 1812 on the western side of the D'Entrecasteaux Channel, south of Hobart, the capital of the island state of Tasmania. Encroached on by a British penal colony from 1803, Tasmanian Aboriginal people suffered the genocidal effects of colonization earlier than many other parts of Australia. She lived through the brutal frontier wars that began when she was a child and culminated in 1830 when the governor ordered over two thousand soldiers and armed civilians to march across the entire island in a line, killing or capturing any Aboriginal people they found. The survivors were confined to a settlement on Flinders Island in Bass Strait. In parallel with the military campaign of extermination, builder and lay preacher George Augustus Robinson established a "Friendly Mission" in partnership with Truganini, whom he had befriended, aimed at coaxing all surviving Aboriginal Tasmanians to Flinders Island. She managed to live out most of her later years at a new settlement at Oyster Cove on her traditional Country. Over the course of her tragic life, all her family, her husband, and her fellow displaced settlement residents died in frontier violence or from disease (Pybus 2020; L. Ryan 2012).

At the time of her death in 1876, Truganini was internationally famous as the "last Tasmanian." The "mixed-race" descendants of Truganini's generation who would be recognized as Indigenous Tasmanians one hundred years later were at that time completely invisible. This convenient myopia allowed Truganini's death to be understood as the first racial extinction to be observed by scientists, a demonstration of the doomed race theory.[30] Before her death Truganini was well aware that scientists would seek to study her, telling a priest, "I know that when I die the Tasmanian Museum wants my body" (quoted in Rae-Ellis 1976, 123). She requested her body be placed in a bag with a "stone inside" and thrown into the D'Entrecasteaux Channel to avoid scientific dissection and display. Although initially buried, her body was disinterred by the Royal Society of Tasmania. By 1904 it was indeed put on display at the Hobart

Museum until, in response to public protest, it was locked in museum stores in 1947. Controversy haunted her body for decades, with scientists, white Tasmanians, mainland Aboriginal people, and later Aboriginal Tasmanians joining the fray to argue for her reburial, entombment, or scientific study (Turnbull 2017).

As the centenary of Truganini's 1876 death approached, the issue was once again raised. For the first time, Aboriginal Tasmanians were part of the discussions, represented by the newly formed Aboriginal Information Service. By the 1970s the "mixed-race" descendants of Aboriginal women and the sealers that abducted them in the first decades of the nineteenth century began to be recognized as Aboriginal Tasmanians and a political force (L. Ryan 1977).

In 1974 the director of the Tasmanian Museum and Art Gallery, D. R. Gregg, wrote to his peers around the country to garner their support against a new wave of concern about Truganini. In his letter to the principal of the AIAS, Peter Ucko, he attributed the activism to "mainland Aboriginal organisations," snubbing the fledgling efforts of the Tasmanian Aboriginal community to exert their rights over their ancestors: "Prompted, in part, by agitation from mainland Aboriginal organisations the Tasmanian Chief Secretary has recently proposed that the skeleton be placed in a mausoleum erected as a monument to Truganini and the Tasmanian Aboriginals. He has emphasized that the skeleton must be preserved for possible future scientific study, but it seems certain that it would not be readily available for such study."[31]

Gregg's concern was that the mausoleum proposal would inhibit scientific access to the bones. He went on to explain that in previous times of intense public discussion about Truganini, in 1953 and 1970, his predecessors had sought advice from leading anatomists and physical anthropologists, who had all agreed the skeleton must be retained for science. Following past practice, he was now writing to "Directors of the major museums in Australia and New Zealand to seek their views on the matter" to assist in his response to the chief secretary.[32]

The unanimous support that the Tasmanian Museum and Art Gallery had likely expected from the museum community was not forthcoming from the AIAS. The Human Biology Advisory Committee discussed the issue at their September 1974 meeting and resolved that "Truganini's own wishes should be established if possible, as a matter of urgency. If her wishes can be established, in this particular case they should be followed. If her wishes cannot be established without doubt, the Institute should explore, through discussion with Aboriginal groups, the problem of the fate of skeletal remains of historical, social and scientific interest."[33]

This was a turning point in the case. Within months, the Tasmanian state government had agreed to rebury Truganini in cooperation with the Aboriginal Information Service, a major win for the repatriation movement and for Aboriginal Tasmanians, who had been considered a ghostly presence, an illegitimate remnant, for the century since Truganini's death. Her second burial brought them to political life.[34]

THE INTERVENTION OF THE AIAS in Truganini's reburial was a defining moment for repatriation. Thousands of other bones were repatriated and reburied in the following decades, largely removing the material substrates of physical anthropology and archaeology.[35] For this inquiry into the haunting presences of past scientific research, it is notable that the Human Biology Advisory Committee took decisive action on bones, while the blood collections that some committee members maintained remained unquestioned.

This relationship between bone and blood collections is strangely mirrored by the relationship between cadaver and embryo collections in the history of embryology in the United States (Morgan 2009). Medical anthropologist and science and technology studies (STS) scholar Lynn Morgan's account focuses on Franklin Mall, an anatomist at the Johns Hopkins University School of Medicine who pioneered American embryology. Embryology emerged as a subfield of anatomy, and the collection of embryos, fetuses, and stillborns in the early twentieth century was led by anatomists, who were accustomed to the complex and often dubious chore of acquiring dead bodies for their research and for medical training.

By the 1920s there was widespread public outrage about the practices of cadaver procurement, including grave robbing and crime syndicates that murdered marginalized people by suffocation so their bodies would be sufficiently unmarked to fetch a high price in the medical school market. Franklin Mall was well connected to state and federal authorities and assisted in reforming laws and regulations for the movements of dead bodies that aimed to end unethical and illegal practices. At the same time, as Morgan explains, "his efforts to regularize the acquisition of cadavers helped to facilitate his access to embryo and fetal specimens" (2009, 68). His long-standing attempts to coax family physicians and gynecological surgeons into sending him specimens of embryos and fetuses, and city officials to send abandoned stillborns, were further enhanced by his reputation as a responsible researcher who prioritized ethical concerns above the desires of scientists for dead bodies to study. While restricting the availability of cadaveric material, Mall's collection of embryos, stillborns, and infants who had died in the neonatal period grew dramatically.

This situation differed somewhat from that of the Human Biology Advisory Committee scientists, who sought to regulate bones while overlooking blood samples. For a start, the two examples are separated by fifty years and take place on different continents. The archaeologists and physical anthropologists examining bones were generally not the same people as those examining blood, in contrast with early twentieth-century anatomist-embryologists who studied both bodies and embryos. However, the principle of a degree of regulatory activism toward one kind of specimen and silence toward another holds across both examples. In both cases, the effect, if not the intention, of this uneven scrutiny was to increase confidence in the scientists as moral actors in ethically dangerous territory. If these morally upstanding scientists made efforts to ensure that skeletal remains and cadavers were treated with the respect due to former persons but saw no need to extend the same concern to blood samples and embryos, who would disagree?

This illustrates how the social life of the material substrates of science determines the fate of the disciplines that use them. In the case of the disciplines represented on AIAS committees in the 1970s, the cultural objects and human remains studied by archaeologists were potent symbols of colonial theft and desecration and were usually held in public museum collections. The substrate of the serological disciplines was blood samples maintained in university freezers. While battles raged over bones, frozen samples raised no concerns.

This is not to say that blood samples and the discipline of human biology were unaffected by the political changes that began in the late 1960s but that the full effects were *delayed*. Osteology, the study of bones, was the first of the biological disciplines to be explicitly excluded from the funding goals of the committee, in the mid-1970s. It took a decade longer for all the biological disciplines to become stigmatized and the committee to turn its focus away from human biology and toward health research. I don't believe that members of the committee intended it this way, but by excavating itself from physical anthropology and archaeology, the committee was able to delay the demise of the blood-based serological disciplines. And crucially, it was able to save its biospecimen collections.

This invites an extension of Kevin Hetherington's framework to analyze the disposal of disciplines, adapting the concepts of first and second burial. Consider an interpretation of the first burial of a discipline as the time when it falls into disrepute, and the second burial as the time when its substrates are disposed of, ending the possibility of reestablishing scientific study.[36] Following this framework, we can say that the work of the committee helped to delay both the first and the second burial of human biology. In fact, the second burial is delayed to this day. Frozen archives of blood samples collected in the 1960s and 1970s, including Kirk's collection, are stored in medical research institutes in the major Australian capitals.[37] Their continued existence means that Kirk's collection, along with a few other key collections of Indigenous bodily substance, have the potential to serve as a reference sample of genome variation across Australia for use in provenancing skeletal material.[38] The preserved blood could help to complete the return of the bones.

Genetic provenancing has been discussed in the museum sector at least since scientists at the University of California, Berkeley, first extracted DNA from a museum specimen in the 1980s (Higuchi et al. 1984). As methods of amplifying DNA improved, human genetic material was recovered from ancient bone, teeth, mummified remains, and paleofeces (Pääbo 1986). The new field of paleogenomics has expanded rapidly in the twenty-first century (Llamas, Willerslev, and Orlando 2017). Genomic information from thousands of ancient humans has now been obtained, allowing more complex reconstructions of historical population movements. Very little of this work has involved Australian samples because of the cultural and ethical barriers to genomic research with Indigenous people. The "first Aboriginal genome" was sequenced in 2011 from a hair sample collected in 1923, a story I tell in the next chapter (Rasmussen et al. 2011). In 2016 the analysis of eighty-three genomes from living Indigenous and human remains greatly increased the data available for understanding evolution in Australia, as I discuss in chapter 5, although the data are not freely available (Malaspinas et al. 2016; Kowal, Llamas, and Tishkoff 2017).

All this makes it technically possible to use genomic information from living people, or from well-provenanced remains, to provenance human remains of uncertain origin. This involves extracting DNA from a human remain and comparing it to existing genomic information. As discussed in the previous chapter, Danish geneticist Eske Willerslev dramatically achieved this for Kennewick Man/the Ancient One, leading to the repatriation of the skeleton to Native Americans (Rasmussen et al. 2015). As that repatriation took place, Joanne Wright, from Griffith University in Queensland, was leading a study that explored whether genetic information could be used in the same way for human remains in Australia. Working with several traditional owner groups as part of her PhD research, she demonstrated that whole genome information could accurately link human remains to the communities they were most closely related to (Millar and Lambert 2019; Wright et al. 2018). While this method has not yet been attempted with unprovenanced human remains, Wright has proven the concept.

This possibility could matter a great deal to Romaine Moreton in her quest to quiet Mackenzie's ghost. After her haunting she began to track down the ancestral remains that once populated the building she now worked in. It turned out they had not traveled far. When the Institute of Anatomy closed in 1984, the human remains were transferred into the custody of the still-new National Museum of Australia.[39] Most of them remain stranded there to this day. They sit in containers in the museum's storage facility in Mitchell, a light-industrial area north of Canberra, named after the nineteenth-century explorer and surveyor general of New South Wales. They are unable to be repatriated as they are inadequately provenanced. Like many of his generation, Mackenzie was an avid collector but only a haphazard labeler. His eagerness to accept human remains collected by others exceeded any classificatory qualms he might have had about regional, community, or language group—the racial designation "Aboriginal" was enough. In other cases, labels that once existed were eaten by silverfish in the institute's basement (T. Griffiths 1996, 81).[40] Museum staff continue to comb through historical records, hoping to find information that will link a bone to a place, but the best hope for identifying the source of each skeleton and returning them home may be the blood that was saved.

HOW CAN WE UNDERSTAND the various hauntings of the substances and actors that populate the interwoven stories I have told here?

As I have already suggested, collections of Aboriginal human remains, such as Mackenzie's, are the most clear-cut instances of unfinished burials. In most cases, those who dug up graves or removed bones from burial sites in caves and trees deliberately intercepted burial. Subjects were turned into objects, sometimes in a grisly fashion, as flesh was stripped from bones to produce a clean scientific specimen fit for a museum collection (W. Anderson 2012; T. Griffiths 1996; MacDonald 2010; M. Thomas 2014). From the point of view of the present, that the skeletal remains of Indigenous people whose departure from the world of the living was interrupted should be haunted hardly seems surprising.

The case of blood samples is less clear. Do blood samples also haunt? To many, the collection of a regenerating substance from living humans is very different from digging up graves. Blood is easily collected with a needle and syringe, and notoriously difficult to do without the cooperation of the research subject.[41] Samples stored in collections that originated in the 1960s, such as Kirk's, are in tiny glass or plastic vials containing a range of substances, only some of which resemble clotted blood. Frozen serum samples are pale and opaque; extracted DNA samples are clear and colorless. These objects may appear less like subjects than bones do, and less able to haunt.

Compared to Romaine Moreton's vivid description of Mackenzie and his scalpel, Kirk wielding a syringe might seem an unlikely ghost. Among the various phenomena recognized by anthropologists of monsters (Musharbash 2014), it is vampires, not ghosts, that have most commonly been attached to geneticists. The vampire-scientist became a well-worn trope when the Human Genome Diversity Project (HGDP) triggered international opposition from Indigenous people, who called it the "vampire project" (Haraway 1997; M'charek 2005; Reardon 2005). As discussed in the previous chapter, this 1990s effort by population geneticists to record and analyze genetic diversity from groups they insensitively called "isolates of historical interest" backfired, to say the least. The Indigenous Peoples Council on Biocolonialism is a US-based organization that united Indigenous critics of the HGDP from across the world, including the Indigenous law professor and Aboriginal and Torres Strait Islander social justice commissioner Michael Dodson (Dodson and Williamson 1999; Harry, Howard, and Shelton 2000). The council took a broad approach to biocolonialism, relating its critique of the HGDP to the exploitation of other Indigenous biological assets, such as natural resources and traditional botanical knowledge. Indigenous lawyer Terri Janke's influential 1998 report *Our Culture, Our Future* included human genetic material alongside Indigenous environmental, plant, and animal resources as in need of legal protection.[42] Progressive legal scholars soon called for the United Nations Convention on Biological Diversity (1992)—which provides an extensive international framework to protect Indigenous cultural property—to extend its scope to human genetic research (C. Hamilton 2000).

Given this history, it is no wonder that in the twenty-first century, Indigenous groups in the Americas have begun to argue that blood samples are no different from bones. As discussed previously, the Yanomami and other groups have sought to have samples returned on grounds that include the need to complete burial rites. These claims suggest that in the past decade or so, blood samples have begun to be seen as something akin to human remains.

The "vampire project" had direct effects on Kirk's sample collection. Kirk had retired in 1987, the same year that the Human Biology Advisory Committee of the AIAS folded. By then, the collection had grown to 100,000 samples from around the globe, including a subset of around 7,000 collected from Indigenous Australian communities. When Kirk retired, custody of the samples fell to Sue Serjeantson. Born in Adelaide, Serjeantson had completed a PhD in human genetics at the University of Hawaii and spent five years working in Papua New Guinea before joining Kirk at the Australian National University (ANU) in 1976. She and her departmental colleagues used the samples for further research into genetic diversity, extracting DNA from a few hundred of them. When the HGDP began in 1993, Serjeantson was appointed as regional coordinator for Southeast Asia, Oceania, and Australia. At first, she defended the project in the media, while behind the scenes she raised concerns with project organizers about cultural insensitivity and lack of Indigenous consultation (H. Anderson 1994). In the following months, the bad press intensified. Spokespeople from the community-control Indigenous health service in Alice Springs, the Central Australian Aboriginal Congress (known simply as Congress), spoke out in the media against the project. The magazine of the Australian and New Zealand Association for the Advancement of Science, widely read by Australian scientists and the educated public, printed an article she penned defending the project alongside an article from Congress attacking it, accompanied by a cartoon of a vampiric researcher (figure 2.9) and another cartoon that appeared to depict her (Central Australian Aboriginal Congress 1994; Serjeantson 1994). This upset her deeply, and within a few months she had stepped down from her HGDP role and from her lab science, taking on a senior administrative role in the university.[43]

Scientists working with Kirk's collection were well aware of the vampire project. They were equally aware of the growing movement to repatriate human remains: their university colleague and Kirk's collaborator, Alan

FIGURE 2.9. Cartoon from *Search*, the publication of the Australian and New Zealand Association for the Advancement of Science, April 1994.

Thorne, had been central to the return of Mungo Lady in 1992.[44] They began to wonder if the blood samples they handled daily might be similarly implicated in the changing ethical norms of Indigenous control over biological materials. By the end of the 1990s, the ANU had decided the collection should be closed to scientific use. At this point, no Indigenous Australians had made any claims on the samples. Rather, the shifting political context of Indigenous rights over scientific research and human remains now had wider effects on various kinds of biological matter, including frozen samples. No longer simply a valuable raw material of science, the collection was now potentially subject to a set of interests beyond the laboratory.

We get a sense of this shift from the head laboratory technician recruited by Kirk in the early 1970s. He was responsible for maintaining the collection from when he started working at the lab, fresh out of university, until his retirement thirty-five years later. In an interview he recounted his mixed emotions when research on the Indigenous samples was halted. "I didn't know what I should do," he told me in an interview. "Do I quietly take it out and autoclave it all [destroy it through vaporization]? Do people want it back?" The identity of the samples as *Indigenous* abruptly became significant and unsettling for lab staff. "From a management point of view its identity [of the samples] is well hidden," he said. "Aboriginal is hardly ever mentioned [on the lists of samples]. But all the names . . ." he trailed off, referring to the detailed lists of names and other information on people who contributed samples kept in filing cabinets elsewhere in the building (quoted in Kowal and Radin 2015, 73–74).

The lists of names, kin, and language groups that gave the samples their provenance also irrevocably marked them as *Indigenous*, even if their material presence, boxes of glass tubes with aluminum stoppers and newer plastic cryovials, seemed no different from any of the thousands of other laboratory samples. At that time, the Indigenous component of Kirk's collection ontologically shifted from scientific specimens to a potentially repatriable substance.[45] The relative stability of the frozen samples was overturned as, in Hetherington's (2004, 163) terms, "the aporial absent presence [of] the unfinished disposal" reappeared. In short, the blood became haunted.

As it turns out, Kirk's collection has had a somewhat different fate than the sample collections claimed by the Yanomami and other Indigenous groups in the Americas. After Sue Serjeantson left the lab for an administrative position in 1994, custodianship of the samples fell to Simon Easteal. Brought up by English parents in Sri Lanka, Easteal spent time in Australia as a young man and returned to complete his PhD in cane toad genetics at Griffith University in Queensland in the early 1980s. He was then recruited to the position Kirk vacated when he retired. In the years leading up to the voluntary moratorium, and for a decade afterward, he repeatedly approached university management to develop a management strategy for the samples, with no success. The ethical and political challenges posed by the sample collection were simply too big to face.

Late in 2010, I cold-called Simon Easteal. By then, I was several years into an ethnographic project with the few geneticists working in Indigenous communities, and I had been told multiple times about a large collection of blood samples stored in Canberra. They encouraged me to look into it, and when I finally took the time to call Easteal, things quickly fell into place. Within the first ten minutes of our conversation, he asked for my help. This began a long process of consultation with Indigenous leaders and community members. With the support of my former PhD supervisor, Professor Ian Anderson—the University of Melbourne's first Indigenous medical graduate—an Indigenous Consultative Committee was established in 2012 to advise the ANU on what to do with the samples. I was engaged as a consultant and wrote a book-length report for the committee on the history of the collection, the potential cultural and ethical issues raised, and the management options (Kowal 2012a).

Eventually, the Indigenous Consultative Committee advised the university to set up a managed collection and genome facility under Indigenous governance, and the National Centre for Indigenous Genomics (NCIG) was duly formed in 2013 (Kowal, Easteal, and Gooda 2016). I served as the first deputy director before leaving the center in 2017. An Indigenous-majority governance board led by an Indigenous chair controls the collection and oversees the consultation process (figure 2.10). In the years since it began, the governance board has included many leading Indigenous Australian professors from fields within health, science, and the humanities. The caliber of Indigenous governance was set very high from the start, with Mick Gooda, Michael Dodson, and Misty Jenkins (whom we met in chapter 1) among the first Indigenous board members.

Mick Gooda was the first chair of the board. Gooda is a Gangulu man who grew up in a large Catholic family in Central Queensland. After leaving school, he worked on the railways, then fixed telephone towers around the state. His leadership skills were finally recognized, and he began working in government, rising to a series of senior positions in national Indigenous organizations: chief executive of the Aboriginal and Torres Strait Islander Commission, chief executive officer of the Cooperative Research Centre for Aboriginal Health, and Aboriginal and Torres Strait Islander social justice commissioner at the Australian Human Rights Commission. Later he was appointed co-commissioner

FIGURE 2.10. Members of the inaugural Governance Board of the National Centre for Indigenous Genomics, Australian National University, 2013. *Back row, left to right:* Professor Michael Dodson, Professor Simon Easteal, Professor Don Chalmers. *Front row, left to right:* Professor Margaret Harding, Mr. Mick Gooda, Dr. Misty Jenkins. *Source:* Australian National University.

on the Royal Commission into the Protection and Detention of Children in the Northern Territory and has led the national campaign for the recognition of Aboriginal and Torres Strait Islander people in the Australian Constitution. A quiet and warm man, he described the establishment of the NCIG as "a watershed moment for Indigenous health research": "The National Centre will provide the framework where Indigenous people can finally get the benefits of this kind of research" (quoted in Australian National University 2014).

Also on the inaugural board was Professor Michael Dodson, a Yawuru man who grew up in Katherine in the Northern Territory. He attended boarding school in Melbourne and went on to be the first Indigenous person to receive a law degree in 1974. He started working in the Victorian Aboriginal Legal Service in 1978 and later directed the Northern Land Council, served on the Royal Commission into Aboriginal Deaths in Custody, and was appointed as the first Aboriginal and Torres Strait Islander social justice commissioner in 1993. This was the time when the HGDP was capturing the attention of Indigenous activists globally. As I discuss in chapter 5, Dodson included a scathing assessment of the HGDP in his annual Social Justice Report (Human Rights and

Equal Opportunity Commission 1996). After further years of legal activism in Australia and internationally with the United Nations Permanent Forum on Indigenous Issues, he moved into academia, establishing and directing the National Centre for Indigenous Studies at the ANU. To have him on the inaugural Governance Board of the NCIG was highly significant: Australia's premier critic of the vampire project had become an advocate for Indigenous-governed genomics.

Indigenous staff continue to travel to communities from which blood was taken, speaking to the donors or their families to ask what should be done with their samples. The vast majority have chosen to have the sample retained by the NCIG, and many have provided saliva samples that have extended the collection. Full genome sequences have been produced from saliva samples, and the data will be available in the future to researchers who can demonstrate to the governance board that their project will offer direct benefits to Indigenous people. As the NCIG is based in the John Curtin School of Medical Research, where Kirk built his collection, the primary focus of the NCIG is health and medical research, but Indigenous people have expressed interest in using the resource to reconnect members of the Stolen Generations with lost family and to provenance human remains (Booth 2016).[46]

The NCIG has also directly repatriated samples. In the Northern Territory community of Galiwin'ku, from which 1,200 samples were collected after a typhoid outbreak in the late 1960s, community members requested the return of 200 samples taken from relatives who had since passed away (Dyani Lewis 2020). In November 2019 repatriation ceremonies were held in Canberra and in Galiwin'ku in front of assembled community members, scientists, and enthusiastic journalists. The Indigenous rationale for the return was similar to that expressed by the Yanomami. "It was something that is our culture. We have to take it in our way and bury it—cultural way. It's part of the person," explained Ross Mandi Wunungmurra, an Indigenous leader who co-organized the repatriation (quoted in Wellington 2019). This repatriation, however, was materially different from the Yanomami return of samples. Galiwin'ku community members consented to have DNA extracted from the samples before the remaining material was desiccated, combined together, separated into portions for each major clan in the community, and returned in specially designed wooden boxes. The blood samples of living community members were all retained by the NCIG, and hundreds more community members gave fresh saliva samples. As the NCIG website explains, "Culture and tradition are respected, but the people of Galiwin'ku are also participants in modern life. In considering the blood samples in the NCIG Collection, they have been ingenious in their navigation between the traditional and the contemporary. The samples of those who have passed away will be sequenced **and** repatriated. The samples will contribute to Indigenous medical research and discovery that aims to benefit current and future generations, **and** they will be returned to Country, reconciling the physical and spiritual dislocation" (National Centre for Indigenous Genomics 2020).

The Galiwin'ku sample repatriation was an overwhelming success for the ANU. Simon Easteal and his team succeeded in turning a highly contested sample collection into a "powerful symbol of reconciliation" (National Centre for Indigenous Genomics 2020), a good-news media story, and a win for science communication.[47] The willing participation of Indigenous Australians in a large genome project would have seemed unimaginable twenty-five years earlier, when Easteal's predecessor, Sue Serjeantson, had to extract herself from her close association with the vampire project.

It is still early days for the NCIG, despite its extensive media profile. No data sharing has yet occurred, and all the health and social benefits that the NCIG claims will flow from Indigenous genomics are still hypothetical. However, it is already clear that the very possibility of imagining and then enacting such novel fates for Indigenous biospecimens is a matter of spacing and timing. The fate of Kirk's collection reflects that it became a subject of attention of Indigenous people in 2011 rather than 2000 or 1990 and that this occurred in Australia, where Indigenous governance in research was relatively well developed. The ability to develop an Indigenous-governed genome facility has meant that many Indigenous people have felt confident that their interests will be protected by the governance board and have consented to participate.

Now we can more clearly see the significance of the *delay* of the second burial of human biology's substrates. If the fate of Kirk's collection had been contemplated at an earlier point, Indigenous Australians may have interpreted their samples in a similar way to the Yanomami: as an unfinished disposal haunted by ancestors who unequivocally demanded reburial. The delay of human biology's second burial has meant that when the time came, Indigenous leaders—a category that now includes Indigenous scientists like Misty Jenkins—could see the potential benefits of using the samples for genome science, under their control and on their own terms.[48]

How can we understand the choice of some Indigenous people to allow genome research on blood samples taken from them or deceased relatives? This choice is understandable if we take blood samples to be objects (to return to the discussion at the beginning of the chapter). Kirk's collection went out of scientific circulation in the late 1990s, a form of temporary disposal. Now that the second burial of the samples is contemplated, Indigenous people are invited to weigh the value of these unique objects. The great majority have allowed the lab in Canberra to extract, sequence, and store their DNA, believing that this will bring benefits to their families and communities.

If the samples are viewed as subjects, the choice made by Indigenous people to defer second burial—in some cases indefinitely—becomes more problematic. The living and the dead donors may haunt their corporeal traces left behind in the freezer, and even the digital traces of sequence data they produce. For those who participate in the NCIG, and perhaps other Indigenous people and minorities, engaging in genome science may be best understood as living with ghosts.

No one could expect Romaine Moreton to live with Colin Mackenzie's ghost, violent as he was. The ancestral ghosts contained in the Institute of Anatomy's bones insistently urged her to help them get home. For Indigenous people in Galiwin'ku and elsewhere in Australia, Kirk with his syringe and starch gels may be a more hospitable spectral presence. Indigenous people's sampled ancestors might want to be returned to Country but might also contribute genome data to a national, Indigenous-controlled resource that promises a bright technological future.

Facing ghosts without fear is a troubling prospect, and I am fully implicated in it. In embracing the haunting legacies of twentieth-century biology through Indigenous-governed genome science, my colleagues and I are far from guaranteed a happy ending. Comprehending the choice to salvage Kirk's collection demonstrates that living with ghosts has, through unique historical circumstances, become a necessary condition of human biological science in a twenty-first-century settler colony. There is no escaping the haunting presence of the past lives of biological research, but we can seek to better understand the ghosts we live with.

A Century in the Life of an Aboriginal Hair Sample

A single hair presenting the average form
characteristic of the age might
serve to define it.
—Franz Pruner-Bey, "On Human Hair as a
Race-Character, Examined by the Aid of the
Microscope," 1864

One mild September afternoon in the Goldfields region of Western Australia in 1923, an aging British ethnologist encountered a young Aboriginal man. They met at Golden Ridge station, twenty kilometers east of Kalgoorlie, named after a short-lived gold mine.[1] It was the second stop on the Trans-Australian Railway (figure 3.1), from Kalgoorlie to Port Augusta, completed just six years earlier.[2]

The older man was Alfred C. Haddon (1855–1940) (figure 3.2). A Cambridge zoologist turned anthropologist, he is best remembered for the groundbreaking 1898 Cambridge Anthropological Expedition to Torres Straits he led with a multidisciplinary team of ethnologists. A leading scholar of race in the early twentieth century, he believed hair was the primary marker of race, and he collected large numbers of hair samples in his lifetime.

A Typical Roadside Railway Station

FIGURE 3.1. Image from a booklet printed for the opening of the Trans-Australian Railway, 1917. *Source:* National Library of Australia.

We know nothing about the man he encountered at Golden Ridge station beyond Haddon's description of "Young Man" inscribed on the collection card accompanying the sample (figure 3.3). The Trans-Australian Railway, half a century in the making, brought hundreds of Aboriginal people living in the region into contact with European society for the first time. By the time Haddon passed through in 1923, the remote railway stations in the Goldfields had become intense sites of trade and other forms of encounter between Indigenous people and passengers during their brief stops (figure 3.4) (Bates 1966, 243; Paisley 1997; Rowse 1986, 185–87). Speaking in 1937 of stations in South Australia, Western Australian commissioner for native affairs A. O. Neville described, in his deprecating way, the exchange economy that saw passengers give Aboriginal people "money, fruit cake and other things": "The train stopped at the station for about twenty minutes and these natives swarmed round like flies" (Commonwealth of Australia 1937, 28).[3]

Hair would have been an unusual trade item. It is likely Haddon offered money, food, or tobacco to the man in exchange for snipping "one complete double long lock and one short lock" (figure 3.3) and adding it to his luggage. This was not specifically a collecting trip for Haddon. At sixty-eight, he was near retirement and in Australia for the second Pan-Pacific Science conference, held in Melbourne and Sydney (August 13–September 3, 1923). It was his

FIGURE 3.2. Alfred C. Haddon (1855–1940), painted by Philip Alexius de László (1869–1937). "Commissioned by the sitter's friends and pupils for the Museum of Archaeology and Anthropology at Cambridge on the occasion of his 70th birthday," 1925. *Source:* Wellcome Collection.

second trip to southern Australia and his first time in the west. Consistent with the time, the conference featured the discourse of salvage anthropology. Delegates were urged to contribute to the task of salvaging Indigenous knowledge "before it was too late" (MacLeod and Rehbock 2000).[4] Haddon doesn't appear to have collected any other hair samples on his westward journey. I imagine what happened at Golden Ridge was an "opportunistic" collection, the convergence of a persistent collecting impulse and a particularly impressive head of hair.

The thousands of cultural artifacts, bones, and hair samples Haddon collected formed the bulk of the Cambridge Museum of Archaeology and Anthropology. The encounter at Golden Ridge would have remained an obscure moment in a long collecting career if not for the interest of a Danish evolutionary biologist named Eske Willerslev. In a prominent example of twenty-first-century science bringing new life to neglected twentieth-century biological collections, this lock of hair was elevated to iconic proportions within the

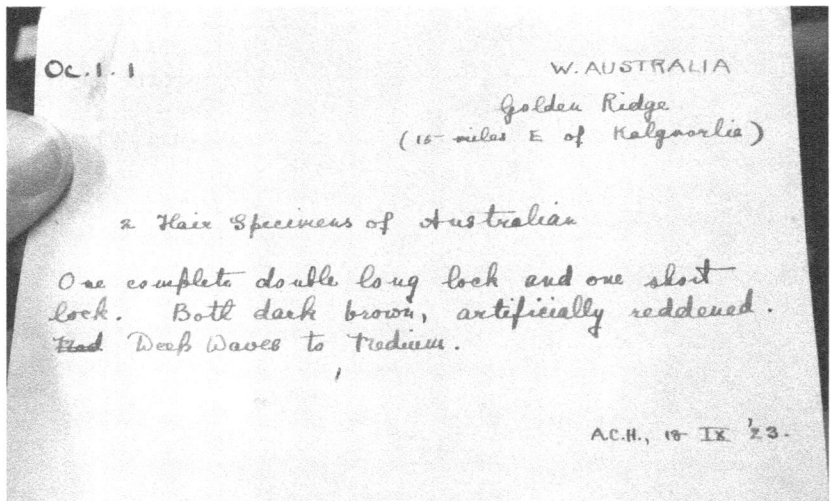

FIGURE 3.3. The specimen card for the Golden Ridge sample, Duckworth Collection, Cambridge University, UK, 2017. Photo by the author.

scientific community in 2011 as the source of the "first Aboriginal genome" ever to be sequenced. This chapter traces the life of this particular piece of human biology from a remote railway siding to Cambridge, Copenhagen, and Kalgoorlie. It explores the material entanglement of interwar race science, postwar scientific antiracism, and twenty-first-century postcolonial genomics.

Below I first focus on Haddon and the importance of hair in his account of race. Recalling the discussion in the previous chapter, I then describe how hair, and anthropometry in general, was generally abandoned as the mid-twentieth-century rise of serology, and later genetics, promised more direct and accurate measures of racial difference. In the twenty-first century, innovative scientists applied ever-advancing methods of DNA extraction and gene sequencing to museum collections of Indigenous biological materials. I explore in detail the use of the Golden Ridge sample to sequence the "first Aboriginal genome" in 2011, including the complex, contested story of how and why Aboriginal endorsement of the research was obtained.

There will be more to say about the haunting properties of that piece of hair, sheared from its owner in exchange for a few coins or piece of fruitcake, then carried in Haddon's luggage to Cambridge to lie dormant for eighty-eight years before a Danish scientist with the right tools and ambition could make its degraded genomic information speak for the entire "Aboriginal race." However, there is another, more procedural question I need to pose in this chapter.

FIGURE 3.4. Group of Aboriginal people identified as "detribalised Aboriginals," Ooldea, ca. 1920s. Photographer: John Henry York. *Source:* State Library of South Australia.

The "first Aboriginal genome" to be sequenced was a scientific achievement worthy of assured publication in a top international journal. As we will see, the research was completed with no Indigenous involvement whatsoever, until journal reviewers and editors raised a crucial question: How is it that this groundbreaking research with huge potential implications for Indigenous people could occur without talking to any Indigenous people? Particularly when using a biospecimen that was collected in circumstances very different from contemporary standards of consent and that some would consider to be a human remain?

For Australian researchers, such a lack of consultation for such controversial research was unthinkable in 2011. However, the ethical norms of Indigenous research had yet to penetrate beyond the national borders of the settler colony. The case of the first Aboriginal genome illustrates the mechanics of how emerging ethical norms gain momentum and spread. A Danish scientist, previously untroubled by the implications of his research for Indigenous people, was touched by these spreading ethical norms and, by his own account, "evolved" to incorporate them. Like the fate of bones and blood discussed in the previous chapter, the fate of the first Aboriginal genome was a matter of spacing and timing. Australian population geneticists have been aware of the ethical sensitivities of Indigenous research—and Indigenous genetic research in particular—since the 1990s and have made various efforts to spread the word among international colleagues. A point of no return for the principle of community approval came in 2011, and as we will see, a letter of endorsement from the Goldfields Land and Sea Council was duly included in the article's supplementary materials.

Charis Thompson's (2013) concept of "good science" is useful to help unpack the questions raised here. In her analysis of the ethical machinery of stem cell science, she parses various potential meanings of "good science." The first two are undoubtedly familiar to contemporary Western readers. A "good" scientific experiment is well designed and answers the questions it sets out to answer or leads to further, even more productive questions. Good science can also mean science that meets disciplinary and institutional standards of research integrity such as accountability, transparency, and replicability. Although these normative senses of "good" are clearly important, they are not the focus of her—or my—interests.

Thompson introduces a further meaning of "good science": a descriptive term for fields that raise complex societal issues and so develop their own ethical apparatus to engage interest groups beyond science itself. Although all research has been subject to bioethical regulation in most countries in the past few decades, the sciences that "have ethics" pose risks above and beyond the usual ones. Some of these fields are seen to potentially threaten critical aspects of human experience and society, such as stem cell science, gene editing and cloning, and artificial intelligence. In the case of stem cell research in the early twenty-first century, the need to procure human research materials from aborted fetuses and donated eggs created a wide network of interest and regulation. Antiabortion activists, patient groups, politicians, disability activists, and scientists argued over whether and how these valuable biospecimens should be obtained and used.

Another category that "has ethics" is research with groups that are seen as "vulnerable" or "high-risk," such as people engaging in illegal behavior, children, or people in dependent or unequal relationships with the researchers (National Health and Medical Research Council [NHMRC] 2018b). Adding "Indigenous people" to this shopping list of vulnerabilities immediately requires qualification. Some Indigenous scholars would dismiss the idea of themselves as "high-risk" as succumbing to a "deficit model," instead underlining their sovereign right to control research that affects them (Fforde et al. 2013).[5] Others might argue further that the idea of vulnerability overlooks years of Indigenous activism, discussed in the first chapter, that forced Western researchers to take their demands seriously. While I agree with these critiques, our existing models of ethics undeniably place Indigenous people alongside other "vulnerable" groups (NHMRC 2018b).[6]

However you conceptualize the exceptional nature of Indigenous research, it is clear that research with Indigenous Australians "has ethics," at least since 1991, when the first specific ethical guidelines for Indigenous research were produced. These require researchers to demonstrate that their work actively involves Indigenous communities and is likely to benefit these communities (NHMRC 1991, 2018a). For health researchers in four out of eight Australian jurisdictions, there are also separate Indigenous health ethics committees that consider research applications. Indigenous research fits within Thompson's definition of "good science" in the sense that, in response to Indigenous critiques of Western research, the "separation between ethics and science" became "increasingly untenable" (2013, 29).

The life history of the Golden Ridge hair sample intersects with the good-science framework of contemporary Indigenous research but also skirts around it. Haddon and Willerslev, the two major characters in this story, eluded these ethical requirements. For Haddon, it was simply a matter of time and mortality. He died years before revelations of the horrors of Nazi science led to the Nuremberg Code, the Helsinki Declaration, the discipline of bioethics, and the concept of informed consent, universal principles that were taken further by Indigenous research guidelines (Annas and Grodin 1995; Jonsen 1998). For Willerslev, national borders allowed him to spatially elude the ethical requirements that Australian scientists could not avoid. Nevertheless, both scientists were (and in Willerslev's case still are) considered "good" in their time. Haddon coauthored a book, *We Europeans* (J. Huxley, Haddon, and Carr-Saunders 1935), which bravely attempted to counter Nazi racial ideology. Willerslev experienced his Australian research as an epiphany of ethical enlightenment and proceeded to deliver the most contested Indigenous skeleton, Kennewick Man/the Ancient One, back to Native American tribes. The twists and turns of the Golden Ridge hair sample tie together these disparate tales and illustrate the queer fortunes of "good" Indigenous science in the twenty-first century.

THE SON OF A London printer, Haddon rejected the family business and took evening classes at King's and Birkbeck Colleges before gaining entrance to study natural science at Cambridge. He taught zoology and comparative anatomy at Cambridge before being appointed chair of zoology at the Royal College of Science Dublin, where he focused on marine zoology. Dissatisfied with deep-sea dredging off the Irish coast, he took up a suggestion from his patron Thomas H. Huxley and visited the Torres Strait in 1888. His research there inspired a switch to anthropology, and on his return he published anthropological articles, retrained in anthropology at Cambridge, and was eventually appointed to that department after many years of academic precarity (Mullins [1996] 2006). His pioneering Torres Strait expedition is credited with establishing the practice of anthropological fieldwork.[7]

Hair was a crucial tool for classifying human races within the natural sciences of the eighteenth and nineteenth centuries and was especially important to Haddon. As an object of collection and study, hair had many advantages: it was easily observable (even from some distance), easy to collect and transport, and preserved well over time. Skin color and hair form are generally listed first within rubrics of racial classification, but hair as a *primary* marker of race is relatively neglected in the historical literature. George Stocking, for example, has little to say about hair, except that already in Georges Cuvier's time "it had long been known that human races differed as to the color of their skin and the quality of their hair" (1968, 29).

There were many categorizations offered by natural scientists in the nineteenth and early twentieth centuries based on hair color, hair form, and microscopic appearance. French naturalist Jean-Baptiste-Geneviève-Marcellin Bory de Saint-Vincent (1827) is often credited for the first dual classification of *Liotriques* (straight haired) and *Oulotriques* (woolly haired).[8] Decades later, German anthropologist Franz Pruner-Bey claimed "a single hair presenting the average form characteristic of the age might serve to define it" (1864, 23). This line was subsequently quoted by many, including Haddon, who believed that hair was *more* important than skin color as a marker of human difference.

In his widely read 1909 monograph, *The Races of Man and Their Distribution,* Haddon first argues that physical methods of distinguishing the races of man are superior to culture and language because they cannot be passed horizontally between groups. Of all the physical methods available,

> hair appears to be the most useful character in classifying the main groups of mankind. . . . The three main varieties of hair are the straight, wavy and so-called woolly. The first is lank hair that usually falls straight down, occasionally with a tendency to become wavy; it is apt to be coarse in texture. The second is undulating, or may form a long curve or imperfect spiral from one end to another, or may be rolled spirally to form clustering rings or curls a centimetre or more in diameter. The third variety is characterized by numerous, close, often interlocking spirals, 1–9 mm. in diameter. These three varieties are now termed leiotrichous,

cymotrichous, and ulotrichous. It must be remembered, however, that all intermediate conditions occur between these three types.[9] (2–3)

The *cymotrichi* group included Australians, Polynesians, Indonesians, Dravidians, and Ethiopians but also Afghans, Armenians, Mediterraneans, Nordics, and the Alpine race. This classification aligned with the archaic Caucasian hypothesis (discussed in chapter 4), although Haddon (1909, 13) preferred the term *pre-Dravidian* to classify Australians, Veddas, Dravidians, and several Southeast Asian populations.

Throughout the 1920s and 1930s, systems of anthropometric classification proliferated with much internal contradiction between them, not to mention the problems of interobserver variation in measurement and the increasing recognition that "race mixing" had a long history that hopelessly complicated the measurement of race. The leading researcher of hair at that time was Mildred Trotter, a trailblazing forensic anthropologist and professor of anatomy at Washington University. Inspired by her science professors at the exclusive girls' college Mount Holyoke, she excelled in biology and was subsequently hired by Washington University anatomist C. H. Danworth to conduct research into excessive hair growth (hypertrichosis). She completed her master's and PhD degrees in the early 1920s and became a world expert in the physical anthropology of hair. Later in the 1920s, during a fellowship at Oxford, professor of anatomy Arthur Thomson—best known for "Thomson's rule" predicting that people in colder climates will have longer noses that function to warm the cold air—persuaded her to switch to skeletal biology. In the aftermath of World War II, she directed the Central Identification Laboratory at Schofield Barracks, O'ahu, Hawaii, identifying the bodies of US soldiers who had died in the Pacific. In the mid-1950s she became the first female president of the American Association of Physical Anthropology and then fought for a long-overdue promotion, making her the first female full professor at Washington University (Conroy et al. 1992; Emily Wilson 2019).

The switch from hair to bones might have been somewhat of a relief to Trotter (who was universally addressed as Trot). In a 1938 review of the physical anthropology of hair, she lamented that a poor understanding of the relationship between microscopic and macroscopic appearance was hampering the development of a comprehensive taxonomy. Later, during fieldwork in Hawai'i, she developed a groundbreaking method of estimating height from the length of leg bones that became a mainstay of forensic anthropology (Emily Wilson 2022).

Meanwhile, hair as a scientific substrate also faced competition from serology. As the twentieth century progressed, blood group research became attractive to anthropologists as a more objective measure than hair or skin color, although they often found the results difficult to interpret using existing models of race. By the 1940s the importance of hair and other anthropometric measurements began to wane as blood groups, and later other serological tests, stole the limelight. Adelaide comparative anatomist A. A. Abbie (discussed in chapter 4) concluded in 1951 that hair form varied greatly among Aboriginal people and was "a very poor guide to ethnic affiliation" (1951, 92).

In the 1930s progressive European anthropologists like Haddon realized they had a bigger problem on their hands than scientific arguments about racial taxonomy. Adolf Hitler's appropriation of racial classifications for his notion of an Aryan master race of predominantly Nordic stock, and corresponding *Untermensch* (subhuman) status for Jews and Romani, caused some alarm in Britain. The Royal Anthropological Institute formed a Race and Culture Committee in 1934 to respond to the disturbing developments in Germany, but their resulting report was vague and ineffective, largely thanks to the efforts of Nazi sympathizers George Pitt-Rivers and R. Ruggles Gates (Barkan 1992; Hart 2013; Schaffer 2008). In parallel with the official Royal Anthropological Institute process, Haddon, demographer A. Carr-Saunders, and Julian Huxley—the grandson of Haddon's old mentor Thomas H. Huxley and major architect of the modern evolutionary synthesis—speedily wrote and published *We Europeans*, a book that accomplished what the Race and Culture Committee failed to do.[10]

We Europeans, published in 1935, was a crushing critique of "the vast pseudo-science of racial biology . . . which serves to justify political ambition, economic ends, social grudges, and class prejudices" (J. Huxley, Haddon, and Carr-Saunders 1935, 7). At least within Europe, they argued, extended intermingling of groups made it meaningless to discern different races. Instead, the "non-committal term ethnic group" should be used (115). They reserved their strongest critique for the idea of a Jewish race. "Jews do not constitute a race, but a society forming a pseudo-national group with a strong religious basis and with peculiar historic traditions. Biologically it is almost as illegitimate to speak of a 'Jewish race' as of an 'Aryan race'" (274). The idea of Nordic or Aryan racial superiority was, in their view, profoundly unscientific, "based on nothing more serious than self-interest and wish-fulfilment" (276).

The book was immediately and predictably criticized by Pitt-Rivers, who dismissed it as "Jew propaganda" and accused Huxley of exploiting the aging Haddon (Hart 2013, 316).[11] Haddon's coauthorship certainly lent scientific weight to Huxley's arguments, as Huxley himself left academia fairly early in his career to write science books for a general audience with the prolific H. G.

Wells. Elazar Barkan (1992, 303–4) details Haddon's private ambivalence about being involved in such a radical project in the face of harsh criticism from Ruggles Gates.

Despite the radical framing of the book, the chapters that Haddon most likely penned on the ethnic groups of Europe are very similar to his previous work (a point not lost on historians and contemporaneous reviewers; Barkan 1992; E. G. R. T. 1936), except that the term "race" is replaced by "ethnic group," "people," or "type." In his descriptions of the ethnic groups of Europe, Haddon maintains his loyalty to hair, listing it as the most important method of classification.

Whatever Haddon's real contribution was to *We Europeans*, his association with the book fits with his broader congenial persona. His collecting practices are recounted as culturally respectful, at least in comparison to his contemporaries. One example is a review of the second edition of his popular book on his experiences in the Torres Strait, *Headhunters: Black, White, and Brown* (Haddon [1901] 1932). Haddon never specifies in the book what he means by the "white headhunters" of the title. The reviewer argues it was a critique of the unscrupulous scientific collecting practices of other scientists. In contrast, "Dr Haddon's scrupulous respect for native ideas and religious customs prevented at times his getting the skull or the object of veneration he was after" (Ivens 1932, 147).

The many thousands of items he did manage to collect, including his hair samples, made a major contribution to the Cambridge Museum of Archaeology and Anthropology.[12] Haddon maintained an active role in the museum and was the acting curator in the early 1920s (Quiggin 1942). In 1945 most of the hair and skeletal material from the museum, including Haddon's collection, was moved across campus to the newly established Duckworth Collection, which focused on biological anthropology.

The Duckworth was named for W. L. H. Duckworth, at that time recently retired from a readership in anatomy and an important figure in the earlier development of internationally standardized anthropometric measurement (J. Boyd 1956). The first director of the Duckworth Laboratory was the Oxford-educated physical anthropologist J. C. Trevor (1907–67). Trevor spent much time in southern and eastern Africa as a child and later during World War II. After graduating, he received a Eugenics Society fellowship to study race mixing and was subsequently appointed to anthropology at Cambridge in 1938 ("Leonard Darwin Scholarship" 1936). His analysis of anthropometric data (head and facial measurements) was eventually published as *Race Crossing in Man* (1953), by which time his statistical methods were outdated (as noted even by his obituary writer) (Brown 1954; Lawrence 1967). After the war he contributed to drafting the revised UNESCO Statement on Race as part of the British contingent, along with prominent geneticists J. B. S. Haldane and Arthur Mourant (UNESCO 1952). This revision was a direct response to the perceived inaccuracies of the first statement, which was seen as too radical by many geneticists and physical anthropologists (Barkan 1992; Maio and Santos 2015; Stepan 1982).

Trevor continued to work on cataloging and preserving the Duckworth Collection until his premature death in 1967. He constantly lobbied for more space and resources to curate the vast skeletal holdings; it is likely he never considered Haddon's hair samples, easily stored as they were in cardboard boxes. During this time the center of intellectual gravity in the science of racial differences continued to shift from physical anthropology to human biology and then to population genetics following the discovery of DNA's molecular structure. By the early 1960s, advances in statistical methods highlighted the deficiencies of physical features as reliable taxonomic markers in humans. For example, while anthropometric data placed Australians closer to Africans than any other group, analyses of genetic distance using serological markers found that Australians and Africans were the furthest apart, with Europeans and Asians in between (Cavalli-Sforza and Cavalli-Sforza 1995, 97–101).[13] Serology undermined the authority of the anthropologist's gaze and calipers. The "new physical anthropology" (Washburn 1951), of which the UNESCO Statements on Race were an important part, eschewed discredited concepts of discrete racial groups and embraced population variation (Reardon 2005).

AFTER TREVOR'S TIME, DIRECT genetic methods began to emerge. As I discussed in the previous chapter, in the late twentieth century, advances in DNA extraction and amplification techniques opened up new fields of inquiry into human variation and evolution, the very questions that animated the research of Haddon, Duckworth, and Trevor. Scientists began to extract DNA from recent and mummified museum specimens (Higuchi et al. 1984) and, after the development of the polymerase chain reaction method in the late 1980s, ancient bone, teeth, paleofeces, and other materials. By the turn of the twenty-first century, ancient DNA (aDNA) had become a prestigious area of science, populated by evolutionary molecular biologists, anthropological geneticists, and paleogeneticists. In 2005 massively parallel sequencing, also known as *next-generation sequencing*, emerged and was immediately taken up by the aDNA field (E. Jones and Bösl 2021; Knapp and Hofreiter 2010).

As DNA methods rapidly developed, so did the political and ethical environment of the late twentieth century. First, the Indigenous repatriation movement led to a reversal of the colonial flow of skeletal remains from the colonies to the metropole, backed up by national legislation and museum policies on human remains in North America, Australia, and Aotearoa/New Zealand. Increasingly throughout the 1990s, the destructive analysis of bone required to extract DNA was seen as a violation of Indigenous peoples' ancestors (Fforde 2004). At the same time, the Human Genome Diversity Project was creating negative press for population geneticists, who sought to research human movements and evolution by analyzing Indigenous blood samples (Harry, Howard, and Shelton 2000; Reardon 2005).

The combination of these political and ethical shifts was to make first bones and then blood originating from Indigenous people less available to scientists. It makes sense that aDNA researchers would look to other, less controversial biological substances. However, these alternatives might not be ideal sources of DNA. Hair, for example, does not contain cells, apart from the root of the hair, which is absent from cut hair samples. While mitochondrial DNA (mtDNA)—the DNA outside the nucleus of the cell that is passed directly from mother to child—is small, very robust, and thus well preserved in hair, nuclear DNA rapidly decays into tiny fragments. Fortuitously for these scientists, improvements in genetic technologies in the 2000s made it possible to extract, amplify, and assemble nuclear DNA from materials with only trace amounts present.

It was inevitable that hair samples left over from anthropometric studies would eventually attract the attention of aDNA researchers.[14] The evolutionary geneticist who won the race to extract the hardier mtDNA from human hair was Alan Cooper, a New Zealander and former student of leading evolutionary geneticists Svante Pääbo and Alan C. Wilson. In 2004 Cooper's lab at Oxford successfully extracted mtDNA from 3,000-year-old Pazyryk horse hairs, 64,000-year-old bison hairs, the hair of an Andaman Islander, and six samples purported to be from Isaac Newton (at least three of these were not).[15] The study concluded, "The successful amplification of high yields of uncontaminated mtDNA indicate that hair represents a useful and under-utilized source of aDNA" (M. Gilbert et al. 2004, R463).

The race was then on to sequence the first ancient human genome (that is, information from all the nuclear DNA). It was won by Eske Willerslev, a former postdoc in Cooper's lab. Born in 1971, Willerslev is a Danish evolutionary biologist who forged his interest in Indigenous people during Siberian expeditions in his twenties with his twin brother, prominent cultural anthropologist Rane Willerslev. Eske Willerslev was made full professor at the University of Copenhagen at thirty-three and is revered in Denmark. He has pioneered aDNA research into the peopling of the Americas, Europe, and Australia. He sequenced the first ancient nuclear human genome using a hair sample of a 4,000-year-old man from the Saqqaq culture of Greenland (Rasmussen et al. 2010). Willerslev recalls that Cooper's work finding the Andaman hair sample and, around the same time, obtaining Andaman teeth from London's National History Museum (Endicott et al. 2003) was the inspiration for his approaches to the Duckworth Collection.

Willerslev visited the Duckworth Collection in 2010 to find his sample. When I went there a few years ago, the director, Marta Mirazón Lahr, recalled showing Willerslev the available samples of hair, which, by chance, were kept in J. C. Trevor's army trunk. According to Lahr, Willerslev chose the Golden Ridge dreadlock as it was the largest one with the best chance of extracting DNA. He took it to his lab in Copenhagen, and his team sequenced 60 percent of the genome to a depth of 6.4X (meaning each part of the genome was sequenced an average of 6.4 times)—quite respectable for an aDNA study. Their various statistical analyses comparing the genome to others from around the world concluded that the population that would become the First Australians split off from the population that would become Europeans and Asians around seventy thousand years ago. This fit with the archaeological record at the time of publication, which dated the earliest Australians at around fifty thousand years old.

Finding the sample, extracting DNA, and analyzing it appears to have proceeded fairly smoothly. Although sequencing a full genome from an eighty-eight-year-old hair sample could not be easy, ambitious projects of this scale are Willerslev's specialty. It was when his team submitted the manuscript to *Nature* that things got complicated. The varying stories I have been told by geneticist colleagues and gleaned from media reports provide an (admittedly incomplete) "backstage" view (Goffman 1959), which illustrates the circuitous and dramatic process through which Willerslev—and, by implication, all of international paleogenomics—was initiated into the "good science" of Indigenous research.

The paper eventually came out in the top international journal *Science* after first being submitted to the equally prestigious journal *Nature*. During the review process with *Nature*, the question of permissions was raised. Had Willerslev secured ethical approval for the study? Had anyone in Australia given approval? When the paper was eventually published, Willerslev told *Nature* reporter Ewan Calloway (2011) that the University of Copenhagen had told him ethics approval was not required because it was an "archaeological" sample and not a "biological" one.[16] He also told me that he believed the tribe that the hair derived from was "extinct" (advice that may have come from Lahr), so no approval was possible.

At some point, after receiving feedback from *Nature*, Willerslev made contact with a collaborator based at Curtin University in Perth, forensic biologist and hair expert Silvana Tridico. She referred him to her Curtin colleague and environmental geneticist Michael Bunce. Bunce put Willerslev in contact with archaeologist Joe Dortch at the University of Western Australia, who in turn contacted Craig Muller. Muller was a historian who was then research manager for the Goldfields Land and Sea Council, the native title representative body with jurisdiction for Kalgoorlie and surrounds—the area where Haddon obtained the Golden Ridge sample. Muller and Willerslev hit it off, and Muller began researching the 1923 collection encounter and talking to the board of the Land and Sea Council about the possibility of Willerslev visiting them.

Muller concluded from his research that because the stop at Golden Ridge station was no more than forty minutes, and because Haddon was old and therefore not physically intimidating, the sample of hair was "freely donated." It is not irrelevant that all of these people who helped Willerslev get to Kalgoorlie are named authors on the paper, and Muller, the key gatekeeper and facilitator, left the Land and Sea Council in 2013 for a postdoctoral position in Willerslev's lab and is an author on five of the lab's highly cited publications.

The stories of this period told by some of Willerslev's collaborators are significantly different. Michael Bunce claimed Willerslev consulted with the council *before* he analyzed the DNA. "Initial tests confirmed DNA could be extracted from [the hair sample]," the *Australian* newspaper reported. Bunce told them, "That's when Eske got on a plane and came straight over. He's acutely aware that this is a politically charged area" (Dayton and Rintoul 2011). In a *New York Times* profile of Willerslev, University of California, Berkeley, collaborator Rasmus Nielsen is given credit for prompting Willerslev's visit. "'It didn't seem right to circumvent the wishes of the aboriginal community by using that sample,' Dr. Nielsen said. 'I was about to remove myself from the study due to these concerns'" (Zimmer 2016).

Whatever the actual sequence of events and motivations, it is clear that Willerslev visited Kalgoorlie in June 2011 to present his findings to the board of the Land and Sea Council. The visit went well. In the resulting letter, published alongside the paper, the council both "endorsed" and "approved" the research. Muller's conclusion that the hair sample had been "freely donated" to Haddon was crucial to the board's approval. "Once that was made clear," Muller told a reporter, "nobody [on the board] was bothered that there might be some underlying problem" (Calloway 2011). The final version of the paper, published in *Science*, indicated that Willerslev had obtained ethics approval in Denmark, and the project was not submitted to any Australian ethics committee. That there are at least three competing stories of how and why Willerslev went to Kalgoorlie is intriguing. Of course, the truth may be a combination of these stories or lie somewhere in between. It appears very likely, however, that the DNA analysis was conducted before seeking approval from the Land and Sea Council and that the journal *Nature* rejected the paper on these, or similar, grounds.

The paper was announced on the lab's website in an article entitled "Aboriginals Get New History," with a generic image of an Aboriginal man (Centre for GeoGenetics 2011). The wording of the title clearly marks it as *not* Australian: Aboriginals is an outdated term, and it would be presumptuous and racially insensitive for an Australian scientist to purport to give an Indigenous group a "new history." The coverage in the magazine accompaniment to the journal *Science* was not as clunky but still highly resonant of Pruner-Bey's mid-nineteenth-century observation: "A single hair presenting the average form characteristic of the age might serve to define it" (1864, 23). Multiple images of the hair at different levels of magnification are included in the multimedia materials that accompanied the article. The reader clicks through images of the hair at higher and higher magnification until they finally reach the electron microscope view (reproduced on the cover, figure 3.5) that depicts the uneven, craggy surface of the cut edge. These otherworldly images are not part of the scientific article: they are purely aesthetic, an allegory of the scientific wizardry that crushed and dissolved the hair to extract DNA and then sequence it.

The most significant *Science* and *Nature* articles are accompanied by a piece in their respective magazine sections, written by a journalist to explain the findings in plain terms and gain media attention. In the magazine article accompanying the "first Aboriginal genome," a photograph of the sample is placed alongside an image of a generic Aboriginal man and the hypothesized migration route of "his" ancestors (Gibbons 2011). In combination, the three-part image and the caption invite the reader to imagine the owner of the lock of hair ("an Aboriginal Australian like the one pictured above"), to wonder at an image of the decontextualized specimen, and to behold the ancient population routes revealed by scientists (figure 3.6). The viewer is invited to collapse together the fetishized piece of hair, the nameless "traditional" man, and a 70,000-year history of the "Aboriginal race."

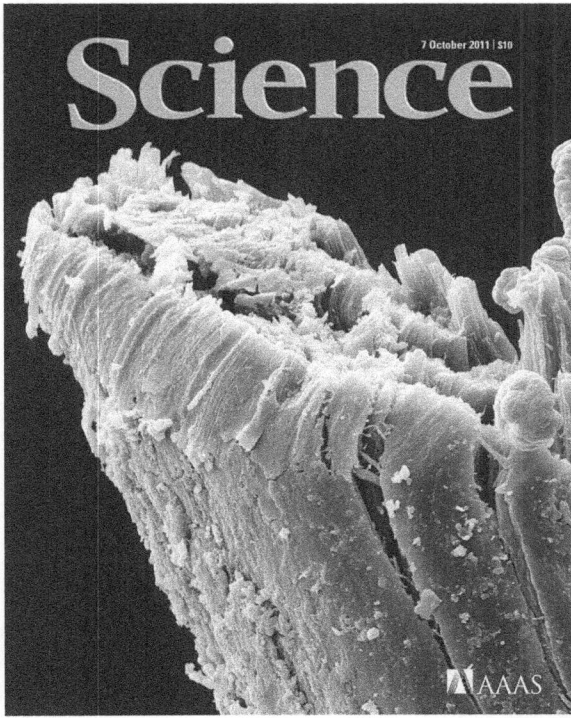

FIGURE 3.5. Electron microscopy image of the Golden Ridge hair sample on the cover of *Science*, October 7, 2011. *Source:* Science Magazine.

The stock photograph of "an Aboriginal Australian like the one pictured above" that stares out from the pages of *Science* is heavy with ghosts. For a start, it invokes a tradition of the depiction of races that stretches back at least to Carolus Linnaeus's *Systema Naturae* ([1735] 1964), where he identified four races: white Europeans, "tawny" Asians, red Americans, and black Africans.[17] By the nineteenth century, the concept of racial type had been adapted from botany to apply to subspecies classifications of *Homo sapiens* (Daston 2004; Stepan 1982; Stocking 1968). When applied to humans, its biological meaning was hazy but was represented by a set of "typical" physical traits including skin color, hair form, and facial features. Throughout the nineteenth century and into the twentieth, images of racial types were central to ethnological and anthropological knowledge and practice, allowing students to learn and scholars to categorize. A key advancement in the 1860s and 1870s was the use of photographic portraits as a more accurate depiction of race (Edwards 1990; Edwards and Morton 2005). This resulted in several new genres of visual anthropology. The most important was a seemingly enhanced representation of

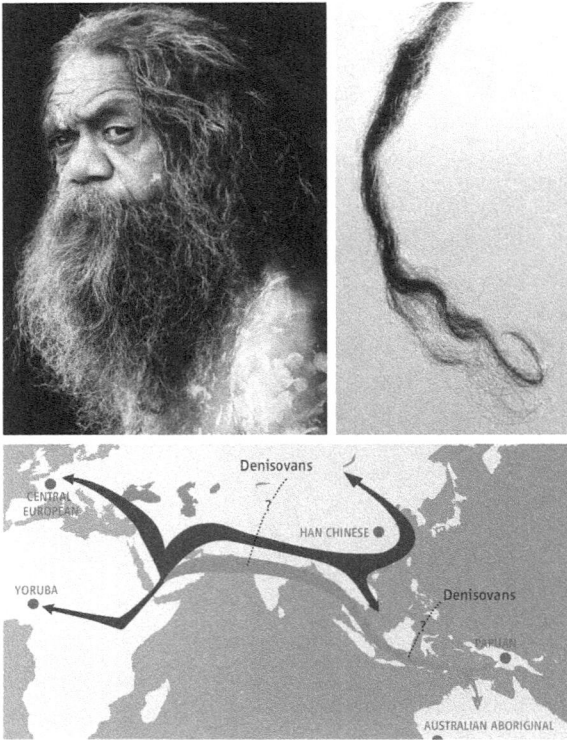

FIGURE 3.6. Illustration for *Science* magazine article (Gibbons 2011). Figure caption: "Great migrations. DNA from a lock of hair from an Aboriginal Australian like the one pictured above shows that Aboriginal ancestors left Africa and quickly traveled south (orange [lower] line) to Melanesia and Australia, interbreeding with Denisovans along the way. Other modern humans (brown [higher] line) headed to Asia in a second, later wave." *Source:* Science Magazine.

racial type. Apart from type photographs, other related genres of the late nineteenth century included the popular cartes de visite (calling cards) of "typical natives," often photographed with studio backgrounds and props that supposedly matched their racial type; and the scientific photograph, carefully staged to enable accurate anthropometric measurements (Edwards 1990).[18]

The "type" photograph was seen as a vast improvement on the previous method of artistic sketches. Supported by the Berlin Anthropological Society, photographer Carl Dammann and his brother Frederick amassed nearly six hundred photographs of people of fifty different races, published in a groundbreaking reference volume, *Anthropologisch-Ethnologisches Album in Photographien* (Dammann 1873–76; see Edwards 1990). Writing in *Nature* in 1876, founding father of British anthropology Edward B. Tylor enthusiastically reviewed the book and the smaller coffee-table version. Tylor complained that the "race-portraits" of a previous era were mostly "worthless, either wanting [that is, lacking] the special characters of the race, or absurdly caricaturing them." Photography was clearly a superior technology, faithfully capturing racial features. The remaining challenge for the collector, he advised, "lies in choosing the right individuals as representatives of their nations" (1876, 184). Once chosen, they were no longer individuals but stood in for their race.

Three decades later, the use of photographs of racial types was still standard in anthropological research. Haddon's *The Races of Man and Their Distribution* (1909) was no exception. He included ten plates to illustrate some of the racial types discussed in the text: "A Jicarilla Apache," "Two Koiari men," "An Arab (Semite)," "An Ainu," "An Old Chinese Man," "A Maori Chief," "A Negrillo," "An Eskimo," and "Two Patagonians." The final plate in this set features the head and torso of a young man staring into the lens (figure 3.7), captioned "A Northern Australian, with curly hair, a broad nose, through the septum of

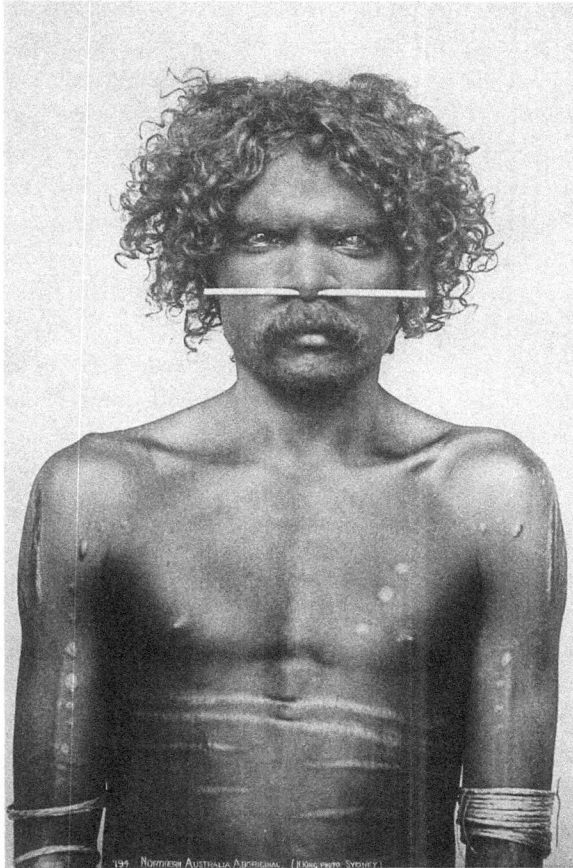

FIGURE 3.7. "A Northern Australian." *Source:* Plate VI from Haddon 1909, 22.

which is inserted a long bone (probably a wing bone of a wild swan); the body and arms are decorated with cicatrices and cheloid" (22).

The man in the *Science* figure and Haddon's "Northern Australian" appeared in print 102 years apart but seem like companion images, uncannily similar. They are both decorated with cultural items, although for the *Science* man this is only ochre body paint. They both stand in for their race and thus do not require names or specific tribal affiliations (Edwards 1990; Qureshi 2011). In the case of the *Science* man, we have access to an alternative narrative that challenges the racial type. The image was purchased from Sydney-based photographer Sheila Smart, whose work is available through multiple international art websites.[19] In response to a Facebook message I sent her asking about the man, Smart used the outdated term "full-blood aborigine" to describe Cedric, who she said was otherwise known as Mudda Mudda and lived in Redfern. A telecommunications executive and photographer who had also taken pictures of Cedric told me via LinkedIn that Cedric was a homeless Aboriginal man who performed dances with a small informal troupe in Sydney's iconic tourist destination, Circular Quay, in the 2000s. Other images of Cedric available to purchase from Smart are titled "Cedric, Aboriginal busker" and feature him smiling and wearing a souvenir T-shirt from ZagrebDox, a Croatian documentary film festival (the image is available to purchase as a pillowcase, a tote bag, stationary, a T-shirt, baby clothes, or a phone case). These brief attempts to scratch the surface of the image using internet searches and social media immediately spawned multiple Cedrics. I don't know if any of them overlap with how Cedric sees himself, but all of them push against the generic representation of "an Aboriginal Australian like the one pictured above" in *Science* (figure 3.6): Mudda Mudda from Redfern; Cedric the homeless man dancing for a few coins at Circular Quay; Cedric the lover of European documentary film.

The ease with which Cedric becomes a racial type is explained by long-standing scholarly critiques of literary and visual practices that essentialize, homogenize, and dehumanize Indigenous people (W. Anderson 2002; Clifford and Marcus 1986; J. Fabian 1983; Kuper 1998; Moreton-Robinson 2004; Russell 2001b; Said 1978). From a scientific perspective, the main challenge, as Tylor pointed out, is choosing the appropriate racial representative. Willerslev and his colleagues also chose a racial representative to produce scientific knowledge, in this case the opportunistic selection of the lock of hair from Trevor's war trunk. The man once physically connected to the lock of hair until his encounter with Haddon at Golden Ridge station is unknown to us, but "an Aboriginal Australian like the one pictured above" (figure 3.6) provides a handy racial script to fill in the blanks. The scientific prowess of extracting the 70,000-year history of an entire race from a lock of hair is strangely tied to a 300-year-old discursive practice of racial types and 150 years of colonial photography. Nineteenth-century racial science haunts twenty-first-century evolutionary biology through the gaze of the "representative" Aboriginal man.[20]

There was not even a whisper of such postcolonial critiques in the public reception of the research. On the contrary, Willerslev was seen as a hero for seeking and gaining endorsement from an Aboriginal organization. In the lead-up to the paper's publication, geneticists working in Australia feared a massive backlash against genetics not seen since the Human Genome Diversity Project. Many I know were hugely relieved when they saw the Goldfields Land and Sea Council had been consulted.[21] This episode is already immortalized in Willerslev's accounts of himself as the moment he realized he needed to engage directly with Indigenous people. His *New York Times* profile tells us, "His experiences in Australia have changed the way Dr. Willerslev and his colleagues investigate DNA from Indigenous people. 'I've evolved,' he said" (Zimmer 2016).

He has gone on to engage Native Americans in his research. Most famously, as discussed in chapter 1, he sequenced the skeleton that was perhaps the most contested of all—Kennewick Man/the Ancient One—proving the remains are related to present-day Native Americans. Months after the findings were published, the Ancient One was repatriated. Although Willerslev again sequenced the genome of the remains in Copenhagen, without prior permission from Native people and consulting with them only afterward, he emerged from the episode as an antiracist scientific hero.[22] His curriculum vitae on his website includes his adopted name from the Crow tribe of Montana among his many honorary doctorates and awards.[23]

AMONG THE LITANY OF bad news emanating from highly disadvantaged Indigenous communities in the Australian settler colony, aDNA stories are usually received as good news. So far, Indigenous Australians have not expressed any of the concerns of some Native Americans that scientific accounts of population migration (in the case of the Americas, across the Bering Strait) undermine their sovereignty (Harmon 2010). Indigenous Australians have incorporated the date of forty thousand years of human occupation—the limit of radiocarbon dating—into their political slogans since the 1980s. Ancient DNA and archaeology research findings have slowly but steadily pushed that date back to fifty thousand, sixty thousand, and now perhaps seventy thousand years (B. Griffiths 2018).

Amid all this good news, it is easy to lose sight of the layers of settler co-lonial violence, both the fast and slow kinds, that permeate every part of this story. We could start, for example, with Kalgoorlie, where the constant racial tension between white and Aboriginal residents spilled over into riots after a white man in a car chased, ran over, and killed a fourteen-year-old Aboriginal boy riding a bike in 2016 (Toohey 2016). The Aboriginal people who endorsed Willerslev's DNA study—referred to in his paper as "cultural (and possibly biological) descendants" of the hair sample "donor"—got their day in the in-ternational science media spotlight and perhaps a sense of their historical im-portance. I doubt, however, that this is much comfort when Facebook groups of white male Kalgoorlie locals openly encourage violence toward Aboriginal teenagers, including the grandchildren and great-grandchildren of the Land and Sea Council board members.

Willerslev might reasonably object that these issues I raise are not within his sphere of expertise. This bracketing of expertise is a long-standing tactic to "purify" science from the contamination of society (Latour 1993). A biologized accompaniment to this strategy is the bracketing out of what geneticists call "admixture" in a scientifically justified quest for racial purity. Haddon was not interested in modern Indigenous cultures, and certainly not biologically interested in those Aboriginal people who appeared to him to be of mixed race. As he succinctly put it in the introduction of *The Races of Man*, "The effects of European colonization are entirely omitted" (1909, ix). When Haddon snipped a hair sample on the Trans-Australian Railway, this omission required even more work than during his time in the Torres Strait three decades earlier. By the 1920s there was public alarm about begging and miscegenation along the train line, but for Haddon this was not a matter of concern (Latour 2004).

Bracketing off "the effects of European colonization" is not an option for twenty-first-century social scientists like myself. The rocky publication his-tory of the first Aboriginal genome shows that it may no longer be an option for evolutionary biologists. The reviewers of the version of the article sub-mitted to *Nature* brought Indigenous concerns out of their bracket and into the sentence proper. I'm sure that some thought the request for Indigenous approval of the research would stop Willerslev in his tracks, but he showed that with conviction, sincerity, and a generous serving of charisma, anything is possible. The cunning of recognition is at work here (Povinelli 2002).[24] In-digenous interests were folded into science as usual (Harding 1986), merely a speed bump, causing a few months' delay, an urgent international trip, and a change of publication venue from one top international journal to another. Willerslev simply evolved.

While Haddon was insulated from the bioethics of Indigenous research by decades of nonexistence on the planet, the small piece of the young Aboriginal man Haddon took from Golden Ridge station quietly persisted in Trevor's war trunk. Little known to Willerslev, by the time he salvaged it for genomic study, it had become an object of concern to its "cultural (and possibly biological) descendants" halfway around the globe. Willerslev discovered the hard way he was dealing with a "good science" (in Thompson's sense of the term) and that the "ethics" of Indigenous research could reach beyond Australian borders, all the way to Copenhagen via the *Nature* editorial office in London.

This story illustrates how the ruins of one scientific era can become the spoils of the next. Anthropometry was discredited by serology as blood was a more reliable substrate for molecular biology. As time went on, though, old hair collections posed a solution to the politico-ethical problems of accessing bones and blood. This return to hair contains other returns within it. Despite the political and semantic shifts from "race" to "population" in the mid-twentieth century, the "first Aboriginal genome" to be sequenced in 2011 was received as a racial story. The particulars of the encounter at a railway station in 1923 are relevant only as a media-friendly backstory highlighting the cultural sensitivity of the scientist and the racial purity of the subject. Somehow, once more, a single characteristic hair exemplifies a race (Pruner-Bey 1864).

We can understand the uncanny nature of the Golden Ridge hair sample as a folded object, a concept I discussed in chapter 1 (Serres 1995, 60). Amade M'charek describes folded objects as "gather[ing] heterogeneous spaces and temporalities together" such that "history can be recalled in objects" (2014, 33, 31). In the folds of the hair sample, time is kinked and curled. The perils of the long twentieth century are written into its keratin and its traces of DNA: mineral exploration, settler infrastructure, colonial photography, the postwar repudiation of race, and the treasures that Trevor's war trunk contained for "evolved" evolutionary biologists who came to recognize that "good science" requires recognition that Indigenous people and scientists have shared interests in stories about the past.

In the autumn of 1889, a group of Aboriginal people walked into a remote cattle station on the northwestern coast of Western Australia. On seeing the only white man on the station, Alexander "Sandy" McPhee, they were shocked, not because he was the first white man they had ever seen, but because he was the second. They told him of a white man that they had seen at a large ceremony further inland months before. Believing that "some unfortunate European was dragging out a miserable existence among the blacks," McPhee resolved to find him (*North Australian and Northern Territory Government Gazette* 1890).[1]

Sandy McPhee was born in the Western District of Victoria to Scottish migrants. He moved to the remote north of Western Australia in his early twenties and made his name as a drover, station manager, pearler, and prospector. By the time he was told of the white man in the desert, he was well established as the manager of Ninety Mile Station at Lagrange Bay, south of Broome, owned by prominent pastoralists Edward and Frank Wittenoom.

McPhee's late nineteenth-century journey in search of a white man in the desert serves as my starting point for a consideration of settler belonging from McPhee's time to the present. As discussed in chapter 1, non-indigenous occupation of the Australian continent is an inherently ghostly mode of inhabitance. Legally, British colonization was based on the principle of terra nullius: the legal fiction that Australia was a land belonging to no one. It was well established that Indigenous people lived there, but the eighteenth-century British legal system considered that Aboriginal people were too "primitive" to be capable of ownership (Reynolds 2021). This was always a convenient settler fantasy, contradicted by much anthropological scholarship (perhaps most famously Norman B. Tindale's 1974 magnum opus, a summary of half a century of research into Aboriginal tribes and their boundaries) and finally overturned in *Mabo v Queensland (2)* (1992), when the High Court of Australia accepted that Torres Strait Islander Eddie Mabo was a traditional owner of Murray Island.[2] Various legal systems of traditional landownership have operated in different states, leading to Indigenous ownership of approximately 40 percent of the Australian landmass (almost all in very remote areas) (Bartlett 2019). Nevertheless, the falsehood at the heart of British occupation haunts the nation to this day. Australian statehood is built on a legal lie, an injustice deepened by the ongoing oppression of Indigenous people and the denial of their sovereignty.

As Avery Gordon (2008) reminds us, ghosts thrive under conditions of racialized violence. The inconvenient truths underlying the settler state must be repressed for non-indigenous Australia to function. Forgetting is thus a key strategy for making settler lives tenable (Attwood 2005; Gelder and Jacobs 1998; Gooder and Jacobs 2000; C. Healy 1997, 2008; McKenna 2002). But the violent past is always threatening to reappear. How is settler belonging to operate under these extreme psychic conditions?

From the beginning, the main strategy of settler Australia has been to depict Indigenous people as "primitive," "savage," and thus subhuman (Bennett 2004; Russell 2001b). As in many other parts of the colonial world, the idea that colonized people were lower in the hierarchy of "races"—the theory of social evolutionism—justified the denial of their sovereignty and their freedom (Asad 1973; Wolf 1982; P. Wolfe 1999). In this dominant mode of settler defense, the ghosts of extinguished or displaced Indigenous people, languages, and lands are discredited and disregarded. Like all attempts at collective repression, this form of psychic defense is never-ending and takes different forms in each generation.[3]

This chapter considers a less common but no less important strategy for managing the uncanny disquiet of living on stolen land: Indigenous whiteness. A persistent, striking, audacious strategy of quieting ghosts is to make them white. Throughout the nineteenth century and well into the twentieth, various colonial powers around the world considered whether certain "races" under imperial control might be white, or white in specific and limited ways.[4] In Australia this preoccupation has taken a variety of forms that I weave together in this chapter. I begin with McPhee's quest to find a white man who might be a descendant of a shipwrecked sailor or lost explorer, a member of long-lost white tribe, or perhaps a settler who had "gone native" or was being held against their will. I then move to the first "authenticated" Indigenous person with albinism, a young girl called Lorna who featured in the medical and national media spotlight in 1969. An image of Lorna was the frontispiece for a popular book on Indigenous Australians by professor of anatomy and Board for Anthropological Research scientist A. A. Abbie. Abbie was an advocate of the "archaic Caucasian" (or "dark Caucasian") theory of Aboriginal racial origins that classified them as part of the Caucasian race: white, in a sense. The white-skinned Aboriginal girl cradled in her mother's black arms illustrated Abbie's broader biological point that the darkness of Indigenous Australians was only shallow and could easily erode. I show how the rise of serological methods seemed to confirm the archaic Caucasian theory but eventually led to its undoing.

The career of this theory spilled out into the policy and public spheres. I explore how it provided a scientific basis for state policies of Aboriginal absorption from the 1930s, theoretically supporting the findings of anthropologist Norman B. Tindale's and geneticist Joseph B. Birdsell's research that the progeny of white settlers and Indigenous people were biologically fit.[5] I then consider why the idea of Indigenous people as a kind of ancestor to European settlers was particularly appealing at that time of heightened white nationalism. In that period the dominant notion of Australian nationhood shifted from a white man's country witnessing the vanishing of the Aboriginal race (Lake and Reynolds 2008) to forms of Australian identity that appropriated, and then "assimilated," Indigenous people. The work of writer Xavier Herbert and publisher P. R. "Inky" Stephensen contemplated the relationship between settlers and Indigenous people, desperate for coherent racial narratives to support settler belonging and quiet colonial ghosts. For Stephensen, Indigenous people were the ancestors of *all* humanity. Colonial dispossession, therefore, was a homecoming. Herbert took a different approach. For him, settler belonging could be obtained only by fathering a "hybrid" race of "half-castes" whose mixed parentage would make them the true Australians.

The chapter returns once more to Abbie's frontispiece to illustrate a third mode of imagined racial kinship—an Aboriginal mother to the white race. This last configuration can be read as an allegory for the Stolen Generations: those disastrous, multigenerational practices of child removal that went on for much of the twentieth century. Children of mixed ancestry were targeted for institutionalization—snatched from their Aboriginal mothers' arms—in an effort to absorb Indigenous "blood" into the white population and eventually forget Australia's black history altogether. I argue that these endeavors—cast as "saving" lighter-skinned Indigenous children and making them white— were really about making a place for whiteness.

Ultimately, none of these varied attempts to quiet the inconvenient, haunting truths of Australian nationhood succeeded. In the last part of the chapter, I consider the ironic failure of Indigenous whiteness. Far from becoming white, the Indigenous polity today is highly diverse and includes many people who could pass as "white" but do not. Population numbers are rapidly growing owing to high birth rates and tens of thousands of Australians who begin identifying as Indigenous after discovering their heritage. They are reclaiming the Indigenous ancestors who came before them and keeping them close.

I approach the diverse and intersecting histories outlined in this chapter as sites of white desire for identification and belonging in a continent that resists settler efforts to feel at home. My analysis of scientific and popular speculation on the relationship between Indigenous people and settlers reveals the plays of sameness and difference, attraction and repulsion, that Ken Gelder and Jane Jacobs argue are spectrally generative:

> "Ghosts" simply could not function in a climate of sameness, in a country which fantasizes about itself as "one nation" or which imagines a utopian future of "reconciliation." . . . But neither can they function in a climate of nothing but difference, where the one can never resemble the other, as in a "divided" nation. A structure in which sameness and difference solicit each other, spilling over each other's boundaries only to return again to their respective places, moving back and forth in an unpredictable, even unruly matter—a structure in which sameness and difference embrace and refuse each other simultaneously: this is where the "ghosts" which may cause us to "smile" or to "worry" continue to flourish. (1998, 42)

In this spirit this chapter will move back and forth in an unruly manner, across space and time, in pursuit of worrisome and comforting ghosts.

LET US BEGIN THIS inquiry into Indigenous whiteness by speculating on what McPhee might have been looking for on his desert journey. He set off in the cooler month of July with Bunga and Yuarrick—two young Aboriginal men who worked for him at the station—six horses, provisions, and several firearms.[6] As the three of them traveled south along the coast and then east into the desert, McPhee might have entertained the possible origins of the mysterious white man. The white man may have been a descendant of seventeenth-century shipwrecked sailors. Four ships belonging to the Dutch East India Company were known to have been wrecked on the West Australian coast between 1629 and 1727, with hundreds of Dutch sailors unaccounted for and suspected to have assimilated into Aboriginal society (Gerritsen 1994, 2006; McCarthy 2003). The explorer Ludwig Leichhardt may have also been on McPhee's mind. Leichhardt had gone missing on his third expedition in 1848 while attempting to cross the continent from east to west. Three expeditions had already been launched to discover what had happened to him and between them had found only four trees marked with "L" and little evidence of their authenticity. Leichhardt's fate had gripped the imaginations of white Australians across the country, and many reported seeing his ghost in their dreams, together with his men, "thin and ragged . . . accompanied by a pack of gaunt and transparent dingoes" (Darrell Lewis 2013, 379).

It is also possible McPhee knew of the famous "white tribe" of Gambaragara contacted by explorer Henry Morton Stanley in 1876 and widely reported in newspapers around the world. These fair-skinned people with "European" features reportedly lived on the steep slopes of Mount Gambaragara in the Rwenzori mountains of Uganda, herding cattle and living on milk and bananas (Robinson 2016, 14).[7] In reporting the curious discovery, the Adelaide press pondered "whether these pale-faced Africans are merely albinos of the negro race or belong to a distinct family" (*Adelaide Observer* 1876). By the mid-1880s other explorers were attempting to find the Gambaragara. The theme of lost white tribes was amplified by the worldwide success of H. Rider Haggard's novel *King Solomon's Mines* (1885) and the sequel *Allan Quartermain* (1887). In the latter book, the trio of explorers from the first novel assemble to search for a kidnapped white girl in darkest Africa and discover a subterranean world inhabited by a lost white society.[8]

He may even have reflected on the story of William Buckley, the convict who escaped from the Port Phillip colony in 1803 and lived with the Wadawurrung people, west of present-day Melbourne, for thirty-two years. Buckley became a respected elder and fathered at least one child. He was presumed dead by colonial authorities until he walked into the camp of John Batman, the entrepreneur who was about to found the city of Melbourne. Perhaps the man McPhee now pursued was deliberately lost, escaping the law.

McPhee had had his own legal troubles just two years before, having been charged with the murder of two Aboriginal men who lived on the station, known as Nelson and Coola Coola. McPhee was released immediately on bail, and the following year the case was discharged by the Roebourne court. His violent history was the rule rather than the exception on the colonial frontier. Lagrange Bay itself had been the site of an infamous massacre in 1865 following a punitive expedition to investigate the disappearance of three settlers who were scoping out new pastoral runs that would displace and dispossess Aboriginal owners (Forrest 1996). McPhee's behavior would have only been endorsed by his employers, the Wittenoom brothers—especially Frank—who were notorious for their belief that settlers should be allowed to deliver retribution to Indigenous people "in their own way" (Birman and Bolton [1990] 2006). While it was highly unlikely that a white man would be convicted of violence toward an Aboriginal person (especially with powerful benefactors on his side), McPhee couldn't have enjoyed the legal exposure. This could partly explain why he decided to direct his energies toward finding an elusive white man who he imagined was a potential victim of Aboriginal captivity.[9] The white perpetrator of crimes against Indigenous people sought to reverse the script.

As their journey progressed, McPhee's small party heard more reports of the white desert man from the Aboriginal people they met, indicating they were on the right track. A month later, after traversing over four hundred kilometers to Joanna Springs, a place named by the explorer Peter Egerton Warburton, McPhee found what he was looking for (Rundell 1934).

He approached a camp of around forty Nyangumarta people.[10] A man rose and walked toward him. The two men were roughly the same age, both in their late twenties. The man's skin was "light brown, almost copper colour, hair a light brown" (*West Australian* 1890). He had blue eyes and a red-brown beard, and a layer of fine white hair covered his body. McPhee quickly saw that this man, rather than being a descendant of sailors or explorers, or an escapee, likely had albinism. He was the only light-skinned person there and, besides his skin and hair color, looked similar to the rest of the group. He was named Jungun, a word that may mean "moon" (Darrell Lewis 2013, 189). Jungun agreed to come with McPhee but asked that they visit his parents first: McPhee could thus report that his parents and siblings were uniformly dark skinned. The four walked back to Lagrange Bay and proceeded by boat to Perth. Jungun was exhibited in the Mechanics' Hall, flanked by McPhee's "boys," and the three performed traditional songs later described as "extremely simple, of curious emphasis and haunting effect" (Gustafson 1893).[11] Nearly a thousand of Perth's residents, both distinguished and ordinary, flocked to view this remarkable "racial paradox" (West Australian 1890).[12]

McPhee had returned with not just Jungun but also a story that might explain the fate of the lost explorer Leichhardt. Baron Ferdinand von Mueller, the most eminent scientist on the continent, heard of this and arranged passage to Melbourne so that he could examine Jungun and so that McPhee could present his story to the Royal Geographical Society of Australasia (Darrell Lewis 2006; Royal Geographical Society of Australasia [Victoria] 1890). McPhee applied to the Aborigines' Board for permission to take Jungun and the two "boys" across state lines and paid a security deposit of ten pounds. Hearing the stories that McPhee had been told about white men and horses who had died years earlier, Mueller was inspired to organize an expedition to find evidence of Leichhardt's fate and asked McPhee to lead it. McPhee declined and instead extended the Jungun tour to Sydney. In any case, the expedition returned empty-handed.[13]

In Melbourne Jungun was examined by Mueller, Anthony Brownless (a physician and chancellor of Melbourne University), and Rev. Dr. Llewelyn Bevan, who each considered whether he was Leichhardt's descendant. They concluded that he was an albino with "no white blood in him" (West Australian 1934).[14] He was exhibited in the heart of the city at the Waxworks, a venue where patrons could enjoy music and magic shows while viewing wax models of the royal family and politicians. Upstairs, so-called freaks were shown to the public. At the time Jungun was there, the other live attraction was General and Mrs. Mite, an American couple of short stature exhibited as the shortest couple in the world. By February 1890 the Melbourne newspapers reported that "Jun-gun maintains his popularity, and his efforts to entertain his visitors are evidently as agreeable to him as they are novel to the audience" (Table Talk 1890).

Jungun's popularity came at a time when Australian nationalism was building to fever pitch. In 1901 the Commonwealth of Australia, a self-governing Dominion of the British Empire, was formed from the six colonies. As Marilyn Lake and Henry Reynolds (2008) outline, those who worked to found the nation contributed to an emerging "global whiteness" that promoted the international brotherhood of white men. Indigenous people, then believed to be on

FIGURE 4.1. Portrait of Jungun, ca. 1890, by John William Lindt. *Source:* National Library of Australia.

a path to extinction, did not feature in this particular phase of national anxiety, and legal restrictions focused on preventing Asian immigration (regardless of whether the nonwhites in question were British imperial subjects, to the annoyance of Britain). Racial homogeneity was seen as crucial to the success of the fledging Australian nation: anything else would be "race suicide."[15]

The Commonwealth of Australia acted decisively to whiten itself in its first legislative act, expelling thousands of Pacific Islanders who had been recruited to work in the Queensland cane fields. The Immigration Restriction Act—part of what became known as the White Australia Policy—soon followed, prohibiting new nonwhite immigration (Markus 1994). As Lake and Reynolds put it, "Australians drew a colour line around their continent and declared whiteness to be at the very heart of their national identity" (2008, 138).

McPhee went searching for whiteness in the heart of the continent just as transnational ideas of "white men's countries" were emerging. Jungun was an exception, a "racial paradox" that proved the rule of white nationhood. His popularity might have partly lain in his implausibility—viewers could be reassured that under no circumstances other than a rare genetic condition could Indigenous people be white. As we will see, only a few decades later the confidence of white Australia in the whiteness of its heart was severely tested. Indigenous people failed to die out, as racial theories had predicted, and the mixed-race Indigenous population proliferated. The bulk of the chapter focuses on this second round of national identity crises in the 1930s, a period when racial theories of Aboriginal whiteness and the "fitness" of Indigenous-European "hybrids" had pressing policy implications.

Jungun was the most famous Aboriginal albino but not the only one to come to public attention.[16] One local politician named J. M. Perry was reported to have seen an albino Aboriginal woman while prospecting for gold in the Lake Cowal region of western New South Wales in the 1870s (*Newcastle Morning Herald* 1932). An albino woman in southeastern Queensland was apprehended by the Normandy police in 1887 and later died (*Daily News* 1887). In the 1920s a girl born in Terrey Hills, north of Sydney, was exhibited at the Maitland Show at age eleven. A local journalist described that she "possesses features of undoubted negroid type. Her skin however is perfectly white, and her hair is as white as snow with the scalp of a natural pink colour." Her pink eyes were said to "alter their colour in the changing climate in a remarkable manner" (*Maitland Daily Mercury* 1924).

It wasn't until 1969 that the first "authenticated" Aboriginal person with albinism was reported in the *Medical Journal of Australia* and the national media. The child was from Nulbulwar, a community in southeast Arnhem Land in the Northern Territory. Alan Walker, the first permanent pediatrician in Darwin, had sent blood samples from the two-year-old girl—called Lorna—and her parents to Roy Simmons at the Commonwealth Serum Laboratories in Melbourne. Extensive blood group testing confirmed she was not of European origin and almost certainly the biological child of her parents. Journalists asked Walker how the girl was being treated. "Dr Walker said the girl seemed to be getting special treatment from her parents. 'She's thoroughly spoilt,' he said. 'In Africa, albinos were sometimes treated as gods—or killed. This child is treated almost normally, though there is some evidence of more care than usual'" (*Canberra Times* 1969).

Albinism—known to scientists as "oculocutaneous albinism"—is a rare genetic condition causing a reduced or complete lack of pigmentation in the skin, hair, and eyes. Those with albinism are highly susceptible to skin cancers and have a variety of eye problems. Most are legally blind. It occurs in every known population but rarely—between one in twenty thousand and one in forty thousand people in most countries. Selected groups have a high incidence:

the Guna people of Panama have the highest rate at one in seventy, and the many young people with albinism are known locally as "children of the moon" (Bjornberg 1960).

In Tanzania, which has the highest incidence of any country—one in 1,400—people with albinism are called *zeruzeru*, meaning "ghost"; *mzungu*, meaning "white person"; or *dili*. This last Kiswahili word means "deal" and refers to the black-market trade in the body parts of people with albinism, which are thought to be powerful ingredients for amulets that bring luck and prosperity (Brocco 2016; Bryceson, Jønsson, and Sherrington 2010). In the past decade, foreign nongovernmental organizations have worked to provide safe school and living facilities and medical care to Tanzanians with albinism. They helped to secure the country's first prosecution for the murder of a person with albinism in 2009, although vanishingly few perpetrators will ever be brought to justice.[17]

Meanwhile, a global network of NGOs promotes a positive image of albinism, showcasing African American model Diandra Forrest and two Melbourne teenagers, Lucy and Sammy, whose fashion-oriented Instagram account has a worldwide following. Parliamentarians, judges, scientists, and athletes with albinism all feature on the Office of the United Nations High Commissioner for Human Rights' (n.d.) albinism website, which is titled People with Albinism: Not Ghosts but Human Beings.

Exhibited as freaks, murdered and mutilated for their body parts, or revered as models and Instagram stars, people with albinism are human beings, but the place they hold in many cultures continues to be ghostly. They mingle in the remainder of this chapter with lost explorers, elusive white tribes, dark Caucasians, and pale-skinned Indigenous people who refuse to be white.

I FIRST BECAME AWARE of Aboriginal albinism while interviewing the late John Mulvaney, widely recognized as the father of archaeology in Australia, at his modest but comfortable home in Canberra in 2015. After we had talked for over an hour about the history of the Australian Institute of Aboriginal Studies (discussed in chapter 2), we stood and chatted in front of one of his many bookshelves. All the major twentieth-century texts on Aboriginal Australians were there. My eye was caught by a copy of A. A. Abbie's *The Original Australians* ([1969] 1976). It was a later edition than the one I had previously read. This second edition was published in the year of Abbie's death, 1976. Opening to the first page, I was confronted with an image of an albino child in the arms of her mother (figure 4.2). I recognized Alan Walker's name printed underneath. I had known him in Darwin in the early 2000s as a medical elder, always interested in discussing Indigenous health with young doctors like myself, newly arrived from southern capitals.[18]

It was startling to see the name of someone I had personally known in Abbie's book. In my mind, Abbie was someone of a previous era.[19] Born in Kent and educated in England, A. A. Abbie (1905–76) moved with his family to Australia and trained in medicine at the University of Sydney. He married a fellow medical student, Frieda Ruth Heighway, who pursued a successful career in obstetrics and gynecology despite the demands of raising three daughters and the sexism of the medical profession. After completing PhD research with Grafton Elliot Smith in London and war service, Abbie took up the Elder Chair of Anatomy and Histology in Adelaide, and the family moved there in 1944.[20] Abbie was personally distant, "fastidious in dress and meticulous in every matter," and an enthusiastic teacher, using two hands simultaneously to draw complex blackboard illustrations of neuroanatomical structures in his medical lectures (Elmslie and Nance [1993] 2006).

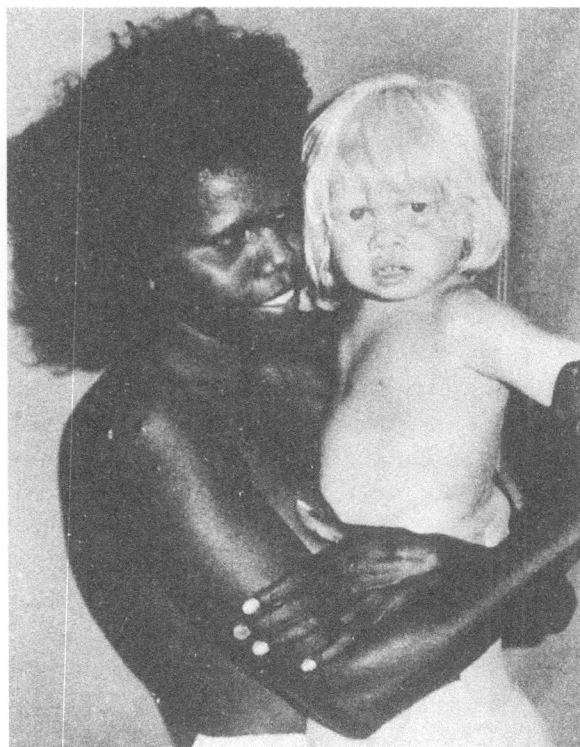

FIGURE 4.2. Lorna and her mother. *Source:* Abbie (1969) 1976, frontispiece.

In the 1950s he turned his attention to the anatomy of Aboriginal people and joined several Board for Anthropological Research expeditions. His *The Original Australians* was among many popular twentieth-century monographs written by anthropologists, linguists, archaeologists, and human biologists that offered a synthetic view of Indigenous Australians. Herbert Basedow's *The Australian Aboriginal* (1925) was perhaps the first, but Sydney professor of anthropology A. P. Elkin's *The Australian Aborigines* was by far most successful, first published in 1938 and reprinted and reissued multiple times until the fifth edition in 1974 (Elkin 1974).[21]

Competing theories of Aboriginal and Tasmanian origins, hotly debated in the first half of the twentieth century, play out in the pages of these books.[22] Herbert Basedow, a South Australian government geologist, anthropologist, and explorer, proposed the archaic Caucasian theory in his 1925 monograph. He was influenced by his mentor, Breslau anatomist and anthropologist Hermann Klaatsch, a polygenic Darwinist who conducted three years of field research in Queensland from 1904. Klaatsch believed that modern humans first evolved from nonhuman apes in Australia before spreading to the rest of the world: Indigenous Australians as the wellspring of all humanity. Basedow made the less radical argument that Aboriginal people and Europeans should both be classified as Australoids, without specifying the direction of travel: "This line of anthropological relationship connects the Australian (including the proto-Australian) with the Veddahs and Dravidians of India, and with the fossil men of Europe, from which the Caucasian element has sprung. In other words, the Australian aboriginal stands somewhere near the bottom rung of the great evolutional ladder we have ascended—he the bud, we the glorified flower of human culture" (Basedow 1925, 58; see also W. Anderson 2002; Collette 1987; McGregor 1996; Zogbaum 2010).

In Basedow's view, the clearest evidence of Aboriginal-Caucasian shared ancestry was "the shallowness of the pigmentation in the aboriginal's skin, and . . . the fair hair of the children found among certain tribes of central Australia" (1925, 59). The hair-based racial classifications discussed in chapter 3 were also a convenient fit with the archaic Caucasian theory. W. Ramsay Smith (1932), another Adelaide physician turned anthropologist, expressed the common belief that "the wavy hair of the Australian, as contrasted with the straight hair of the Mongol and the 'wool' of the Negro, is a characteristically Caucasian feature." In the first half of the twentieth century, then, the dominant view of Aboriginal racial origins saw them as distant cousins of the colonizers.

The archaic Caucasian theory had nineteenth-century antecedents. Thomas H. Huxley, famous for being the principal promoter of Charles Darwin's theory of evolution, first suggested a connection between Australians and "the so-called hill-tribes who inhabit the interior of the Dekhan, in Hindostan" (1870, 404-5). Two decades later, British biologists and racial scientists William Henry Flower and Richard Lydekker (1891, 748-49) proposed that Australia was first "colonized" by a Melanesian race and the mainland population was later replaced by a black Caucasian race. Alfred Russel Wallace, co-discoverer of natural selection, claimed in 1893 that Australians were a pure primitive Caucasian race (W. Anderson 2002).

These theories coalesced in a proposed global "Aryan race" promoted by German-born Oxford philologist Max Müller (1823-1900) (Robinson 2016). His model attempted to synthesize the many reports of pale-skinned, blue-eyed, or long-nosed peoples in India, Japan, the Pacific, the Americas, and even the arctic circle. Müller's theory was grounded in his Sanskrit scholarship and had at its heart the idea that the Brahmin caste descended from Aryan invaders who displaced "native" Dravidian tribes, a theory later exploited by Hindu nationalists (Subramaniam 2019). Müller's ideas were taken up widely to argue that Maori in New Zealand, Ainu in Japan, Inca in Peru, and populations in the Philippines, Indonesia, Hawaii, and Greenland were all branches of the Aryan racial family, variously seen as descendants of one or all of Noah's sons or, alternatively, one of the twelve lost tribes of Israel (Robinson 2016, 153-54). Australian pioneer of geography Griffith Taylor (1921) echoed this work in his ambitious secular theory of the progressive migration of five races across the Earth, although he classified Australians as Negro rather than Caucasian. On hearing of blond-haired Aboriginal tribes in the northwest in 1924, he went to investigate, subsequently adjusting his theory of Australian origins to include a later migration of narrow-nosed, fair-haired people (Taylor 1925). The golden locks he witnessed proved to Taylor that the Aboriginal people indeed had Aryan origins.

In parallel with the various racial theories of anatomists, anthropologists, and geographers (based on anthropometry, hair form, and other physical characteristics), the rise of serology—discussed in chapter 1—began to contribute to the debate. When blood group research began in Australia in the 1920s, it appeared to confirm the biological relationship between Aboriginal people and Europeans, a major windfall for the archaic Caucasian theory. At the time, it was believed that ABO blood groups provided a convenient serological marker of race (Bangham 2014, 2020). Group A was considered European, group B was Asian, and group O was American. A major figure in the Australian arm of this research was J. B. Cleland, a professor of pathology in Adelaide and an active member of the Board for Anthropological Research. Building on blood group research with Indigenous Queenslanders that had found a very low incidence of group B, Cleland bled people across central Australia and found no group B in any "full-bloods" he encountered (W. Anderson 2002, 200–202; D. Thomas 2004).

It is hard to overstate the significance of this finding for scientists seeking to understand the origin of the Australians. Blood group research was widely lauded as the first "objective" measure of race that would transcend the biases of anthropometric analysis that may, in the words of leading blood group researcher Arthur Mourant, "plausibly though wrongly hold that fair or dark hair is the nobler" (1954, 1; quoted in Bangham 2014, 74). Although Cleland himself was skeptical that Aboriginal people and Europeans were "related" (W. Anderson 2002), his blood group findings were widely cited as the smoking gun of the archaic Caucasian. However, many of the culturally oriented anthropologists remained unconvinced. Elkin (1974, 4) was among those who preferred to add "Australoid" as a fourth racial category alongside "Caucasian," "Mongoloid," and "Negroid." Julian Huxley, Alfred C. Haddon, and A. M. Carr-Saunders's landmark 1935 critique of race (discussed in chapter 3) held fast to the notion of three historical races while admitting that the place of the Australians in this schema was "quite problematical" (116).

As the anthropologists and other scientists debated whether there were three, four, or five major racial groups and how they related to each other, the serological side of the story grew in complexity. While research using the initial ABO system seemed to present a straightforward racial story, a stream of new blood group antigens were discovered from the late 1920s (including the Australian scientist R. J. Walsh's discovery of Factor S/s; Walsh and Montgomery 1947). Even the ABO groups were eventually divided into many subgroups and rare types. The clear relationship between blood groups and race soon fell away, and serological endorsement of the archaic Caucasian theory soured.

A key figure here was Roy T. Simmons, a technician at the National Blood Group Reference Laboratory at the Commonwealth Serum Laboratories in Melbourne (and the man who confirmed the kinship of white-skinned Lorna with her black-skinned parents). With access to the latest technology for discerning ABO, MNS, and Rh subgroups, not to mention a plethora of eponymous blood group antigens such as Duffy, Kell, Kidd, and Diego, he became central to Aboriginal blood group research and received samples from across the continent and the region.[23] After analyzing results from over ten thousand samples, he concluded that Aboriginal blood groups differed from those of Caucasians and the other racial groups that were supposedly part of the "Australoid/Archaic Caucasoid" group: the Dravidian people of India, the Veddah of Ceylon, and the Ainu of Japan. By the 1970s he sadly concluded he was none the wiser on Aboriginal biological origins: "Our 35 years of blood group genetic research have unfortunately failed to provide us with any clues, at least obvious to us" (Simmons 1976, 319).

Attesting to the conservatism, or perhaps loyalty, of the Adelaide scientists, Abbie remained faithful to the archaic Caucasian hypothesis in the monograph I saw on John Mulvaney's bookshelf in Canberra. The theory was already outdated when he included it in the first edition of his book in 1969, perhaps contributing to the few and unenthusiastic reviews it received (Joseph B. Birdsell's 1972 review was predictably scathing as he defended his own tri-hybrid hypothesis).[24] Despite this, Abbie made no amendments to the second edition, adding only a preface that provided a few updates, including mention of the finally authenticated case of albinism that was venerated in the frontispiece.

Abbie's particular take on the archaic Caucasian gives some clues to his interest in albinism.[25] His account of the physical features of the Aboriginal population in his opening chapters sets the reader up for the origin theory to come. Updating Basedow's account of Aboriginal physical characteristics, he documents the "flaxen," "reddish-gold," and blond hair that also caught Griffith Taylor's attention, noting it occurs across the continent and in up to 80 percent of children in some central Australian "tribes" ([1969] 1976, 15).

He describes the wide variability of skin color, "from sienna and umber through light and medium to dark vandyke," indicating "that pigment shows less 'penetrance' in Aborigines than in some other coloured peoples."[26] Infants are noted as universally "pinkish-yellow" at birth and lacking the Mongolian spot "that seems to characterize the newly-born of what might be called the 'more committed' coloured peoples."[27] The "blackness" of Aboriginal people, Abbie surmises, "is far from fixed—that they may be on a sort of borderline between black and white." He entertains the possibility that their superficial blackness supports Klaatsch's theory: "that the Aborigines are a basic human type that gave rise—under the pressure of natural selection in different environments—to the whites on one hand and the blacks on the other." To definitively say one way or the other, he notes, "more evidence is needed" ([1969] 1976, 12–16).

In a later chapter, Abbie quickly dispatches Klaatsch's and Birdsell's theories to arrive at his favored archaic Caucasian hypothesis. "Proto-caucasians" from Central Asia gave rise to the Australians—Klaatsch's theory of Australian origins, he explains, but the other way around (figure 4.3). Once they migrated to Australia, he continues, their evolution stalled in a "primitive" stage while Caucasoid descendants advanced elsewhere. For Abbie, two critical pieces of evidence for his theory were the success of biological absorption and blood groups: "It is obvious on a number of grounds, such as the ready physical absorption of Aborigines into a white population and the close similarity of blood groupings, that the Aborigines appear to be closer to Caucasians generally than to any other people. It is possible that the Aborigines may even represent a basic physical type from which the Caucasians in their many varieties were evolved, and it is therefore quite logical, in our present knowledge at least, to class the Aborigines as 'proto-Caucasoids'" ([1969] 1976, 201–3).

The 1974 memoir of physiologist C. Stanton Hicks (whom we met in the introduction and who features in the next chapter) similarly illustrates the Adelaide scientists' commitment to the archaic Caucasian hypothesis, long past its use-by date. He reflects that "the Centralian tribes have a longer and more pure pedigree than the recent European intruders who (in a manner of

FIGURE 4.3. Map showing the purported migration of "proto-Caucasians" from Central Asia to Europe, the Middle East, South Asia, East Asia, and Australia. *Source:* Abbie (1969) 1976, 20.

speaking) happen to be their own civilized descendants" (1974, 11).[28] Australians were the original Europeans, and the colonists their progeny.

MY ENCOUNTER WITH ABBIE'S book that afternoon in Mulvaney's Canberra living room was the irresistible provocation for this inquiry into white belonging and the ghosts of colonial violence. The frontispiece (figure 4.2) and the map depicting the travels of the archaic Caucasian (figure 4.3) seemed to exist in relation to each other, but what was that relation? To answer this puzzle requires an exploration into racial desire, Australian nationalism, and reproductive politics.

As hinted by Abbie's mention of "physical absorption" as a key piece of evidence for the theory, the archaic Caucasian hypothesis was important to colonial reproductive policies of the early twentieth century. For the first century of European colonization, it was widely believed that Indigenous people would become extinct due to contact with a "higher" race.[29] As it became clear that the population of mixed-race Indigenous people was increasing in the early twentieth century, the White Australia policy was threatened from within. The proposed solution was the biological absorption of "half-castes" into the white population: "full-bloods" were still thought to be heading toward extinction. It is from this period that we see visions of a future Australia devoid of Indigenous people. A. O. Neville, the Western Australian commissioner for native affairs and a key assimilationist thinker, famously posed the rhetorical question in 1937: "Are we going to have a population of one million blacks in the Commonwealth or are we going to merge them into our white community and eventually forget that there were any aborigines in Australia?" (Commonwealth of Australia 1937, 11). A white Australian future required the successful absorption of the "aborigines."

But was biological absorption possible? Would the miscegenation of Indigenous people with Europeans (as this was the only ethnic mixture of interest) lead to degeneration and "throwbacks"? In the United States, such concern had led to the "one drop rule," otherwise known as "hypodescent" (Hollinger 2003). A person with any African ancestry at all was at risk of "throwback"—of blackness reemerging in their descendants—and was therefore most safely classified as black. Miscegenation was illegal in several states and frowned on throughout the Union. Was it safe for Australia to take a different path?

Policy makers turned to science for the answers, and Norman B. Tindale provided them. Known to friends and colleagues as "Tinny," Tindale was a precocious collector who was born in Perth in 1900 and moved with his family to Adelaide at seventeen. Soon after, he joined the South Australian Museum as an entomologist's assistant and published widely, only later going on to gain a science degree at the University of Adelaide (P. Jones 1987, 2008). He married a shop assistant, Dorothy, at twenty-four, and they stayed together until her death in 1969. Like Alfred C. Haddon and Baldwin Spencer, he came to anthropology through biology, and it became his main fare. When he visited physical anthropologist E. A. Hooton at Harvard University in 1936, Tindale was introduced to Hooton's graduate student Joseph B. Birdsell, who was looking for a dissertation topic. With similar interests in Aboriginal culture and origins, and complementary areas of expertise, Tindale and Birdsell struck up a lifelong friendship. Their research partnership led to the Harvard-Adelaide expedition of 1938–39, a major study of "race mixing" on behalf of the South Australian state government and funded by the Carnegie Institution. They were joined on the expedition by Dorothy and by Birdsell's wife, Bee, who had gone to the exclusive women's college Vassar and worked as an interior decorator in New York before marrying (W. Anderson 2002; Davis 2009; McGregor 2011).

Tindale and Birdsell measured and bled thousands of "mixed-race" Aboriginal people on missions and government stations (including a collection of five thousand hair samples still held in the South Australian Museum) (O'Brien 2007). Dorothy and Bee cooked, helped with the equipment, and collected crayon drawings from children (A. Roberts, Fowler, and Sansbury 2014). Tindale published his conclusions two years later, affirming the biological fitness of the "half-caste" and prescribing education, training, and integration. Preempting critics of race mixing, he carefully justified his position on scientific grounds: "Complete mergance of the half-castes into the general community is possible without detriment to the white race. Their aboriginal blood is remotely the same as that of the majority of white inhabitants of Australia, for the Australian aboriginal is recognised as being a forerunner of the Caucasian race. . . . There are no biological reasons for rejection of people with a dilute strain of Australian aboriginal blood. A low percentage of Australian aboriginal blood will not introduce any aberrant characteristics and there need be no fear of reversions to the dark aboriginal type" (Tindale 1941, 67).[30]

Then, as now, scientific and policy timelines are often out of sync, and although this scientific endorsement of biological absorption would have been reassuring to some, a new policy approach was already in the making. After World War II, the rise of assimilation policies and the quest for Aboriginal citizenship began to make questions of biological absorption obsolete. The new vision for Indigenous Australians was as full citizens regardless of their skin color or degrees of heritage (Elkin 1944; McGregor 2011).[31] In the 1930s, however, progressive scientists argued that people of mixed heritage were no danger to the body politic as their color would naturally dissolve over generations. As Warwick Anderson puts it, drawing on the language of the time, "'half-castes' would sink and show no trace" (2002, 222). Some scientists even dared to suggest that an archaic Caucasian injection would enhance the Australian race, introducing advantageous adaptations to the harsh climate that would assist white survival in the tropical north (W. Anderson 2002).

Policy problems and their scientific solutions are always more than they seem. They reflect collective needs and desires. For a settler colony like Australia, the problem of settlement always exceeded the (already substantial) practical challenges of climate, infrastructure, disease, and the need to "disperse" (a euphemism for dispossession or murder) remaining Aboriginal people who opposed the appropriation of their lands. From the point of view of the settler, the problem of settlement was also the problem of belonging: what Tom Griffiths calls "emotional possession" (1996, 4). While legal instruments of terra nullius, maritime technology, and firearms allowed Europeans to physically inhabit the great southern continent, how would they mentally inhabit it and feel at home?

A great many social science and humanities scholars have considered the mechanisms and consequences of white belonging.[32] Paul Carter's *The Road to Botany Bay* was a milestone in this literature. He described how Europeans made the land "theirs" through mapping and naming places, building dwellings and fences, and writing, painting, and seeing the land through a European lens. For Carter, landscape is "not a physical object: it is an object of desire, a figure of speech outlining the writer's exploratory impulse" (1987, 81).

From the beginning, Indigenous people were an obstacle to white desires to occupy, own, and belong to Australian landscapes. As mentioned, for the first century of colonization, the project of eliminating the "native" was the major—if unofficial—goal of the Australian colonies and their settlers, and the "doomed race theory" was a handy scientific accompaniment (McGregor 1997). As it became increasingly obvious that the Indigenous race would not expire, the archaic Caucasian theory came into its own, not just as a scientific validation of biological absorption, but as a vessel for varied and unstable archetypes of white-Aboriginal relations. As Warwick Anderson puts it, "Through biological investigation, strangers became kin, and the romance of the nomad became a family romance" (2002, 215). What kind of family was this? There are three possibilities to consider, each with different implications for the broader settler challenge of quieting the ghosts of colonial violence and taking "emotional possession" of the land.

The first possible family relationship between settlers and Indigenous people is "ancestral." Aboriginal people were seen as the distant progenitors and predecessors of "modern" Caucasians. This is a temporally strange kind of family, one that would require a time machine rather than a car to get together. Indigenous Australians were seen as "primitive" remnants of a much earlier stage of human existence, simultaneously present and past (J. Fabian 1983). Such an ancestral relationship, like every construction of marginalized people by their dominating societies, is flexible, contradictory, and highly convenient. These are not the kind of elders you need to listen to or take care of—they are the kind you *replace* and then poignantly remember at appointed times. This form of fictive kinship put Europeans *in place* in Australia. Colonial dispossession could be recast as a return "home."[33] More than that, white people were destined to continue the human story of the Australian continent, arrested as it was in the Stone Age, and bring it up to date.

The complex and multivalent relations contained in the archaic Caucasian theory were particularly potent in the burgeoning Australian nationalism of the 1930s. Many nationalists were fiercely anti-British, and indigeneity provided the perfect ingredient for a truly "Australian" culture. Artist Margaret Preston used Aboriginal motifs as inspiration, arguing for the appropriation of Aboriginal art as "a source of national authenticity" (Rowse 2017, 171). An Adelaide-based writers' collective who called themselves Jindyworobak—a name supposedly derived from a Woiwurrung word for "joining together"—produced poetry that drew on Aboriginal themes and stories in a quest for a unique form of national expression (W. Anderson 2002; T. Griffiths 1996; C. Healy 2008; McGregor 2011; A. Moran 2002).

A key figure in the Jindyworobak movement was writer, publisher, and political activist P. R. "Inky" Stephensen. Queensland born and educated, he studied at Oxford on a Rhodes scholarship in the 1920s, where he became friends with D. H. Lawrence and Aldous Huxley. He joined the Communist Party in England but later developed his own brand of Australian nationalism that embraced both Aboriginal rights and an anti-immigration rhetoric that eventually turned to fascist ideology (Munro 1992; Winter 2005). He published and vigorously promoted his friend (and later foe) Xavier Herbert's first book, *Capricornia* ([1938] 1972), an epic, transgressive novel depicting the violent and intimate interracial relations in the country's north.

As both Ellen Smith (2014) and Dan Tout (2017) have explored, the archaic Caucasian hypothesis was a perfect fit with Stephensen's eclectic vision. In embracing the hypothesis, his nationalist magazine, the *Publicist*, could support Aboriginal rights, reject nonwhite immigration, and forge a white Australian identity through the "Aryan Aborigine." As Smith puts it, "The Aryan Aborigine was really just the settler cast backwards, grounded in a million-year tradition" (2014, 104). In his unpublished novel "The Settlers," one of Stephensen's main characters endorses Klaatsch's theory of Australian origins: *The Aryan race began in Australia. Australia is the original home of the white man. In coming to this land we are returning home. . . . [We] are Australian Aborigines of a million years ago; gone white in the cold latitudes*" (quoted in E. Smith 2014, 105, italics in original).

While Stephensen looked to the deep past for an Indigenous origin for Europeans, Herbert sought to ground white belonging in closer lines of kinship. Herbert was born in Geraldton, Western Australia, in 1901; trained as a pharmacist in Perth; and later moved to Melbourne to study medicine, although he abandoned it once his short stories began to be published. He soon came to view his vocation as informing the highly urbanized Australian public about the reality of the frontier (McDougall 2007). *Capricornia* was an instant classic. It is usually read as the story of the "half-caste" Norman Shillingworth, who comes to know and embrace his maternal Aboriginal heritage. Ellen Smith offers an alternative reading that foregrounds the redemption provided to the troubled figure of Mark Shillingworth, Norman's biological father. By accepting his paternity of Norman, the "Aboriginal son provides the white man with a retrospective claim to autochthonous belonging" (E. Smith 2014, 109). In this vision of Australian nationhood, a deep Indigenous ancestry can only be recognized when white fathers acknowledge their Aboriginal progeny.

Smith illustrates this further through a breathless letter that Herbert wrote to Stephensen on first reading Stephensen's magnum opus, *The Foundations of Culture in Australia* (Stephensen 1936). Herbert told Stephensen of his plan "to found a gigantic organization called the Euraustralian League comprised of so called Halfcastes and Quartercastes and of any white fellas who can bring themselves to believe that there is nothing like Australia and that the culture of the land will grow like the gum-trees from the soil." He lamented that those without Aboriginal ancestry could never be properly Australian ("We are not Australia, Inky. Only those lucky people are") and that the only solution was to father children to Aboriginal mothers: "God help me, and all like me who were conceived by a Dreaming place Spirit and born of foreigners. There is no help for us, except that we place on our poor Aboriginal souls, through a lubra into a yeller feller—a true Australian" (quoted in E. Smith 2014, 110). For Herbert, white paternity of a racially distinct nation was the means to emphatically reject the "Pommies" he disparaged at every opportunity (Probyn 2003, 63). Displacing ties with the white "mother country," the "poor Aboriginal souls" of Australian-born Europeans would find belonging, not through an abstract tie with archaic Caucasians who would conveniently die out, but through the living bodies of a new "half-caste" nation.

A third form of racial family is suggested in the frontispiece of Abbie's monograph (figure 4.2). The black mother cradling her white child offers a maternal configuration of national kinship. I read it as a visual referent of the archaic Caucasian hypothesis—black ancestor to the white race. This haunting correspondence between the image and the map (figure 4.3) provides one explanation for Abbie's decision to include the image in the second edition when he changed nothing else, other than adding a three-page preface. The preface mentions other subjects that could make for inviting images—medicine men and new archaeological findings, for example—but he only chose to show Lorna and her mother. The mother's supportive arms and protective gaze contain the wisdom of the maternal ancestors who promise to care for us and guide us even as we overrun and replace them.

In a limited way, this maternal formulation is an antidote to the stark gender politics of Xavier Herbert's racial nationalism. Smith notes that his "retrospective claim to autochthonous belonging" requires the erasure of Aboriginal women except as reproductive vessels. The "lubra" of his letter to Stephensen is merely a means to produce offspring, after which time they should conveniently exit the historical stage. In *Capricornia*, Smith tells us, "almost all the Aboriginal women die ... and all the Aboriginal mothers die" (2014, 114). At least Lorna's mother is alive and well, even, according to Alan Walker, offering "more care than usual" to her child (*Canberra Times* 1969). Any optimism, however, is immediately crushed by the most obvious referent of the black mother/pale child dyad from a twenty-first-century vantage point: the Stolen Generations. The racial logic of assimilation, captured in the famous "Three Generation" image from A. O. Neville's *Australia's Coloured Minority*, promised that white descendants of Aboriginal people could seamlessly assimilate if raised far from "negative" maternal influences (figure 4.4). If Lorna's whiteness had been due to ancestry rather than a genetic error, she may have been removed from her family by the director of social welfare and placed in an institution such as the Retta Dixon home in Darwin, a place where many residents later reported being abused (Royal Commission into Institutional Responses to Child Sexual Abuse 2015).[34]

Abbie wrote of the rising "half-caste" population in his book, praising the policy shift from absorption to assimilation and asserting that Aboriginal women prefer to marry white or light-skinned Aboriginal men. Although "nobody now wants the Aborigines to disappear," he notes that "already a great

number—probably thousands—*have* disappeared into the white population . . .
[s]o to some extent the Aborigines are contributing to their own extinction"
([1969] 1976, 247). While his view that Indigenous people were embracing
absorption and assimilation—at least "to some extent"—would have been
shared by many settler Australians in the 1970s, the tragedy of what would become known as the Stolen Generations was about to come to public attention.

It was just one year after this book appeared that the traumatic human
cost of racial policies began to be recognized by non-indigenous Australians. An important figure in this shift was Koori activist Margaret Tucker
(1904–96), who grew up on Cummeragunja Mission on the Murray River.
Despite the desperate attempts of her mother to evade the authorities, Tucker
and her younger sister were removed by force from school when she was thirteen and placed in the Cootamundra Domestic Training Home for Aboriginal
Girls, where they experienced abuse. Her autobiography, published in 1977, is
remembered as the first widely read account of the crushing effects of assimilation policies.

IN ONE WAY OR another, all the stories told in this chapter are concerned
with saving the white child. The whitening child of the Australian nation
must be saved from "primitive" blackness by removing "mixed-race" children
from their parents; by white fathers claiming their Indigenous children; by
rescuing the captive or lost white, or their descendants; or by saving the imper-

FIGURE 4.4. Image caption: "Three Generations (Reading from right to left): 1. Half
blood (Irish-Australian father; full-blood Aboriginal mother). 2. Quadroon daughter
(Father Australian born of Scottish parents; Mother No. 1). 3. Octaroon grandson
(Father Australian of Irish descent; Mother No. 2)." *Source:* Neville 1947, 72.

iled albino who might be worshipped but might be killed. Stephensen wants to replace them—allowing Europeans to return to our rightful place, a million years on—and Herbert wants to progenerate a uniquely Australian race. Abbie is simply reassured that the white-Aboriginal child exists, solving a medical anomaly that troubled him, seemingly unaware of the haunting echoes of the archaic Caucasian and the premonition of the Stolen Generations.

A popular account of McPhee's pursuit of Jungun can be read in this light. Zadel Barnes Gustafson (1841–1917), an American writer for the major US news weekly *Frank Leslie's Illustrated Newspaper*, visited Melbourne during Jungun's tenure at the Waxworks. She viewed him and interviewed McPhee in depth, producing a long-form account that was reprinted in many Australian newspapers. Although she employed substantial poetic license, her version of events is still instructive for understanding the reception of Jungun and his story. Jungun was a man, not a child, but he was no less in need of saving: "A savage, indeed, with the habits, the heredity, and the inescapable stamp of the wilderness upon him, but a man with a head more commanding than rests on the shoulders of any known savage king, or of most European potentates; and with brows and temples of a model to match with any in the deliberate conclaves of the civilised world." Her description of McPhee's first encounter with Jungun is one of recognition: "'You are very like me, you see,' said McPhee to him. . . . 'You are not black like your people, you are white like me; you had better come with me and see my people.' . . . Jungun took kindly to white men's clothes, and with a well-cut suit on looked like a prince" (Gustafson 1893).[35]

Despite living with "savages," the white child of the Australian nation is one of us—even a prince—and must be saved. All this searching for, saving, and producing Aboriginal whiteness had a greater, implicit purpose: to make a place for whiteness in Australia.

Michael Robinson's analysis of the widespread fascination with white tribes in the late nineteenth century again provides a useful comparison. He argues it was an expression of "lingering insecurity" about Western culture: "As much as finding lost tribes represented the research interests of scientists and explorers, it also reflected a deeper, less articulated concern of the Western world: the desire to find itself" (2016, 255).

The desire to find oneself and one's culture in the Other was only more urgent for the settler, who had a pressing personal and collective need to feel at home. Indigenous people themselves were only of interest as tools to tell the stories that white society needed to hear. As Warwick Anderson notes, the doctors turned anthropologists who studied Aboriginal people in the early decades of the twentieth century were spectacularly uninterested in "the normal and abnormal functioning of Aboriginal bodies. The epidemiology of Aboriginal 'extinction' was hardly known." Settler scientists studied the Other in order to learn about themselves. In constructing the archaic Caucasian hypothesis, "scientists and amateur naturalists had unintentionally produced a displaced, allegorical account of white racial history in Australia" (2002, 193).

Ultimately, the whiteness of Aboriginal people—even those with albinism—turned out to be superficial and fleeting. McPhee had planned a London leg of their tour, but instead Jungun went back to his family in 1891 (McPhee 1891). McPhee's account of the return journey doesn't mention why their touring lives were cut short, but other accounts of Indigenous traveling performers suggest Jungun was probably enacting his own agency in returning home (Thrush 2016). Newspaper reports suggest another reason: Jungun "gradually turned black, and thus lost his attraction as an exhibit" (*Bulletin* 1929). Although we can't know exactly why Jungun returned, let's consider this dermal explanation. Jungun appeared to be "white like me" when McPhee met him in the desert, but his whiteness may have been ephemeral: his skin turned dark. He may have had a form of albinism that conferred some pigment, as suggested by his "reddish-brown" hair (*West Australian* 1934). In those cases, the skin can darken over time as melanin is belatedly produced.

The fantasy of Aboriginal assimilation also turned dark, in the sense of bleak and sinister (see C. Elder 2009). After Margaret Tucker's autobiography was published in 1977, other survivors and historians compiled evidence of the scale and nature of what had occurred across the country (Haebich 1992, 2000; Pilkington 1996; Read 1982). This culminated in *Bringing Them Home*, the landmark report of a national inquiry into the Stolen Generations, eventually followed by a national apology from Australian prime minister Kevin Rudd in 2008 (Human Rights and Equal Opportunity Commission 1997). The reality of child removal and its multigenerational aftermath are now well known, and many organizations exist to reconnect families affected by the Stolen Generations to their history and kin. This dark history of absorption and assimilation haunts Abbie's frontispiece.

Abbie, Basedow, and others believed that Aboriginal blackness was only superficial, their dark pigment barely penetrant. Theories of racial absorption viewed Indigenous people as white-in-waiting: exposure to white culture, miscegenation, and the passage of time would allow their inner whiteness to blossom (figure 4.4). As it turns out, the opposite is true: it is the whiteness of light-skinned Indigenous people that is only skin deep. The sweeping political changes from the late 1960s led to a notion of "pan-indigeneity" that embraced all Indigenous Australians as equally Indigenous, regardless of skin color or physical appearance (Beckett 2014). Today the Aboriginal and Torres Strait Islander population of over 800,000 is highly diverse and rapidly increasing. In nearly 80 percent of Indigenous families, one of the two biological parents is non-indigenous, and over 90 percent of their children go on to identify as Indigenous. On top of the substantial natural population increases from births to Indigenous and mixed couples, over 120,000 people identified as Indigenous for the first time in the 2016 census, a status known by statisticians as "newly identified."[36] Nearly all of them were from the large cities of southeastern Australia. Simultaneously, forty thousand switched their identification the other way, from Indigenous to non-indigenous, leaving a net number of around eighty thousand new identifiers (Australian Bureau of Statistics 2016). Already in 2012–13, almost ninety-two thousand Indigenous Australians (17 percent of the then Indigenous population) reported that the people they "mix with" were unlikely to know they were Indigenous, supposedly because their physical appearance did not indicate it (Crawford 2015). All of this points to an Indigenous population that is increasingly merging visually with the non-indigenous population while holding fast to their Indigenous identity (Kowal 2017).

The ephemerality of Aboriginal whiteness contains many ironies. White fathers (and white mothers) are far from the redemptive figures Herbert dreamed of: their racial identity is spurned by many of their Indigenous descendants, who reject white identification (Kowal and Paradies 2017). The choice that A. O. Neville proposed in 1937—"one million blacks in the Commonwealth" or mergence into "our white community"—was a false choice. Both things are occurring, and without any "forgetting" of Indigenous Australia (Commonwealth of Australia 1937, 11). The "ultimate objective" of biological absorption, aided by the archaic Caucasian hypothesis, was "the complete disappearance of mixed-bloods as a distinct ethnic group" (McGregor 1996, 16). While many Indigenous people have effectively "disappeared" as a visually distinct ethnic group, they are no less Indigenous for it. Meanwhile, many non-indigenous Australians continue to struggle to feel at home. The migrant, and particularly the refugee, has become the primary scapegoat for white anxieties (Hage 2003).

Despite the failure of each of these attempts to recognize whiteness in Indigenous people, or to entice or force them to be white, the intricate play of sameness and difference continues in the Australian settler colony. One telling place we see this is the website of the largest ancestry company in the world, Ancestry.com. For just AU$129, anyone can send a saliva sample for DNA analysis and receive a report of how their results compare to the 15 million customer samples in their database. Melanesia, just one of the thousand "regions" that make up their ethnicity database, is the category that encompasses Indigenous Australian ancestry.[37] Under a short section in their customer information on Melanesia, entitled "Additional Genetic Facts about the Melanesia Region," the company chooses to highlight blond hair: "Among the interesting characteristics of Melanesian and Aboriginal Australian populations is the evolution of blond hair, which is believed to have developed independently of the blond hair seen in Europeans" (Ancestry, n.d.).

Here blond hair is an Indigenous trait, not indicative of lost explorers, shipwrecked sailors, or white tribes. Behind the identification of this "interesting" feature by a multinational genome corporation lies over a century of scientific speculation and popular fascination about Aboriginal whiteness. The play of sameness and difference continues, providing fertile ground for ghosts.

Indigenous Physiology

Metabolism, Cold Tolerance, and the Possibility of Human Hibernation

Isolated, a continent inhabited only by hunters and gatherers at the time of contact with Europeans, [Australia] presented a unique kind of laboratory for testing evolutionary hypotheses.
—Joseph B. Birdsell, "Physical Anthropology in Australia Today," 1979

The ephemeral and elusive whiteness of Indigenous people haunted the intersecting stories told in the previous chapter. In this chapter it is spectacular forms of Indigenous biological difference that entice a range of historical and contemporary actors to pursue ghostly presences. The Indigenous bodies of interest in this chapter are framed by scientists not as uncanny echoes of whiteness, but as vessels of novel biological capabilities. The perception of the Australian continent as geographically isolated from the relatively contiguous continents of Africa, Europe, mainland Asia, and America led scientists to believe that Australians were biologically unique, which all too often meant "primitive." In the twentieth century, and particularly since the vast antiquity of Indigenous occupation of the Australian continent began to be understood by archaeologists in the 1960s, this characterization morphed into a belief that thousands of years of adaptation to unique environments had marked the bodies of Indigenous people with unique evolutionary signatures.

This chapter follows the history and potential future of one such supposed evolutionary signature and its obscure phenotype. The phenomenon of temporary hibernation—called "torpor"—is believed by some to be possessed by at least one group of Indigenous Australians. These speculations began with the physiological experiments of C. Stanton Hicks on Aboriginal men of the central desert in the 1930s, as briefly described in the opening of this book. Hicks made the unexpected observation that these men could tolerate sleeping naked in the freezing conditions of the desert night and wondered if they achieved this by entering into a hibernation-like state. Hicks's odd premonition was followed up in the wake of World War II by the investigations of Swedish American physiologist P. F. "Pete" Scholander on behalf of the US Office of Naval Research and the Air Force.

Human torpor is a spectacular example of Indigenous biological difference—especially if it is true. The unlikely afterlives of Hicks's research illustrate the stakes involved in either taking purported biological differences seriously or dismissing them as (at best) fanciful or (at worst) racist. As we will see, there are good reasons to rebuff settler stories of Indigenous superpowers that might one day assist with interplanetary travel as a noble-savage subgenre of science fiction. Nevertheless, the possibility that biological fictions might actually be true can haunt even the most skeptical critic. Once accepted into the realm of the possible, the story of human torpor can reveal the strange entanglements that bind twentieth-century physiology, US defense objectives, a remorseful bioprospector, and a twenty-first-century anthropologist struggling to make sense of it all. The strange bedfellows inhabiting this chapter include two ghostly presences. The first is the man who alerted me to this story, whom I knew only as DT. The second haunting presence is the potential ability of some Aboriginal men to reduce their basal metabolism to better tolerate cold desert nights. These metabolic powers may reflect the interaction of environment and genes over millennia, persisting as genetic or epigenetic signatures in their descendants.

Let us dwell on this second haunting presence for a moment. As discussed in chapter 1, the possibility that some Indigenous Australians could have biologically meaningful differences attributable to their Indigenous ancestry is disturbing for many. Historically, the notion that Indigenous people, Africans, women, or any other oppressed group had "biological differences" was often used as a weapon of domination. At different times and places, science was used to justify why certain people couldn't own property, attend school, use a certain drinking fountain, in other words, why they were not properly human. Globally, Indigenous people in Australia have been among the groups most maligned by assertions of biological inferiority. From 1788 to the mid-twentieth century, scientific assertions of the "primitive" nature of Indigenous people were important in justifying the many forms of dispossession and genocide wrought by colonial occupation.

This has directly led to a strong aversion to the idea of inherent Indigenous biological difference for anyone interested in social justice, a group that includes many in the social science and humanities disciplines and many health professionals. I felt and observed this as a young doctor working in Indigenous health. As I recount in the introduction, to say that there were any meaningful biological differences between Indigenous and non-indigenous people—aside from the physical effects of various forms of racism—was seen as suspiciously racist. A geneticist I knew who spent a few years trying to develop research projects in Indigenous communities described a repeated experience of talking about their work in social situations. This person had recently moved to Australia and was keen to meet new people. They soon found that mentioning genetic research and Indigenous people at a party or the pub was a conversation killer, causing people to involuntarily cringe. For progressive Australians, the possibility that Indigenous people might be genetically susceptible to some diseases or resistant to others can make their skin crawl.

This reaction of disgust to the idea of Indigenous biological difference is related to a broader phenomenon described by political theorist Samantha Frost: the difficulties that the social sciences have with the category of "biological processes." She describes a widespread "wariness about including biological processes" in critical social science scholarship due to "the ongoing effort of social and political theorists to challenge the use of biology as an index of social and political status—and the corollary use of sex, race, and ability as the hinge upon which political dignity and freedom rest" (2018, 900; see also Frost 2016).[1] For some decades, this wariness has been managed through a strict division of labor between the sciences and the social sciences. According to this unwritten rule, the sciences will keep out of "politics," and the social sciences will keep out of science on the condition that everyone will affirm that there are no essential biological differences between dominant groups and minority groups: there are only inequalities resulting from disadvantage and oppression, some of which manifest in bodies.

This returns us to the discussion in chapter 1 of Jenny Reardon's analysis of periodic crises of racialized biology. The ability of episodes like the Human Genome Diversity Project (Reardon 2005) and the "Warrior Gene" controversy

(Hook 2009) to cause an international scandal is a "consequence of a system that delineates the social and the political from the biological: sociologists and humanists can only encounter race's return within biology when they fail to see it all along; biologists can only experience a shock of politicization when the ongoing political dimensions of their work are out of view" (Dunklee, Reardon, and Wentworth 2006). When the unwritten rules separating (or in a Latourian idiom, purifying) "apolitical" science from "abiological" social science are transgressed, shock follows (Latour 1993).

This chapter dwells in the shock and disgust provoked by racialized difference through a story of a human superpower that may have been observed in Indigenous people of central and northern Australia nearly a century ago and that may have spectacular legacies in the technological futures of the present. The shadowy nature of this story—Is it real? Is it a hoax?—is instructive for understanding the haunting qualities of Indigenous biological difference. Haunting can be caused by unseen forces but also by the limits of knowledge. Comforted by what we think we know, we are haunted by what might turn out to be true.

What follows begins with C. Stanton Hicks's journey from a small town in New Zealand to Cambridge, Adelaide, and Cockatoo Creek. It outlines his musings on Aboriginal physiological prowess based on his observations in the desert predawn one morning in 1931. The chapter then explains the phenomenon of torpor in mammals and birds, and the speculation surrounding the potential to induce a state of torpor in humans as a medical intervention or to aid space travel. I then describe my digital encounters with DT, an enigmatic character who contacted me a few years ago and claimed to research biomimicry applications for a secret company. He told me he had discovered the secret of the endogenous cooling observed by Hicks and Scholander and was concerned about the ethics of the original experiments and the potential for harm toward Indigenous people once his discovery was publicly known. He believed the phenomenon was the key to unlocking torpor in humans, a discovery that could lead to new cancer treatments, enable space travel, and extend human life but could also allow the embodied transport of biological weapons by terrorists, who could use torpor to mask a fever as they passed through international borders.

DT's wild claims led me to look further into the desert sleepers, uncovering links to US defense research in the Cold War era. P. F. Scholander, a Norwegian physiologist, led research trips to central and northern Australia in the 1950s that appeared to confirm the unique physiological abilities of Aboriginal people to control their metabolism. That research remains a staple of the scientific literature on cold tolerance. I contextualize this postwar research as part of Big Biology, an effort to upscale biological research that substantially focused on the organic information hidden in the bodies of Indigenous people. "Salvage biology" sought to sample and preserve these biological signatures before cultural and biological assimilation made them disappear.

The mystery of cold tolerance in central Australia is firmly bound to the Cold War, a period rife with conspiracies. Was the secret of human torpor contained in Indigenous bodies now being covertly deployed for the strategic gain of foreign powers? Or was this a fanciful product of my paranoid imagination? The chapter concludes with a haunting experience of missing data in a *Nature* paper, prompting me to suspect a conspiracy of silence surrounding Indigenous physiological abilities. While the missing data turn out to be a red herring, the significance of desert sleeping remains highly uncertain, ever threatening to transgress the boundaries of both "apolitical" science and "abiological" social science.

BORN AND RAISED IN a working-class family in the far south of New Zealand, C. Stanton Hicks excelled at school and studied chemistry at the University of Otago. After graduating with honors in 1915, he joined the New Zealand war effort, manufacturing chloramine-T to disinfect the nasal passages of troops and prevent the spread of meningitis. After the war he worked as a police toxicologist to finance his medical studies while continuing his chemistry research. In 1923 he was awarded a prestigious Beit Memorial Medical Fellowship to undertake doctoral studies at Cambridge on the physiology of the thyroid gland (Nash 1996). He used dogs, rats, and rabbits to study the innervation and secretion of the thyroid and the effect of diet on thyroid function (Hicks 1926a, 1926b).

As he finished his doctorate, a friend alerted him to a position in physiology at the University of Adelaide, noting it would suit his "imperialist outlook" (Hicks 1974, 1). Although he had opportunities for employment at Cambridge, as a New Zealander he felt a sense of duty "to return and work for the Dominions" (Nash 1996). He was received in Adelaide by the spirited professor of anatomy Frederic Wood Jones, a key figure in forming the Board for Anthropological Research and the Anthropological Society of South Australia.[2]

Soon after Hicks arrived in Adelaide in 1926, Wood Jones suggested he take up an invitation to collaborate with Francis G. Benedict, an American chemist at the Carnegie Institute for Nutrition in Boston. Benedict had risen to scientific fame in physiology and biochemistry after fasting a "Maltese" man in his lab for thirty-one days in 1911 (Benedict 1912). He was the world-leading researcher of metabolism and was interested in collaborating with Hicks on racial differences in basal metabolic rate (BMR)—a measure of the minimum level of energy expenditure an organism needs to continue living. It is measured in a resting, postabsorptive, and thermoneutral state—meaning that the body is not moving, is not digesting food, and is not cold or hot—and for many years, it was the best way to assess thyroid function. By the mid-1920s, physiologists had demonstrated that "Chinese" people had a lower BMR than Europeans and that women had a lower BMR than men.[3] A study of "paleolithic Aborigines" was clearly an attractive addition to the literature on the "racial factor" in metabolism.[4]

Hicks's first attempt at measuring Aboriginal BMR at Koonibba Mission Station in 1929 proved disappointing. He found the "detribalized natives" there uncooperative and was not able to collect meaningful data. He informed Benedict that a study would not be possible and considered experimenting on Aboriginal prisoners in the Alice Springs jail instead. The field study of Aboriginal physiology was revived when Wood Jones invited Hicks on a Board for Anthropological Research expedition to study "natives in their tribal state" at Cockatoo Creek, 250 miles northwest of Alice Springs (Hicks 1963, 41). The Board for Anthropological Research had been formed by the University of Adelaide after a flurry of anthropological activity that aimed to impress visitors from the Rockefeller Foundation in 1925 who were considering funding Australia's first chair in anthropology. Disappointingly for the Adelaide scientists, the chair went to Sydney, and the Board for Anthropological Research was something of a consolation prize for Adelaide's efforts. As discussed in chapter 2, the board organized more than forty expeditions to remote Indigenous communities before it was dissolved in 1975 (W. Anderson 2002; P. Jones 1987; Peterson 1990; see figures 2.2 and 5.1).

The first expedition that Hicks joined set out in the winter of 1931. The journey to Cockatoo Creek passed through Coniston station, unoccupied at the time. Just three years earlier, this had been the site of the last mass killing of Aboriginal people by the Northern Territory police, retribution for the murder of a white dingo hunter (Bradley 2019; B. Elder 1992). The violence of the frontier would have been known to the scientists, increasing their resolve to record invaluable data before it was too late.

The party of scientists included South Australian Museum anthropologist Norman B. Tindale, biologist Thomas Harvey Johnston, and four founding members of the Board for Anthropological Research: dentist Thomas Draper Campbell, pathologist J. B. Cleland, and physician-anthropologists Henry Kenneth Fry and Robert Pulleine. The agenda was similar to that of previous

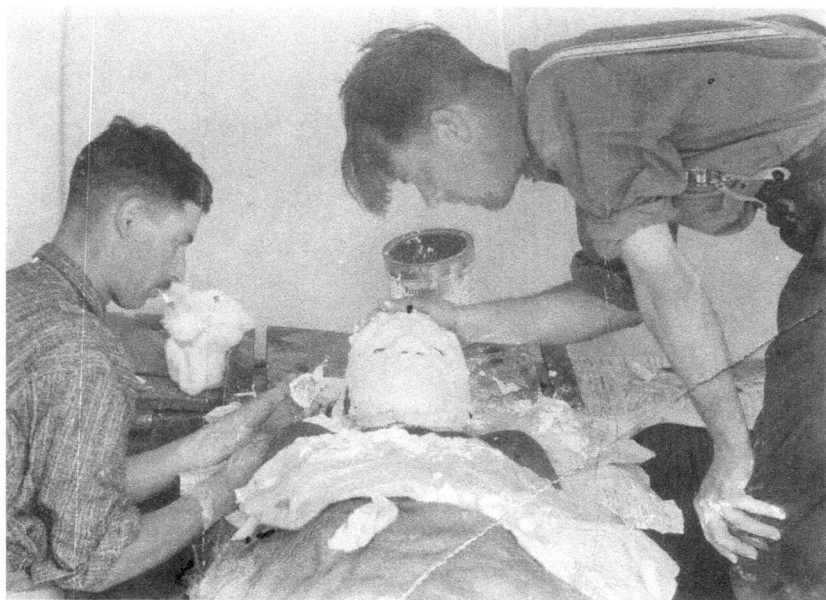

FIGURE 5.1. Herbert John Wilkinson (1891–1963), anatomist, and James Hugo Gray (1909–41), medical student and physical anthropologist, taking a facial cast of an unknown Aboriginal man on a Board for Anthropological Research expedition. *Source:* South Australia Museum.

expeditions: physical measurements, blood grouping, psychological testing, and dental investigations. Hicks's physiological research was a new addition.

The most important instruments carried by Hicks and his two assistants, R. Francis Matters and Ernest Eldridge, were a Benedict Portable Respiration Apparatus to measure oxygen consumption and a Douglas Bag to measure the carbon dioxide in expired air (see figure 5.2). If data were collected early in the morning, just as subjects woke from sleep, BMR could be calculated from these two measurements. As Hicks describes it in the published report of the expedition, "The practical difficulties in the way of conducting such work in the field are considerable, quite apart from the difficulty of conveying instructions through signs or by interpreters of mediocre facility" (Hicks, Moore, and Eldridge 1934, 79). Sensitive instruments did not survive the rough or nonexistent roads navigated in battered vehicles. The instruments that did survive malfunctioned in conditions of heat and humidity they were not designed for (in this case, a Haldane Gas Analysis Apparatus), and buzzing flies interfered with every measurement and tested the mental endurance of the scientists.

FIGURE 5.2. Douglas Bag measurement, Cockatoo Creek, 1931. *Source:* South Australia Museum.

Despite the numerous challenges, Hicks was overwhelmed with the success of the expedition. In contrast with his experiences at Koonibba Mission, the Anmatjera and Ilpirra "natives" at Cockatoo Creek proved to be ideal research subjects, gaining Hicks's respect as "so intelligent, so courteous and good natured, and so willing and interested in co-operating in our experiments despite all the associated discomfort and restraint" (Hicks 1974, 20).[5]

This cooperation was a result of groundwork by the nonscientist members of the expedition, Swiss lay preacher Ernst Kramer and ex-drover and tour guide Fred Colson. Both had liaised with tribes for months beforehand to organize their participation, and Colson had erected makeshift creek crossings along the way to allow the vehicles to reach their destination. Hicks spent much of the journey in the front cab as Colson drove. Colson advised him to present the research as "'big medicine' for men only" and to not attempt to take rectal temperatures, then (as now) the standard measurement of core temperature.

On arrival at Cockatoo Creek, Hicks, his assistant, and his technician set up their equipment in front of an impassive group of Anmatjera men armed with spears. As the scientists demonstrated the experimental procedure, Kramer and his Arunta interpreter, Peter, explained to the group that the scientists "were medicine men, and the ritual they would perform would, if they chose to co-operate, greatly improve their wind" (Hicks 1974, 29).[6] The scientists, Kramer and Peter explained, would arrive very early in the morning at their camp to perform the ceremony, which was only available to fully initiated men, who would have to lie quite still and breathe through a tightly fitting tube with a clip sealing their nose. The group listened and watched intently and then left, leaving Hicks "in a state of shattered, incredulous uncertainty" about what would happen the next morning (30).

As told in the opening of this book, the anxious trio of scientists woke at 4:30 a.m., when the ambient temperature was minus three degrees Celsius, and made their way to the camp by the light of their kerosene lanterns. They encountered nine young men lying perpendicular to a windbreak of small branches and grasses two feet high, and small fires, some still smoldering, at their feet and in between them. The men appeared to be sleeping as the scientists approached and began their experiment on the first man. Although they struggled to get the mouthpiece and noseclips to fit properly, they successfully took multiple measurements on three subjects, who, Hicks recalled, "suffered . . . indignities at our hands without one single departure from the strict requirements of our precise measurement of their oxygen intake!" (1974, 33). Hicks was astounded at their ability to remain perfectly still. Their "respiration and pulse rates," he remarked, "remained regular as clockwork. Did someone mention Yoga?" (32). The comparison of the desert men to yogis is a repeating trope in Hicks's memoir.

Their painstaking measurements found that the BMR of their subjects was the same as it was in Europeans. Hicks interpreted this through the "archaic Caucasian" hypothesis, which had recently been reinforced by the discovery that blood groups were the "same" as for Europeans (as discussed in the previous chapter). "These Centralian aborigines, though living for thousands of years on this isolated continent, had retained their archaic white metabolic character" (Hicks 1963, 45).

Hicks's finding of similarity confirmed the theory of racial origins held by many of the Adelaide scientists but also raised another set of questions. Measurements of BMR in Europeans were made first thing in the morning in a warm bed in a warm room. "These aborigines were in no warm bed. They were naked on the ground with air temperatures well below freezing point" (Hicks 1974, 38). His attempts to explain this phenomenon led Hicks to become an expert in cold tolerance. Subsequent research suggested that rather than increase their metabolism to cope with the cold, as the average human would do, desert Indigenous people lowered their metabolism and vastly reduced the blood flow and temperature of their legs. The coldest subject had a core temperature of thirty-one degrees Celsius with a skin temperature of twenty-three degrees. Hicks speculated that they possessed "some unexpected physiological mechanism which enabled the aborigine to conserve his body heat, which otherwise would have escaped by radiation and convection from the skin surface. In other words, could the aborigines regulate their radiators?" (1974, 38).

Hicks's supposition was influenced by an observation he made on that first morning of data collection at Cockatoo Creek when, still before sunrise, they completed the measurements of their first research subject. "When number one sat up, after we had finished with him, he shivered, quite violently! He then pushed the end of a smouldering piece of firewood at his feet into the middle of the ashes, after waving it about in the air until it began to glow. Obviously he hadn't FELT cold before sitting up. Was it because, when sitting, he exposed his torso to the movement of ground air? So far as we could judge there was no wind, not a zephyr. Or, had he suddenly switched his vegetative (involuntary) nervous system from 'sleep' to 'wake'?" (33).

Hicks's strange, unpublished musings are key to a haunting metabolic possibility that animates this chapter. Did Aboriginal people from desert regions possess the ability to reduce their metabolic rate and enter a state known as "torpor," a diurnal form of hibernation? Hicks apparently thought so. The scientific paper reporting this research describes how "the natives did not shiver or show any sign of discomfort. They were, in fact, torpid" (Hicks and Matters 1933, 178). The conclusion of the paper expresses it more tentatively, observing that in cold as severe as minus two degrees Celsius, "unclothed" natives "living in the savage state" showed "no indication of shivering and the natives lay as if torpid" (180). Another paper refers to the "torpor of the natives" at Cockatoo Creek, who demonstrated "more effective vasomotor control than that possessed by the civilised individual, and consequently a smaller skin circulation in the cold" (Hicks, Moore, and Eldridge 1934, 86). If Hicks was correct that Aboriginal people used torpor as an adaptation to cold, they would be unique among humans.

"HIBERNATION," "TORPOR," AND "ESTIVATION" are all terms for periods of lowered metabolic rate and lowered core temperature. Broadly, animals can be divided into ectotherms, or cold-blooded animals, whose internal temperature varies with the environment, and endotherms, or warm-blooded animals, who maintain a higher and relatively constant internal temperature. Some endotherms—birds and mammals—use torpor or hibernation to survive periods of environmental stress (reduced food or water availability or cold). The most well-known hibernators are bears and squirrels, but many other animals use similar mechanisms to lower their energy requirements for periods of less than twenty-four hours (known as "torpor") or in warmer climates (known as "estivation").[7] In this chapter I use the term "torpor," following the bulk of the literature and my historical actors, while acknowledging the overlapping and contested definitions of these terms.

Torpor involves a reduction in metabolic rate to as low as 10 percent of usual levels, and a reduction in core temperature ranging from just a few degrees all the way down to the ambient temperature. Heart rate, respiratory rate, and oxygen consumption all decrease. At the cellular level, four things are crucial for successful torpor. In a low-oxygen state, cells are programmed to die, a process called "apoptosis." This needs to be prevented to stop tissue damage during torpor. The immune system needs to be reduced, and the clotting system needs to be downregulated to prevent blood clots in an environment of slow blood flow. Finally, when the body emerges from torpor, the rapid increase in the use of oxygen produces "oxidative stress" and tissue damage without the action of antioxidative agents. A complex cascade of physiological processes produces this wide range of effects whenever torpor is initiated (Daanen and Van Marken Lichtenbelt 2016; Lee 2008; Staples 2016).

Each of these physiological features is the holy grail of one or another aspect of medicine and points to a myriad of potential applications in humans. While humans are not known to experience torpor, the genes that govern the process are preserved in all mammals, giving researchers hope that methods to safely induce "synthetic torpor," and to end it, are possible (Pan 2018, 6). If that could be achieved, the range of uses reads like science fiction. Researchers in the field of space travel are said to be actively developing methods to induce torpor in astronauts to reduce their requirements for food, water, and physical space, and reduce radiation exposure, in preparation for travel to Mars (Choukèr et al. 2019). Other torpor-related research includes work on "therapeutic hypothermia," primarily to preserve organ damage from hypoxia (e.g., due to a heart attack or blood loss from injuries) and also as a method of cryogenic preservation and life extension (Cerri 2017). The US Department of Defense, and no doubt others, is a large funder of torpor research given its potential use to enhance what they term "survivability" (Drummond 2009).[8]

Essential to inducing torpor are so-called hibernation induction triggers. There have been reports of successfully transfusing blood from one hibernating animal to another of the same species to induce hibernation, and even to induce hibernation in non-hibernating species (Cerri et al. 2013; Tupone, Madden, and Morrison 2013). Various compounds have been tested for their ability to induce torpor in animals, as well as techniques of inhibiting specific parts of the brain stem. The field remains controversial, with some reports of synthetic torpor in small mammals contested (Blackstone, Morrison, and Roth 2005; Swoap, Rathvon, and Gutilla 2007; Zhang et al. 2006). Meanwhile, the popular science articles continue to talk up the "superpowers" that might be possible if torpor could be harnessed by humans.

I WAS ALERTED TO a possible link between Hicks's experiments and space travel in an unsolicited email from a person—whom I'll call DT—who contacted me for advice. He claimed to work for a secret biomimicry operation that subcontracted to various defense ministries and pharmaceutical companies. He had been working for a decade, he told me, to identify a trigger for torpor in humans and believed he had found the secret—a complex respiratory procedure. The work was inspired by Hicks's research, and DT was concerned that Indigenous Australians would get no credit for their physiological part in it. The research was on the verge of being capitalized on by departments of defense or by "big pharma," he wrote. When that happened, it was highly likely researchers would come looking for those desert people that Hicks had studied, eager to sample their DNA for genetic and epigenetic clues to upscaling what DT had discovered. He had spent some time in Australia when he was young, and he understood the history and legacies of colonization and the unethical nature of Hicks's research by today's standards. He was motivated to contact me after he read my work analyzing twentieth-century biological research on Indigenous people. He didn't want to be a biopirate. What would I advise?

My first thought, of course, was that this was a hoax. The name was clearly a pseudonym, and the domain name of his email didn't appear on the web. His mode of expression seemed strange, but I knew this could reflect my unfamiliarity with the international bioprospecting community. The level of detail he provided made it seem genuine, and the story intrigued me, so I emailed back. We exchanged emails over the next few weeks and eventually talked at length on Skype. After the Skype conversation, I received a final email, which I did not reply to at the time, occupied with many other things. After some time I wondered what had happened and tried to contact DT by email and Skype. The emails bounced back, and the Skype message went unanswered. I was left with a correspondence and conversation that raised many more questions than it answered, to say the least. As I looked further into the story, I found myself following a trail of plausible connections and mysterious coincidences.

I had known about Hicks's research since first reading historian Warwick Anderson's groundbreaking book *The Cultivation of Whiteness* (2002) many years before. Hicks's experiments are mentioned in the magisterial chapter "From Deserts the Prophets Come." More recently, I had delved further into the Board for Anthropological Research as I grappled to understand the sweep of twentieth-century human biology of Indigenous Australians. DT told me that after the war, more research was done into the desert sleepers on behalf of American defense interests.

The protagonist of those postwar efforts was P. F. Scholander, a Swedish American physiologist. Born in Sweden in 1905 and educated in Norway, he had a celebrated career in the United States and served in the army in World War II. He spent most of his career at the Scripps Institute of Oceanography in California; he established the physiological research laboratory there and was instrumental in designing and building the *Alpha Helix*, a floating laboratory that hosted many leading midcentury biological researchers, including Carleton Gajdusek (W. Anderson 2008; Radin 2017). Scholander is known for many discoveries in the physiology of plants and animals of the sea and cold climates, and for his army research on survival at high altitudes and in the cold (Schmidt-Nielsen 1987).[9]

Scholander's work in Australia began when he was a postdoc at Harvard University. Hicks describes how a "pleasant, fair-haired Norwegian" turned up in Adelaide, explaining he was the advance party of an international expedition of twelve scientists from the United States, Norway, and Canada who would arrive a few days later.[10] They had read Hicks's earlier studies, by then two decades old, and wanted to repeat his measurements with their much more sophisticated equipment. Could he help them contact the desert sleepers? (Hicks 1974, 90). Hicks telephoned T. G. H. "Ted" Strehlow, a famous (and infamous) anthropologist of Central Australia who was by then on staff at the University of Adelaide. Strehlow regretfully informed him that "'those tribes you worked with are no longer there. They have all been mustered in the Settlement by the Department of Territories, and are being educated for assimilation into the Australian community.' I [Hicks] felt like Rip van Winkle, and said so. 'Do you mean that they wear clothes?' 'Yes, and go to school. There are no naked aborigines living as you saw them'" (Hicks 1974, 91).

Scholander's party was unperturbed by this news: they had undertaken challenging fieldwork before in the Norwegian mountains and the Kalahari (Scholander, Hammel, Andersen, et al. 1958; Wyndham and Morrison 1958). They set off for the desert with one of Hicks's staff and equipment Hicks described as "everything that could be imagined in one's wildest dreams of scientific afflu-ence" (1974, 92).

They conducted all-night experiments on young Pitjantjatjara men from Ar-eyonga. The men wore clothes during the day but often removed them for sleep-ing at night, rolling them into a pillow. The scientists joined the men, sleeping on the desert floor with a windbreak and small fires, as the Aboriginal men would normally do. The subjects slept with their heads in a hood and thermocouples at various places on their bodies (including rectally). The instruments were connected to a heated tent nearby that held all the equipment. On a night without wind, all subjects maintained their core temperatures. The white men found the conditions intolerable, simultaneously sweating from fires and shiv-ering from cold, and slept little beside the snoring Aboriginal men. Further experiments without fires were a shivering misery for the white men. They compared their results to a previous Scholander study in which white men slept naked with a light blanket in the Norwegian mountains (Scholander, Hammel, Andersen, et al. 1958). After a week of little sleep, those men accli-matized by increasing their metabolic rate to keep their exterior warm. They were able to sleep in the cold by increasing their internal heaters. In contrast, the metabolism of the Pitjantjatjara men fell in the same conditions, and they tolerated leg skin temperatures of ten degrees Celsius. The difference in physi-ological response was striking (see figure 5.3).

Scholander never used the word "torpor," calling the phenomenon "insulative cooling": "The cooling adaptation of the Australian aborigines, which resembles the insulative cooling commonly found in mammals, differs from the metabolic compensation and greater peripheral heating developed in cold-acclimated white man" (Scholander, Hammel, Hart, et al. 1958, 211). The researchers de-scribed this unusual response as "an economical response to cold, resembling the cooling extremities in arctic animals and birds" (217). The published study concludes that "the original and normal latitude of reaction to cold displayed by naked races may have been largely lost as a ready tool by white men, who for generations have thermostated their bodies with clothing and housing." The fact that these subjects usually wore clothes, however, "might suggest more deeply rooted effects inherited from past generations" (218).

The team returned six months later—"Heaven knows at what financial cost," Hicks drily observed (1974, 92)—to investigate if insulative cooling was an inherited or acquired adaptation. They hired a refrigerated meat van from the South Australian Department of Supply and cooled it to five degrees Cel-sius to test if the Pitjantjatjara men maintained their cold sleeping abilities in the summer. They reported that "certain features of this sleeping chamber

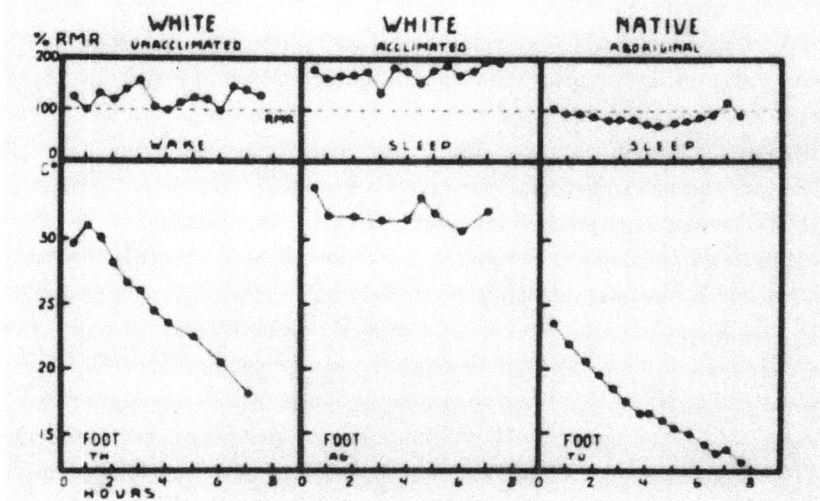

FIGURE 5.3. Figure comparing the resting metabolic rate (RMR) and foot surface temperature of "unacclimated White," "acclimated White," and "Native Aboriginal" subjects after hours exposed to cold. Caption from original: "Examples of 2 known modes of general acclimation to cold in man, as evidenced by all-night bag tests. Left: unacclimated white control. Middle: metabolic acclimation of whites in Norwegian mountain experiments. Right: 'insulative cooling' in Australian aborigines." *Source:* Scholander, Hammel, Hart, et al. 1958, 217.

were objectionable to the natives. . . . The central Australian aborigines expressed, through an interpreter, some apprehension at entering a small chamber, 7′ × 7′ × 6′, and were disturbed somewhat by the vibrations caused by the gasoline engine used for turning the compressor" (Hammel et al. 1959, 606). Somehow, the researchers managed to overcome their subjects' horror at the monstrous cold box and collect their data. They then traveled to Bagot settlement in Darwin to test the cold tolerance of Aboriginal people of the tropical north, whom they thought "much more sophisticated" than the desert people (608).

They found that "tropical natives" exposed to an artificially cold environment had a higher metabolic rate than desert people but lower than whites. They concluded that "the Australian aborigine has an inborn ability to tolerate greater body cooling without metabolic compensation which can be increased by prolonged exposure to cold" (605). In other words, on the question of environment or genetics as the basis of human insulative cooling, they placed a bet each way.

SCHOLANDER'S RESEARCH WAS THE last published attempt to measure cold tolerance in desert Australians. The two articles produced from the research (Hammel et al. 1959; Scholander, Hammel, Hart, et al. 1958) have been cited a few hundred times and are recited in the cold tolerance literature to the present day (for example, Daanen and Van Marken Lichtenbelt 2016).[11] Whether the desert sleepers were entering torpor or not, they appeared to have adaptations to cold that were indeed unique among humans.

Interestingly, while those researching cold tolerance all seem to know about Scholander's Australian research, review articles on *hibernation* and its potential human applications don't mention this literature (Andrews 2007; Cerri 2017; Lee 2008). This could simply reflect good science: some hibernation researchers have been frustrated by the conflation of hypothermia and torpor, two concepts they argue should be clearly distinguished (Geiser et al. 2014). Or maybe these are two scientific communities that are not yet talking to each other. My mysterious correspondent, DT, would argue that this is precisely where the cutting edge of the secret research sector lies, "joining the dots" before anyone else has. There are indications, too, that hibernation researchers looking into synthetic torpor in humans are beginning to cite Scholander: a 2019 review of torpor for space flight mentions the remarkable cold adaptation of "Aboriginal natives" in passing (Choukèr et al. 2019, 824; see also Nordeen and Martin 2019).

The trope of Aboriginal Australians holding the key to biological secrets of humankind has a long history. Research on Indigenous peoples, fueled by colonial exploration and settlement, has driven much of the debate about human evolution and human nature across the past century and a half. In the case of Aboriginal people, dominant racial theories of the nineteenth and early twentieth centuries saw them as "archaic Caucasians" (discussed in the previous chapter), a primitive remnant of Europe's evolutionary past. Europeans and other "Caucasoid" groups were thought to have advanced, while "paleolithic" Australians remained stuck in the Stone Age.

The expansion of "Big Biology" in the mid-twentieth century, most prominently through the International Biological Program, turned again to Indigenous people as exceptionally good subjects for research. This time, the emphasis was not on their arrested social evolution but on their dynamic adaptation to local environments. Midcentury human biology saw Indigenous populations—and the Australian continent in particular—as "a unique kind of laboratory for testing evolutionary hypotheses," as geneticist Joseph B. Birdsell (1979, 417) (who featured in the story of hair collection in chapter 4) puts it in the epigraph to this chapter. Their millennia of adaptation to their environments in relative or total isolation from other racial groups promised novel genetic mutations and somatic signatures. Indigenous populations were understood by scientists to be "more biological" than other humans in both *fundamental* and *exceptional* ways: their apparent lack of social and cultural change made them essentially and uniquely biologically human (Radin and Kowal 2015). Accordingly, Indigenous biospecimens and data became a precious resource (Bangham and Chadarevian 2014; Radin 2017; Reardon 2005; Santos, Lindee, and de Souza 2014).

The most precious resources of all were derived from "uncontacted" or "tribalized natives," who, it was assumed, had not been affected by white society. The challenge for white researchers was to obtain their data and samples before detribalization occurred and death, disease, and miscegenation closed the window of scientific opportunity forever. In an earlier period, scientists attributed this unfortunate fate to the "doomed race theory." This was the belief that the population collapse of Indigenous people was due to the "inferior" race succumbing on contact with the "superior" white race: social evolutionary theory in action (McGregor 1997). By the 1930s Hicks and his colleagues understood it was white pastoralists with guns, and not racial destiny, that threatened desert people. When Scholander arrived in the 1950s, integration and assimilation were the scientists' enemy, threatening to erase thousands of years of adaptation. Luckily for them, the Pitjantjatjara men removed their mission clothes at night, revealing their "true" physiological selves.

Scholander's research was most definitely "Cold War biology," a term that historians of science are increasingly deploying (Chadarevian 2002; Oreskes 2014; Radin 2017). From the 1950s onward, the races for scientific and military dominance were closely intertwined and touched virtually every country on the planet. Within this new research paradigm, long-standing scientific interests in Indigenous peoples were harnessed to benefit the health and security of the Global North. For instance, genetic studies on Indigenous people in South America informed research on the effects of radiation, with the Yanomami people analyzed as a natural baseline for understanding radiation-affected Western societies (Lindee 1994; Santos, Lindee, and de Souza 2014).

Within physiology, populations with special properties like cold tolerance were of vital interest to military-funded researchers. Scholander's group, landing without warning in central Australia in 1957, is a prime example. The hugely expensive exercise was supported by the Physiology Branch of the Office of Naval Research and the US Air Force, which funded research units at the Universities of Washington and Pennsylvania (which were, in turn, monitored by the Arctic Aeromedical Laboratory). In Australia the Aviation

Medical Section of the Department of Civil Aviation and the Royal Australian Airforce funded Hicks to establish an Aeromedical Laboratory at the University of Adelaide in 1954—a piece of Australian Cold War history that deserves more scrutiny (*Advertiser* 1954).[12] Hicks himself had previously been engaged with military research. During World War II he was sent to Washington on a "special secret mission" on "research and development of military clothing for arctic and subarctic survival purposes," an episode his memoir skips over rather quickly (Hicks 1974, 90).

Given this cocktail of scientific and strategic interests, it is not surprising that the history of scientific research on Indigenous people is peppered with conspiracy theories, some of them true. Midcentury researchers of Yanomami people, for example, have been plagued with very public accusations of deliberately spreading measles to the unexposed population under the guise of vaccine research (Tierney 2001). While those particular accusations were disproven, there have been other, more clear-cut cases of misconduct, such as the nutrition researchers in the 1940s and 1950s who experimented on malnourished aboriginal residents of Canadian residential schools without their knowledge (Mosby 2013).

The Arctic Aeromedical Laboratory, a major funder of Scholander's research, has also been embroiled in controversy. The laboratory was based in Fairbanks and focused on research to prepare soldiers who might need to fight in frozen places if the Cold War escalated. It is most famous today for controversial experiments on 108 Alaskan Natives in the mid-1950s. In an investigation of the possible effect of cold tolerance on the thyroid gland, adults and children were given radioactive iodine. An inquiry forty years later found that the informed consent process was flawed, even when judged by the standards of the time: they thought they were receiving medical treatment (Farish 2013; Institute of Medicine and National Research Council 1996; Lanzarotta 2020).

Cold War biology's interest in Indigenous people transmuted into late twentieth-century population genetics, as Jenny Reardon (2005) has demonstrated in her history of the Human Genome Diversity Project of the 1990s. That project was a particularly rich source of conspiracy theories. The Indigenous Peoples Council on Biocolonialism claimed that the diversity project sought Indigenous samples in order to create biological weapons against them (Harry, Howard, and Shelton 2000), an accusation that was reproduced in Michael Dodson's Aboriginal and Torres Strait Islander Human Rights report (Human Rights and Equal Opportunity Commission 1996).[13] While these accusations were not true, they express deep suspicions that are grounded in lived, multigenerational experiences of dispossession and cultural genocide.

As I have already mentioned, the field of human hibernation research has not yet latched on to the unique biological adaptations observed by Hicks and Scholander. If and when it does, I predict it will be a perfect discursive fit. Human hibernation is a field full of futuristic narratives of salvation and hope (Singer 2006). Torpor is seen as an archaic ability that modern humans have lost. Research into genetic (and microbiomic) adaptations that might unlock synthetic hibernation is a small but growing field (Andrews 2019; Blanco et al. 2018; H. Carey and Assadi-Porter 2017; Xu et al. 2013). As a recent news article puts it, "If hibernating astronauts someday wake up to find themselves ready to enter Mars orbit, they can give thanks to a biological superpower that was millions of years in the making" (Hsu 2018). It seems the field is ideally placed to embrace Indigenous "biological superpowers"—their unique genetic variants and patterns of gene expression.

It cannot be known if Hicks (1974, 33) truly observed torpor in subject number one that morning in Cockatoo Creek. To my knowledge, no one apart from Hicks and DT has believed that Aboriginal people could actually enter nightly torpor. But is this a noble-savage subgenre of science fiction, or is it highly classified?

THESE MUSINGS ON THE history of Indigenous biological research and its entanglement with defense objectives and conspiracy theories, however historically correct, did not help me figure out if DT had sent me on a wild physiological goose chase. Military interest in Indigenous people has a long history, but so do wild imaginings about their alleged biological superpowers. Was Aboriginal torpor a conspiracy theory or a conspiracy of silence?

I returned to the emails DT had sent me. In an effort to convince me that Aboriginal genetic adaptations were real and would be of great interest to both public and private sectors, he had sent me a recent link to media reports of unusual thyroid function in Aboriginal people (Gribbin 2014). The origin of that story was in 1980, when pathologists in Perth and Adelaide hospitals showed that 40 percent of those Aboriginal people tested (no doubt using routinely collected pathology samples without specific consent) had substantially lower thyroxine levels than white subjects. Thyroxine, produced by the thyroid gland, is the hormone that most powerfully raises metabolism. Most thyroxine in the blood is tightly bound to proteins—called "thyroxine-binding globulins"—that deactivate the hormone. When the body temperature rises, for example, in response to a fever, these proteins let go of the thyroxine, increasing the metabolic rate. Subsequent research in the late 1980s showed that these lower levels of thyroid hormone were related to two mutations on the gene for the protein that binds to thyroxine in the bloodstream, making it bind more tightly (Dick and Watson 1980; Takeda et al. 1989; White and Morice 1980). In 2014 Cambridge researchers proved that the "Aboriginal" mutations to this protein meant that in comparison to other populations, their circulating thyroxine levels were lower. This allowed them to maintain a lower metabolic rate, even when core temperature increased. The researchers speculated that this was a selective adaptation to the desert, allowing children with fevers to survive in an environment of limited food and water (Qi et al. 2014).

Reading this reminded me of a recent paper led by Eske Willerslev, a major figure in aDNA research. He and his team of collaborators analyzed the most Indigenous genome data produced to date by far: eighty-three genomes from Aboriginal people around Australia (Malaspinas et al. 2016). The massive paper—with seventy-five authors and 172 pages of supplementary material—focuses on the population history of Aboriginal people, confirming and elaborating Willerslev's findings from the sequencing of the "first Aboriginal genome" five years previously (Rasmussen et al. 2011, discussed in chapter 3). A secondary aim of the paper was to identify those points on the Aboriginal genomes that are most different from the genomes of other world populations. If a part of the genome has many differences from the same part in other populations, it indicates that the differences may be the outcome of a process of selection. That is, those DNA variants may produce a slightly different protein that provides an evolutionary advantage: a change in function that makes it more likely someone would survive in the environment where they live.

A table in the paper lists thirty points on the genome that may be the site of selection (see table 5.1). For some of them, the "Function of Gene Product" column is tantalizingly marked "Unknown." This means there is no obvious reason why a change in the gene would be advantageous because Western science doesn't yet know what those genes do. The "Unknown" is a site of the haunting effects of Indigenous biological difference, a kind of haunting that scientists are particularly susceptible to. Tens of thousands of years of evolution have potentially led to the selection of a specific variant of those genes. As the frontier of scientific knowledge has not yet enveloped those particular genes, the significance of those variants remains tantalizingly out of reach, for now.

The other variants in the table involve genes already known to science. Each includes a comment on what the variant might mean for the body based on current knowledge of the gene in which the change occurs. These comments offer hints at the physiological advantages the variant might have been selected for. For most of the variants, the known function of the gene is either so broad or so specific that it is difficult to imagine what selective advantage the variant may provide. The gene *HAUS4*, for example, is "[a] component of a microtubule-binding complex that plays a role in the generation of microtubules in the mitotic spindle," a structure within every cell in the body, and the gene *JKRL* is the "homologue to 'Jerky' gene in mouse" and implicated in epilepsy (Malaspinas et al. 2016, Extended Data Table 2). Neither of these offers a simple story of why variation in these genes might produce a selective advantage for humans in a particular environment.

The story the authors chose to tell from their data was about the desert sleepers: "Increased desertification of Australia during the last glacial maximum (LGM) 19–26.5 kya affected the number and density of human populations. In this context, unique morphological and physiological adaptations have been identified in Aboriginal Australians living in desert areas today. In particular, *desert groups were hypothesized to withstand sub-zero night temperatures without showing the increase in metabolic rates observed in Europeans under the same conditions*" (Malaspinas et al. 2016, 208, emphasis added).

This passage did not help my efforts to disbelieve DT. Of all the possible physiological adaptations to discuss, this large group of international experts on evolutionary genetics with access to the most Indigenous genome data ever produced focused on desert sleeping, citing Scholander's 1958 paper.[14] In the discussion of the table in the results section, the authors understandably skipped over most of the thirty variants listed, zeroing in on just two of them. One was *NETO1*, a gene related to thyroid function and potentially "associated with Aboriginal-Australian-specific adaptations to desert cold" (Malaspinas et al. 2016, 213). I turned to the final page of the article PDF, where a table lists information about *NETO1* and the other genes that topped their selection scan.[15] It was then that I noticed something strange that I hadn't picked up in my previous readings of the paper. The row featuring *NETO1* was mostly blank (see table 5.1).

At that point, my paranoia went up a few notches. Could it be that vital information about a gene critical to thyroid function in Aboriginal people was being suppressed? And this conspiracy involved some of the world's most prestigious genome scientists and a top international journal? By whom and for what purpose was the information withheld? I mentioned the missing line of data to DT. He said that genetics was not his area of expertise, but

TABLE 5.1. Section from "Extended Data Table 2: Selection scan in Aboriginal Australians," showing blank fields in the NETO1 row

Focal Pop	Nearby Gene*	Position†	rsID	Dist‡	$PBSn1$§	F_{12}	F_{13}	F_{23}	Function of gene product#
All	TMEM86B	55,833,076	rs734517	92,444	0.78	0.93	0.99	0.06	Catalyzes the degradation of lysoplasmalogen. Modulates cell membrane proteins.
All	LRRC52	165,621,695	rs4147601	88,510	0.74	0.96	0.91	0.01	Modulates voltage of potassium ion channels. Expressed in testis.
All	MACROD2	15,209,684	rs175279	901	0.70	0.92	0.89	−0.01	Involved in deacetylase activity. Possibly (but not conclusively) causative of Kabuki syndrome.
All	JRKL	96,747,146	rs72959058	507,105	0.74	0.99	0.87	0.15	Homologue to 'jerky' gene in mouse.
All	SPATA20	48,631,324	rs7338243	287	0.70	0.96	0.85	0.09	Spermatid protein.
All	NAA60	3,537,933	rs73503305	970	0.71	0.91	0.91	−0.02	Histone acetyltransferase required for nucleosome assembly and chromosome segregation during anaphase. Human-specific imprinted gene.
All	CBLN2	70,019,066	rs12455116	184,848	0.69	0.92	0.87	0.00	CBLN2: cerebellum-specific protein involved in various signaling pathways. Possibly associated with pulmonary arterial hypertension.
	NETO1			390,482					NETO1: brain-specific transmembrane protein involved in the regulation of neuronal circuitry. Associated with thyroid function.
All	SLC2A12	134,391,056	rs4896021	17,267	0.76	0.96	0.95	−0.01	Catalyzes sugar absorption. Involved in the pathogenesis of diabetes. Associated with serum urate levels.
All	LOC101927657	127,358,509	rs145200081	16,731	0.65	0.94	0.80	0.13	Unknown (ncRNA).
All	LOC102724612	64,466,486	rs11341339	78,446	0.73	0.91	0.95	0.00	Unknown (ncRNA).
NE	ZBTB20	114,530,679	rs9289004	10,658	0.55	0.65	0.82	0.07	Transcriptional repressor associated with Primrose syndrome.
NE	ANXA10	168,646,016	rs2176513	367,671	0.49	0.61	0.61	−0.01	Calcium-dependent phospholipid-binding annexin.
NE	TRPC3	122,905,041	rs4502701	32,132	0.50	0.59	0.64	−0.01	Non-selective cation channel, associated with spinocerebellar ataxia.
NE	HS3ST1	11,634,592	rs7665516	204,055	0.45	0.45	0.71	0.07	Regulates rate of generation of anticoagulant heparan sulfate proteoglycan.

Source: Malaspinas et al. 2016.

Note: A note to the original table reads: "Top 10 peaks of differentiation from genome scans of all Aboriginal Australians combined (All) and two Aboriginal Australians subgroups living in different ecological regions in Australia, the northeast (NE) or southwest (SW)."

several of the institutions where the authors were based were engaged in classified biological research for military purposes. He would not be surprised if my hunch was right.

I consulted some of my genetics colleagues, who immediately emailed the postdoc responsible for the table. It was just a misprint, came the reply. The data were supposed to be there, and the error had somehow escaped the meticulous copyediting of the top international journal. This explanation was not particularly reassuring. Some time later, I had the opportunity to talk in person to another genetics postdoc. I mentioned the missing data and explained that I had not had a satisfactory answer to my concerns. He was alarmed by my story. We stared together at the blank data row on my laptop screen and shared a worried look. He took his smartphone from his pocket and again emailed the author responsible.

After some back and forth, I solved the puzzle. There is another gene, *CBLN2*, that sits on the genome between *NETO1* and the marker used to identify *NETO1*.[16] The information about the marker is a proxy for both *NETO1* and *CBLN2*. Although the text of the article does not mention *CBLN2*—presumably because there was nothing particularly interesting to say about its implications for selection—both genes are included in the table. There was no need to repeat the data in the row for *NETO1* because the data are identical to the row for *CBLN2* directly above it. My fevered imagination had blown an ambiguous data table out of proportion. Yet that doesn't mean the other conspiracy theories *aren't* true.

I have told this story because it illustrates the haunting uncertainty of Indigenous biological difference and the dilemmas this can create for a range of twenty-first-century actors. I remain uneasy about DT's claims and their possible implications for Indigenous people. His fleeting presence in my life arguably allowed him to unload his misgivings and move on with his research as he had before, with no accountability to those who might be affected. For me as a social scientist engaged with Indigenous researchers and Indigenous governance, my responsibilities are more difficult to negotiate. The likelihood of a desert swarming with scientists—another Board for Anthropological Research—seems slim, but is it enough of a risk to raise the alarm?

After my correspondence with DT ended, I didn't know what to do. I overcame my fear of sounding crazy and contacted two respected non-indigenous colleagues for advice. One didn't answer; the other told me to drop it. When they read my message, both probably experienced the reaction of physical recoil my geneticist friend described. What good can come of speculation on Indigenous biological superpowers, even if they turn out to be real?

I didn't feel confident to raise the issue with Indigenous colleagues, who are all thoroughly occupied with the many clear and present dangers to their people. It seemed inappropriate—selfish, even—to burden them with this strange and obscure story.

In the few years since DT contacted me, no flood of scientists has attempted to covertly draw blood from desert people to probe their latent evolutionary powers, as far as I know. Temporary hibernation remains a haunting possibility, dwelling in a liminal space between genres, between disciplines, between rows on a table and markers on a genome.

Spencer's Double   **6**
The Decolonial Afterlife
of a Postcolonial
Museum Prop

In a dark, dark wood there was a dark, dark house;
And in the dark, dark house there was a dark, dark room;
And in the dark, dark room there was a dark, dark cupboard;
And in the dark, dark cupboard there was a dark, dark shelf;
And on the dark, dark shelf there was a dark, dark box;
And in the dark, dark box there was a . . . ghost!
—Traditional English children's story

This chapter is about a ghost in the dark, but it begins in the piercing light of
Alice Springs, central Australia, on May 18, 1901 (figure 6.1). Baldwin Spencer
(1860–1929), foundation professor of biology at the University of Melbourne and
groundbreaking anthropologist of Aboriginal Australia, sits on a bentwood chair
and stares into the lens. Beside him, on another bentwood chair, is his long-
time collaborator, Alice Springs stationmaster F. J. Gillen (1855–1912). Gillen
gazes toward his left. Their legs cross toward each other, the body language reflecting their close friendship. The image was captured outside Gillen's house
at the Alice Springs Telegraph Station near the start of their 1901–2 expedition.
Two days earlier, Gillen's latest child had been born, a son, named Spencer
Gillen to honor his friend. In a standard visual trope of colonial expedition

photography, the supporting actors stand behind: Trooper Harry Chance, the expedition cook and driver, flanked by two Aboriginal "assistants" from Charlotte Waters, Erlikiliakirra and Purula, who handled the twenty horses and at times acted as interpreters. Trooper Chance's regular wage was paid by the expedition, amounting to two hundred pounds for the year; Erlikiliakirra and Purula worked for rations.[1]

This small party had set out from Adelaide two months earlier on a year-long anthropological expedition to the Northern Territory and Queensland. In the wake of the instant success of Spencer and Gillen's book *The Native Tribes of Central Australia* ([1899] 1968), celebrated Scottish anthropologist Sir James Frazer led efforts by leading scholars in the United Kingdom to convince the Victorian and South Australian premiers to support Gillen and Spencer's "work among the tribes who still remain to be examined."[2] They set off from Oodnadatta, the end of the railway line north of Adelaide, laden with food, logistical and scientific equipment, and supplies to offer Aboriginal people in exchange for information—flour, sugar, pipes and tobacco, and hundreds of steel

FIGURE 6.1. Photograph of 1901–2 expedition party, Alice Springs, May 18, 1901. *Back row, left to right:* Erlikiliakirra (Jim Kite), Harry Chance, Purula (Parunda). *Front row, left to right:* F. J. Gillen, Baldwin Spencer. *Source:* Museums Victoria.

axes and knives. They returned with plentiful ethnographic notes, thousands of sacred and profane artifacts, five hundred photographs, thousands of feet of film footage, and two dozen cylinders of phonograph recordings. Thousands of objects Spencer collected remain to this day in the museum he directed for three decades.

In the pursuit of haunting traces, the bulk of this chapter shifts the focus from the history of scientific research on Indigenous people. I focus instead on the efforts of a collecting institution to overcome its colonial past. Museums were and are crucial sites for the production of knowledge about Indigenous peoples represented in their collections. We have already encountered museum collections of bones (chapter 2) and hair (chapter 3) that scientists once used, and in some cases still use, to make biological knowledge about Indigenous people. At Museums Victoria, this has not been the case for many decades.

The museum was one of the earliest to repatriate Indigenous ancestral remains. On a crisp spring day in 1985, thirty-eight ancestors were carried by community members from a range of Victorian Indigenous language groups from the museum to the Domain Gardens, where they were reburied. These remains were collected by the notorious George Murray Black, a pastoralist who dug up Aboriginal grave sites in his spare time and divided them between the Institute of Anatomy in Canberra (see chapter 2) and the medical school at the University of Melbourne. Once Gunditjmara activist and museum employee Jim Berg had secured their release from the university, the newly passed Museums Act 1983 empowered the museum to repatriate the remains (Berg 2010).

Since that first repatriation, the museum has returned nearly all of the Indigenous human remains originally in its collections to traditional owners. However, in that time many more remains have been transferred to Museums Victoria (from sources as varied as universities, private collections, and excavations) in line with legislation that lists it as the holding institute for all Indigenous human remains in the state. As curator Lindy Allen (2014) puts it, the process of repatriation is a "never ending story."[3]

Like all settler colonial museums, Museums Victoria has much difficult history to come to terms with. This chapter tells the story of a strange reproduction of Spencer in his bentwood chair (figure 6.1) that embodies the efforts of twenty-first-century institutions to overcome their colonial pasts and banish their dead white male founders. These efforts, we will see, are plagued by ghosts.

Spencer, Doubles, Museums

Baldwin Spencer had grown up in Manchester in the 1860s and 1870s and studied biology at Oxford before moving to Australia when he was appointed to the inaugural chair in biology at the University of Melbourne in 1887 at the age of twenty-seven. Among his many prominent roles in the fledging Melbourne scientific scene, he became honorary director of the National Museum of Victoria (now Museums Victoria) in 1899, a position he held for nearly thirty years. He was responsible for the acquisition of several thousand Aboriginal objects, including many that he collected himself. He sent numerous pieces of Aboriginal cultural heritage overseas, bartering with museums to build Melbourne's international collections, including, famously, a Samoyed sledge from Leningrad complete with harnessed reindeer and traditional costumes. He pioneered an arrangement with the chief commissioner of police whereby any human remains in their possession that were thought to be Aboriginal were deposited in the museum, swelling the museum's collection of skeletal material (D. Mulvaney and Calaby 1985, 249–54). Today the Spencer and Gillen Collection at Museums Victoria consists of 900 manuscript items, 1,500 ethnographic items, and many other photographs and film and sound recordings.[4]

Spencer enjoyed over forty years based in Melbourne and a lively career in biology, anthropology, museology, and Aboriginal affairs until his death while conducting fieldwork in Tierra del Fuego in 1929. During his lifetime—and for half a century afterward—his scientific achievements were seen in wholly positive terms. He had put the customs of Australian "natives" on the world stage, had salvaged countless priceless artifacts, and was instrumental in the development of remote reserves and urban compounds where Aboriginal people could be protected from frontier violence and be supported to become self-sufficient: all progressive goals for the time.

My story of Spencer's passage from the harsh light of Alice Springs into the dark requires that we focus not on the man himself but on his doubles. By "doubles," I mean images, shadows, and other likenesses and representations of the self—in this case, Spencer's photographic image and, principally, a model of Spencer we will meet shortly. My discussion of Spencer's doubles draws on psychoanalytic theories of the double. Doubling is an inexhaustibly rich topic in psychoanalysis, but two main lines of scholarship are useful for my purposes—Sigmund Freud's ([1919] 1925) notion of the "uncanny" and the work of his close colleague Otto Rank ([1914] 1989) on the double.[5] Each of these notions of the double is relevant to different parts of the story I tell below.

In *The Double* ([1914] 1989), Rank draws on anthropology and literature to make a wide-ranging argument that doubles—in the form of doppelgängers, shadows, spirits, or ghosts—function as a vessel for negative feelings we harbor about ourselves. Projecting negative thoughts and feelings onto the double enables self-love to be maintained. Although some degree of this psychic mechanism is necessary to human flourishing, it can lead to excessive narcissism if we disavow too many of our self-doubts and repress the inevitable contradictions between what we wish we were and what we really are. Like the famous portrait of Dorian Gray in the locked room of Oscar Wilde's (1891) story, a double absorbs negative qualities to preserve the original—in that case, protecting Dorian Gray from the process of aging and the consequences of immorality. I argue that, in the early twenty-first century, a double of Spencer—enclosed not in an attic but in a glass case—became a receptacle for negative feelings that some white people felt toward colonialism.

Freud's famous 1919 essay on the uncanny argues that something is experienced as uncanny when it recalls something that was once familiar to us but that we have repressed. The uncanny is closely related to the double. Building on Rank's work, Freud notes that the double functions as a receptacle for undesirable (or unattainable) aspects of the ego as part of normal psychic development. However, if those qualities projected onto the double are repressed, doubles can become the source of uncanny feelings: "The double has become an image of terror, just as, after the collapse of their religion, the gods turned into demons." This shift to the uncanny is a result of repression, particularly of earlier stages (of life or of evolution) that we believe we have moved beyond: the uncanny is "something which ought to have remained hidden but has come to light" ([1919] 1925, 236, 241). I argue that after Spencer's double was evicted from its case in an attempt to repress colonialism, it shifted from a Rankean receptacle to an uncanny ghost.

My approach to Spencer's double illustrates the historical anthropology methodology used throughout this book. My interest in the history of Indigenous biological difference is driven by questions of how these histories live on in the present. In this chapter I argue that history exerts its effects partly through the negative view of this history shared by many contemporary actors. I saw a similar dynamic in my previous ethnographic project with non-indigenous researchers who worked in Indigenous health in the Northern Territory (Kowal 2015). Although I approached that project as cultural anthropology that aimed to understand the culture of progressive non-indigenous people, it soon became clear that the known or perceived history of Indigenous research played an important role in what it meant for non-indigenous Australians to make knowledge about Indigenous people.

Most scientists who work with Indigenous people have a strong historical consciousness. As the health researcher and historian David Thomas (2004, 2) puts it, they are unlikely to know any details of "past" research (usually meaning anything prior to the 1980s) but still share a "vague certainty" that it was morally corrupt and definitively "racist." My own research found that those working in Indigenous fields, and "progressive" or "antiracist" Australians in general, take great pains to distance themselves from their predecessors. In certain settler colonies, histories of oppression and genocide are routinely evoked by nations and concerned citizens who wish to reconcile with the crimes of the colonial past and their impact on present-day Indigenous populations, a movement influenced by and tied to postcolonialism.[6] The history of scientific research is often considered by Indigenous and postcolonial scholars to be among the worst parts of colonial history: "research" is a "dirty word" for Indigenous people (L. Smith 2012).

Although this story begins with Spencer himself—or at least his photographic image—its real focus is the role of the history of Indigenous research in the postcolonial narratives (and as I argue, the subsequent decolonial narratives) of late twentieth- and early twenty-first-century Australia. As I explained in the introduction, I experienced this period firsthand as an Indigenous solidarity activist while a student at the University of Melbourne in the 1990s, and as a medical doctor, health researcher, and anthropologist in Indigenous communities in the north of Australia in the 2000s. In the social worlds I inhabited, the history of scientific research in Indigenous Australian populations was frequently invoked as something to be embarrassed about and to distinguish ourselves from.[7]

In this chapter it is Spencer's double that is the vessel for the embarrassing scientific past that progressive Australians of the 1990s and 2000s—specifically in this case museum visitors and museum staff—often felt bad about. In fact, by the early 1970s Spencer had already become a focus for negative feelings about the man and what he stood for: white, colonial, masculine domination of the Indigenous Other.[8] His reference to Aboriginal people as "naked, howling savages" in *The Northern Tribes of Central Australia* (Spencer and Gillen 1904, xiv) was not lost on critics of colonialism, who identified him with an evolutionary anthropology that sought to study Aboriginal culture before its inevitable extinction.[9] As Chief Protector of Aborigines in the Northern Territory from 1911, Spencer advocated for the abduction of "half caste" Aboriginal children "for their own good," a practice that continued until the 1970s and produced what is now known as the Stolen Generations (Human Rights and Equal Opportunity Commission 1997).

This rising tide of sentiment against the prodigious white collectors of anthropology impacted the museums that many of them contributed to. Motivated by Indigenous activists both within and outside the museum sector, and by the writings of postcolonial scholars such as Edward Said, Homi Bhabha, and Gayatri Spivak, museum studies scholars and museum practitioners in settler colonial countries in the 1990s began to ask questions about museums' colonial legacies and the possibility for museums to stimulate more positive cultural shifts toward inclusion and recognition, a movement often called the "new museology" (Barringer and Flynn 1998; Bennett 1995; Karp and Lavine 1991; Vergo 1989).[10] Important signs of these shifts include the new Museum of New Zealand, Te Papa, which was legislated in 1992 and opened in 1998, and the National Museum of the American Indian, legislated in 1989 and opened in 2004 (Tramposch 1998; Cobb and Lonetree 2008). As we will see, Spencer's museum was part of this shift. Museums Victoria went through a major redevelopment phase in the 1990s in the lead-up to the opening of a new museum building in 2000. It is within this political context that Spencer's double shifted from the natural light of central Australia to the artificial light of a museum exhibit.

The concepts of *postcolonial* and *decolonial* are important to the arguments I make below about scientific collectors and their collections. I distinguish between postcolonial and decolonial museology on historical and theoretical grounds, while acknowledging that the relationship between the two concepts is contested and varies in different contexts.[11]

Postcolonial studies is a multidisciplinary body of scholarship that examines the impacts and legacies of colonialism. While works identified as seminal postcolonial texts span the twentieth century, as an academic movement it gained momentum in the 1990s and was in part a merging of scholars who identified with subaltern studies and Commonwealth literary studies. Decolonialization or decoloniality, influenced primarily by Latin American scholarship (Mignolo 2011), also has a long history but has come into its own as an academic movement in the past decade. For example, the first journal featuring the term—*Decolonization: Indigeneity, Education and Society*—was launched in 2012, and the term "decolonial studies" is only just emerging. As I explore further below, calls to decolonize the museum have accompanied this decolonial turn.[12]

An emerging feature of the decolonial turn is its frequent opposition to postcolonialism. Science and technology studies (STS) is among the many academic disciplines where arguments for decoloniality and against postcolonialism have recently been made (Harding 2016; Lyons et al. 2017). Decoloniality scholars and activists critique the concept of postcolonialism as not going far enough to "undo" colonialism and as inadequate for analyzing settler colonialism (Grosfoguel 2007; Maldonado-Torres 2011; Tuck and Yang 2012).

My interest here is neither to advocate for decoloniality nor to defend postcolonialism. Rather, they serve as background for my argument that over the past decade or so, at least in settler colonies, a mode of collection and display best described as "postcolonial" has been supplanted by another mode best described as "decolonial." Postcolonial museology refigured the museum as a "contact zone" in which multiple voices should be recognized and reflected (Clifford 1997). This was a space where non-indigenous scholars had clear pedagogical, exhibitionary, and epistemological roles. In the era of decolonial museology emerging in settler colonies, only Indigenous voices are authorized to produce knowledge, and non-indigenous perspectives are strategically deemphasized.

The fate of Spencer's double after he left his museum exhibit in 2011 was intimately connected with this transition in museum practice. The narrative below interweaves archival, ethnographic, historical, and cultural analyses to describe and make sense of Spencer's postexhibition journey from an illuminated glass case to a dark restricted room, deep in the museum. This story of the uncanny end of an unusual museum object illustrates how the decolonial turn, like all cultural shifts, may have unintended side effects. Despite efforts to expunge symbols of colonial knowledge and power from museums, some ghosts refuse to be silenced.

Spencer collected many biological objects, including human remains and hair samples. Unlike in the other chapters of this book, however, the haunting object in this story is not a biological specimen, physiological finding, or racial theory but a museum prop intended as a postcolonial critique of earlier modes of museum collecting. The haunting fate of this uncanny object reveals the opportunities and limits of shifting approaches to Indigenous justice in the late twentieth and early twenty-first centuries. I argue that Spencer's later decommissioning marked the end of a postcolonial mode of museology and the beginning of a decolonial period of collecting and displaying. In including this chapter, I mean to facilitate reflection on how other humanities and social science disciplines might best address the colonial legacies of knowledge making in ways that are more, or less, vulnerable to haunting. Spencer's double illustrates how decolonial approaches to addressing colonial legacies may themselves be haunted.

Finding Spencer

At an anthropology conference a few years ago, I heard a strange story. It was told by Philip Batty, senior curator of central Australian collections at Museums Victoria. Batty had spent part of the 1970s and all of the 1980s in central Australia as a schoolteacher in a remote community and then codirector of a newly established Aboriginal media organization in Alice Springs. He later settled in Melbourne and began working at the museum in the late 1990s, a time when plans were well underway for the opening of the new Melbourne Museum. The revamped museum included an extensive permanent Indigenous exhibit called "Bunjilaka," a Woiwurrung word meaning "the place of Bunjil," the ancestral wedge-tailed eagle.

At that time, Batty was a producer rather than a curator.[13] He worked on the new Indigenous exhibit under three curators, who were each responsible for their own distinct section: Aboriginal academic and writer Tony Birch (a member of the Melbourne Koori community), who curated "Koori Voices"; senior curator of northern Australia Lindy Allen, who curated "Belonging to Country"; and John Morton, an anthropologist specializing in central Australia who was seconded from La Trobe University for two years to curate "Two Laws."[14] The latter section "explor[ed] issues about Aboriginal law, knowledge and property."[15]

Drawing on an idea of Birch's, Morton planned an ingenious climax for his section of the exhibition. In a reversal of the colonial gaze that placed Indigenous people and culture on display, a statue of Baldwin Spencer would be put in a glass case (figure 6.2). The case was specially designed to "parody the large exhibition cases often used in older museums" and measured 3.2 meters high and 12 meters across.[16] Along with Spencer, it contained 112 everyday objects that Spencer and his contemporaries collected, including spears and spear throwers, baskets, smoking pipes, digging sticks, knives, throwing sticks, clubs, neck ornaments, and a canoe. This subsection of Bunjilaka, entitled "Hunters and Collectors," had the statue of Spencer at its heart.[17] He wore his usual fieldwork attire, seen in the photograph of the 1901–2 expedition (figure 6.1): a simple suit and tie, boots, and a wide-brimmed hat, the long lines of his face accentuated by his signature mustache. At his feet were models of two goannas named for Spencer and his collaborator: *Varanus spencerii* and *Varanus gilleni*.[18] Birch's original vision was of a performance piece where an Aboriginal curator would provide commentary on the encased anthropologist. Morton intended to realize this vision with a statue of Irrapmwe, Spencer's main Arrernte informant (otherwise known as King Charlie), standing outside the case peering in, but the idea was dropped by the designers for logistical and financial reasons.[19]

I remember seeing the model when the exhibition opened in 2000. Spencer's expression seemed somewhat bewildered, framed by a quote from the Tasmanian Aboriginal Centre (1997, 21) that made the curatorial intention clear: "We do not choose to be enshrined in a glass case, with our story told by an alien institution which has appointed itself an ambassador for our culture." At a time when Indigenous museology was being reconsidered around the world, the model of Spencer aimed to promote Indigenous agency and a reflexive reading of history against the grain of colonial collecting practice. As explained by Morton in a briefing document, "In this way, the collector (Spencer), has been collected."[20] Enclosed in his glass case, he was also caught, captured "so that you may scrutinise him (and what he stands for) along with the objects."[21] In a set of interlocking reversals, the audience was invited to "study" Spencer's scientific methods and legacy and find them wanting, especially morally. As I explore later in the chapter, reviews of the exhibition indicate that, for many museum visitors, it achieved the intended effect.

The anthropology conference where Batty told me the strange story was held in 2012. He had spent the previous few years working on a major project to digitize thousands of objects and recordings collected by Spencer and Gillen.[22] Batty and I share an interest in the politics of Indigenous-state relations, and I pondered the irony of Spencer the statue trapped in his glass case while the objects he collected and created are granted unprecedented mobility on the internet, all the while under strict Indigenous control through project protocols.

Batty told me that Spencer was no longer in his case.[23] That area of the museum had been rebranded as the Bunjilaka Aboriginal Cultural Centre. The permanent exhibit within the cultural center had been completely redeveloped and was given a separate name—"First Peoples"—that distinguished it from the earlier Bunjilaka exhibition. Created in partnership with a group of local elders, it focused exclusively on Victorian Aboriginal people and Aboriginal perspectives (Broome et al. 2014, 207–9). The Spencer statue was singled out as an example of what the "First Peoples" exhibit was trying to remedy. As an Indigenous curator commented, "I'm not interested in the collectors at all."[24]

What had happened to Spencer? "He's still in the museum," Batty told me, although no longer accessible to the public. At the request of some staff, he had been retained and placed in a receipt room where objects were processed before being accessioned. He sat on a trolley (a dolly or a cart; see figure 6.3), taking up considerable space in a narrow, windowless lab located between staff

FIGURE 6.2. Model of Baldwin Spencer in the "Two Laws" exhibit, Bunjilaka, Melbourne Museum, 2000. *Source:* Museums Victoria.

offices on one side and the museum stores on the other—between profane and sacred areas of the museum. In the terms explored in chapter 2, Spencer was in the liminal space between first and second burial. It intrigued me to think of him on his chair, on a trolley, watching over museum staff as they enveloped objects in the infrastructure of collection—describing, classifying, entering data, labeling, planning maintenance, minimizing risk.

A few years later, I saw Batty again at a museum seminar. The conversation turned to Spencer—was he still on his trolley in the holding room? "That's an interesting story," he said. I was not prepared for what came next. At some point in the previous year, Spencer had been moved from the holding room to the restricted room in the museum stores. Beginning in the 1980s, museums around Australia created restricted or secret/sacred rooms where ceremonial objects that should not be seen by a general audience could be kept securely.[25] Australian museums seek to repatriate these objects to the source communities, but because this is a long (sometimes decades-long) process, and because some communities request that museums retain possession (but not ownership) of their restricted objects, secure storage is needed. At the Melbourne Museum, this is a shed that sits within the museum stores. It is only accessed by the (white) manager of the restricted store, by Batty, and by visiting elders from remote communities in northern and central Australia. Spencer sat on his trolley against the far wall, between the shelves. "He's a bit spooky," Batty told me, "sitting there in the dark."[26]

How did Spencer come to be sitting in the dark inside the restricted room, inside the museum stores, inside the museum offices, inside the museum? Batty wasn't clear on the details, and I didn't have time to probe him further. Another year went by, and I finally took time to email a senior manager at the museum to request permission to look into Spencer's story. Permission was granted, and I began combing through the archives of the exhibition.

Contemporary museums produce mountains of paperwork. Meetings are minuted, policies are revised and circulated, objects are tracked, and exhibition incidents are noted and analyzed.[27] The paper traces of the Indigenous exhibit began with academic essays commissioned in the mid-1990s to provide intellectual guidance for those developing the new museum (Birch 1996; C. Healy 1995); proceeded through hazard reports, design plans, and hundreds of pages of spreadsheets with lists of objects; and ended with a memo announcing the deinstallation of the "large Spencer showcase"—the very first part of the Bunjilaka exhibition to be dismantled—in June 2011.[28]

Two remarkable things about Spencer emerged from these thousands of documents, both of which underline his ambiguity. First, he is called many different things: a statue, a replica, a model, a prop, a mannequin, a set piece, or an exhibition dressing. No one descriptor is more common than any other.

Second, Spencer is not visible in the exhibition management systems.[29] He appears on documents relating to concept development, on prop briefings, and in plans for the exhibition. Once the exhibition was installed, however, Spencer disappears from any lists of display objects or props. The two goannas that sat at Spencer's feet are duly tracked through the entire exhibition and are a proxy for Spencer's archival presence. After deinstallation they parted ways with Spencer and were transferred to the Herpetology Collection, depriving me of even this spectral trace of the statue's location.

Tracing the story of how Spencer came to be an unauthorized occupant of a highly restricted room became partly a question of regulation. His lack of official existence was frustrating to me but was also an important determinant of his mobility. After deinstallation in 2011, individual museum staff could take personal initiative in deciding his location without the scrutiny applied to tracked objects. In other words, he was especially amenable to collection because he was never intended to be collected. To understand why Spencer was not tracked, I needed to learn more about props.

At Museums Victoria, the Exhibition Collection Management (ECM) team is responsible for all items on display. These items can be classified into two groups: items from the museum collection (also called the "state collection" or "heritage collection") and props that are brought into the museum specifically for an exhibition. Props can be items on loan (which must be tracked to ensure they are safely returned), items commissioned from an artist or a commercial prop maker, or items sourced by museum staff themselves. The division between museum collection items and props is not always visually obvious when they are on display (although a discerning visitor might notice that some items have labels and some do not). However, the exhibition management systems maintain a strict electronic separation between collection items and props, a division maintained in physical space through separate off-site facilities for collection items and for props awaiting reuse.

A 2015 Museums Victoria information sheet on exhibition props gives three reasons for their use: "to replace vulnerable collection items,—e.g. facsimile of old letter; to dress an exhibition case or display—e.g. replica jar of preserved fruit; to replicate unusual, rare or important items—e.g. painted cast of Tarbosaurus tooth."[30] These three reasons readily collapse into two: to replace or replicate something that cannot be shown directly (because it is too vulnerable or valuable to show, or because the museum does not have it) and to use "commonly found items and specimens" to provide decoration or illustration.[31] Tellingly, Spencer doesn't fit into either of these categories.

Not all props are tracked with an ECM number. Many minor items like curtains and tables are sourced and recycled as required. The major goal of tracking props is to maintain "a clear distinction between collection items and non-collection items."[32] A manager explained this to me by contrasting a purse bought from a charity shop and a purse in the collection that might look similar. "If something can be confused with the heritage collection, if you anticipate things could get mixed up in the future, it will be tracked." It was Spencer's singularity that kept him out of the ECM records. He could not be mistaken for any object in the collection, was not loaned from anyone, and was not particularly valuable.[33]

This meant that there was no record of disposal at the time of deinstallation. When an exhibition is over, items from the collection are simply returned to their home department. By contrast, props can meet one of several fates. They can be returned to their source, they can be accessioned into the museum collection, they can become part of the "hands-on collection" in the Discovery Centre for handling by the public, they can be distributed to whoever wants them, or they can be destroyed. Again, Spencer defies each of these categories. He was retained but not accessioned: disposed not to one person but to a loose collective of staff. Staff could only vaguely remember the meeting when the fate of Spencer and all the tracked props was discussed, and no minutes were taken. No single person claimed responsibility for the idea to informally collect him, but all those I spoke to were supportive of the decision. Looking back, staff thought the reasons he was retained were that "a lot of work has gone into it," "it's a historical object" marking "the moment of the exhibition," and "people have grown attached to him." Others denied any particular intention or meaning to his retention: "Some things get salvaged, some get ditched. It was an off-the-cuff decision."[34]

Whatever happened at the disposal meeting, it is clear that after June 2011 Spencer was moved to the receipt room (as I have described). No one I spoke to could offer a clear reason or timeline for his next move, to the restricted room. The best explanation I heard was that the lab had to be emptied while LED lights were installed. The restricted room was seen as a safe place for the suddenly homeless Spencer, "out of the way but protected." Staff give conflicting accounts as to how long he was in the room, with responses ranging from several years to two weeks. I noted (without surprise) that my questions about why and how long he was in the room were often taken defensively, despite my best efforts to be casual. "It was *just* a spot to put him," I was told. My anthropological sensibility was never going to be assuaged by reassurances that Spencer's placement in the restricted room meant nothing. Of course, this *just* heightened my belief that it meant quite a lot.

From Postcolonial Prop to Decolonial Ghost

Ever since Bunjilaka opened in 2000, Spencer has asserted his significance. Despite being a mere prop, outside the bounds of museum collection proper, he is universally mentioned in reviews and critiques of the exhibition (Morton 2004). Academic reviews appreciated the intended meaning of Spencer as a postcolonial pedagogical tool that inverted the power relations behind the formation of the museum and its collections. They applauded the "impressive" and "brilliant" "Two Laws" section as the "first time that a major museum in Australia has confronted its past to address the ethics of collecting and constructing non-indigenous versions of Aboriginal history and culture" (Delroy 2001, 149; see also Russell 2001a). In contrast with the warm reception offered by academics and progressive media outlets, the Australian right-wing press was predictably outraged at the indignity of putting Spencer on display. The museum was called a "politically correct Aboriginal gallery" pushing "propaganda" that sullied the good names of its founding fathers (Bolt 2000, quoted in Russell 2001a, 99).

Writing in 2004 in response to various criticisms of the exhibition, John Morton argued for its pedagogical legitimacy and its relevance to contemporary political debates but also made the point that it was intended for Aboriginal audiences as much as, if not more than, the wider public. Bunjilaka was the result of "extensive community consultation" regarding every part of the exhibition (67). Still, the extensive community involvement did not guarantee that all Aboriginal people would endorse the result. As Morton told me, some Aboriginal staff looked on the statue of a scientist in a glass case with suspicion. The intended purpose of collecting the collector did not resonate with them. Why was Spencer at the center, again?

When the Bunjilaka exhibition was succeeded by the "First Peoples" exhibit in 2011, the Spencer statue was removed from public display. The publicly stated rationale for "First Peoples" contained an implicit reference to the presence of white collectors in the previous exhibition. The lead curator, Genevieve Grieves, explained the process of creating an elders' group to co-curate the new exhibition as "creat[ing] new structures which gave authority back to the people who owned the objects and the stories. We tried to make sure stories were not divorced from *their owners* and voices were not silenced" (in Museums and Galleries of NSW 2015, emphasis added). The website text for the exhibition explained that the "First Peoples" exhibit "presents the *Koorie* [a general word for Aboriginal Victorian] experience with immense power, depth and respect in a major permanent exhibition entirely co-created with Aboriginal people" (Bunjilaka Aboriginal Cultural Centre, n.d., emphasis added).

I interpret Spencer's decommissioning as part of the broader cultural shift inside and outside museums toward decoloniality. As discussed above, decoloniality is often seen in opposition to postcolonialism, and as its successor. I see this dichotomy reflected in some museum studies literature as two models of exhibition: the multivocal exhibition model, a model I associate with the postcolonial, and the community-based model, one I associate with decolonial approaches. Leading Native American museum studies scholar Amy Lonetree describes a multivocal approach as characterizing "the effort by the more progressive museums of the 1990s to deal more fairly with [topics related to Indigenous people]. When museum professionals were faced with presenting sensitive topics, especially those of a more controversial nature, they would present a range of perspectives and leave it to visitors to weigh the value of each" (2012, 169–70; see Phillips 2011). The community-based model, in contrast, strives to privilege the Indigenous community's view of an object or collection over other possible views (of curators, scientists, or others). In a decolonial, "indigenized" museum, exhibitions and curatorship should be controlled by Indigenous people because "controlling the representation of their cultures is linked to the larger movements of self-determination and cultural sovereignty" (Lonetree 2012, 1).[35]

Lonetree describes her own passage from a postcolonial, multivocal approach to a decolonial, community-based one through a story of her curatorial practice. At the time, she was working for the Minnesota Historical Society developing the new Mille Lacs Indian Museum, which opened in 1996. In constructing a draft of the historical timeline of the Mille Lacs, Lonetree used a multivocal exhibit model to present Mille Lacs accounts of their origins alongside scientific accounts of population expansion across the Bering Strait. She was "firmly" castigated by community members who told her: "We do not care what other people say about our origins. We want to feature only our story." Similarly, Lonetree sees museum objects as "living entities that remain intimately and inextricably tied to their descendant communities" and that can only be interpreted by these communities, facilitated by museum staff that are also preferably Indigenous (2012, 169, xv). This applies equally to contemporary Indigenous Australian museum practice (O'Sullivan 2016; Simpson 2006).

Given this context, it is not surprising that by 2011 Spencer's double no longer had a place in Bunjilaka. Although the idea was conceived by an Indigenous scholar (Tony Birch), it was widely considered by museum staff to be a non-indigenous object. Birch's idea was implemented, and the statue constructed, by non-indigenous people. Spencer in a glass case was a product of 1990s postcolonial, satirical, multivocal museum practice, and his end had come. This suggests that the passage from postcolonial to decolonial approaches means that collectors no longer have a place in Indigenous museum collections, even as a focus of critical reflection. In the case of Spencer, his exile from the exhibition marked other shifts that had uneven effects on different groups of Indigenous people.

We can see this in the quote a few paragraphs above in which Grieves explains the focus of the "First Peoples" exhibit that succeeded the first iteration of Bunjilaka. When she talks about creating structures that "gave authority back" to the *owners*, she arguably refers to the traditional owners of Victoria—Koorie people—and not the owners of the objects in the museum. The vast majority of the Aboriginal collection is made up of objects from central and northern Australia, with only a small fraction from Victoria. Although the extensive inclusion of remote Indigenous stories in the first Bunjilaka exhibition (particularly the "Belonging to Country" and "Two Laws" sections) accurately reflected the museum's holdings, the focus of two out of three of Bunjilaka's sections on Indigenous people outside Victoria was increasingly seen as a problem. Acknowledging the embeddedness of Indigenous people in the land and the importance of reclaiming Indigenous control of their heritage, by the end of the 2000s many Indigenous curators felt the Melbourne Museum should stick to telling stories about local Koorie communities.

In their eyes, putting Spencer in a glass case was another way to put him on a pedestal. Was the mood lighting, intended to create solemnity and reflection, really a white people's shrine to our revered scientist? Spencer's model, hollow plastic underneath the sand-textured paint, was technically silent. His form, though, spoke volumes and was interpreted as silencing Indigenous voices. John Morton, and certainly Tony Birch, intended for it to be ironic and not reverential, but it could be read either way.

This analysis highlights how, at the Melbourne Museum, the shift from multivocal/postcolonial to univocal/decolonial museology worked to silence not just non-indigenous voices but also nonlocal Indigenous voices. Prior to the decolonial shift, the *national* responsibility of an institution like Museums Victoria to Aboriginal people beyond Victoria's borders was clear, and the importance of the museum's relationships with Indigenous communities in northern and central Australia was taken for granted. Some museum staff believe this is no longer the case. This reflects in part the fact that it is exclusively non-indigenous people who currently work with remote community collections. At the time of writing, there are no Indigenous museum staff who are from the communities that have objects in the restricted room—the place where Spencer's double eventually found a home—so while Indigenous visitors and non-indigenous staff frequent the room, Indigenous museum staff do not pass its threshold. With the decolonization of the museum and the subsequent focus on Koorie communities, the objects and communities that sustain ties to the vast majority of museum holdings have become relatively invisible. The presence of Spencer's double in the restricted room demonstrates both the attempt to exile certain voices from the decolonial museum and the enduring power of that which is repressed but which stubbornly surfaces in ghostly forms.

De/collecting Spencer

Spencer's double embodies the strengths and the vulnerabilities of the postcolonial and decolonial eras. In his time in the glass case, he resembled a Rankean double. He functioned as a cathartic "bad" object for progressive museum professionals, academics, and visitors. To gaze at Spencer in the glass case produced a satisfactory sense of irony and historical distance from the days when the sacred objects of Indigenous peoples, and even Indigenous people themselves, were collected and circulated for the edification and entertainment of Western publics (Qureshi 2011). In place of the dioramas depicting Aboriginal people in "traditional" scenes that were standard museum fare well into the twentieth century, the white audience is invited to gaze at Spencer. If Spencer is in the case and we are outside the case looking at him, then we cannot be Spencer. The glass between us promises we are different—progressive, antiracist, and postcolonial (Ahmed 2005; Kowal 2015).

Despite John Morton's claim that the first Bunjilaka exhibit was primarily aimed at Indigenous audiences, the postcolonial mode of exhibition actively sought to cultivate progressive and reflexive non-indigenous identities. As that mode of collection and exhibition ended around 2010, so did the place for non-indigenous people, disparaging Spencer from outside the glass. In the decolonial era, non-indigenous allies are encouraged to stay silent and try to not take up any space.[36] The local Indigenous critiques of the white guy taking up space in the Indigenous museum exhibit, and the political shifts these critiques represented, were more-or-less well known to non-indigenous museum staff at the time of Spencer's deinstallation in 2011. How, then, should we understand his retention in the "backstage" of the museum? (Goffman 1959). And how do we interpret his later move to the restricted room?

Once Spencer was released from his case and became an honorary museum object (perhaps even an honorary staff member), the Rankean relationship between the non-indigenous viewer and Spencer's double was undone. What exactly he became then is up for debate, and I do not claim to have the definitive answer. I am convinced, however, that part of what he meant to non-indigenous museum staff is captured in the notion of nostalgia, that many-layered relationship to things in our past (Boym 2001). Spencer the ironic postcolonial statue embodied a particular chronotope: a particular time, place, and politics

(Bakhtin 1981). The time was a period in the recent history of collections, approximately 1990–2010, and the place was Australia and other similar settler colonies, particularly Aotearoa/New Zealand, Canada, and the United States. The politics that Spencer embodied was a period when Indigenous interests in (if not outright ownership of) their heritage were firmly established, but some non-indigenous people still had relatively unquestioned roles—significant, positive, and public roles—in telling Aboriginal stories. The Rankean projection that helped maintain the possibility of white antiracism was difficult to relinquish, and keeping Spencer was a coping strategy.

Spencer's uncased double was more than a focus of nostalgia for postcolonial times. He also took on uncanny dimensions, especially when he entered the restricted room. Spencer became the vessel for voices that are silenced in the univocal, decolonial museum, voices including those of non-indigenous and nonlocal Indigenous actors. This analysis recalls a critique of community-based models of museum practice as articulated by Lonetree and other decolonial scholars. As Indigenous scholar Frances Peters-Little (1999) observed long ago, the idea of a singular, uncomplicated "Indigenous community" is a fantasy, especially where state or national institutions are concerned. Privileging the "Indigenous community" requires identifying the boundaries of the community, a move that will inevitably marginalize some Indigenous people.

The hope of the decolonial museum is that local Indigenous voices are allowed to speak without distortion. Yet the presence of Spencer's double in the restricted room illustrates how decolonial approaches may struggle to stifle the many voices that found expression in previous modes of collection. Regardless of the decolonial intentions of museums, repressed traces of past collectors and curators remain embedded in the objects they handled, considered, collated, described, and displayed. This can be seen as the failure of decolonization, remediable through greater efforts to still those stubbornly persistent colonial voices. Spencer's second burial was deferred by people—non-indigenous staff members at the museum—who placed him in the receiving room and then the restricted room. If those people were better trained in decolonial museology, the argument might go, they would not have done this without the specific direction of the Indigenous community.

However, the persistence of Spencer contains important lessons for decolonial practice that may be missed if the episode is attributed solely to incomplete decolonization or racism. An alternate reading I offer is that Spencer's uncanny, obstinate double shows us how the difficult histories of objects cannot be disembedded. Spencer is part of the thousands of objects he collected and cannot be extricated, whether or not Indigenous or non-indigenous curators or community members are interested in his influence. Spencer's model is now also part of the difficult history of Indigenous-museum relations (Attwood 2013; Macdonald 2009). Efforts to silence certain museum histories run the risk of promoting ghostly presences (Gelder and Jacobs 1998; Gordon 2008), even when these efforts are grounded in morally and politically sound principles. Spencer's decommissioning is symptomatic of the decolonial turn, but Spencer's persistent, haunting presence is symptomatic of the decolonial turn's internal tensions and contradictions.

Collecting Spencer in the restricted room reunited him with the objects he collected. Seated on his chair, on his trolley, between the shelves, he was shrouded in darkness save for rare occasions when museum staff or visiting remote community members entered the room and turned on the lights. Staff told me that both they and community members were startled by Spencer's gaze: "You get a shock; it's unsettling." "Most community members do not recognize him, but it makes sense to people that he is there when you explain who he is," I was told. Tony Birch also told me that visiting Indigenous community members approve of Spencer's presence, watching over their sacred objects.[37]

Restricted rooms in Australian museums are a kind of shrine to a form of knowledge that Western scientists believed was on the verge of extinction from almost the first moment of contact. In his lifetime Spencer the man sought to remedy this supposed demise by protecting Indigenous people and culture through isolation on reserves. The critically important efforts of the contemporary museum to counter the fallacy of extinction and promote living Koorie cultures may ironically be marginalizing other Indigenous knowledges all over again. In a sense, Spencer belongs in this dark pseudoshrine, a spectral presence eluding museum categories and databases, a mascot[38] for a mode of postcolonial politics whose time has passed but that refuses to remain hidden. The continued presence of Spencer's double—with no official existence in the museum collection but considerable gravity—is a reminder that decolonial efforts to extricate colonial histories and remake museums from an Indigenous perspective risk providing fertile ground for the ghosts of previous eras of knowledge production.

Epilogue

On my first archival visit to the museum in February 2017, I was taken to see Spencer. Earlier that day I had sat in the office of a department manager explaining my interest in the story of the statue. Like many of the older curatorial staff, he was an academic and was sympathetic to my project. He confirmed that Spencer was stored in the restricted room, a place strictly prohibited to women.[39] "We've taken him out so you can view him," he said with a grin. "You're going to love where he is now."[40]

Later, a curator with access to the restricted room came to pick me up at the desk I had been allocated for the day. I followed him through the open-plan office, through the holding room where the statue had spent a few years, and into the museum stores. At each stage his swipe card gave us access. The stores felt like a suburban library, packed with rows of shelves that held objects instead of books.

He gestured toward the first aisle on my right, and I peered between the shelves. Spencer was there, facing me on his trolley, with a large painted Papuan statue towering over him—another disturbing and humorous juxtaposition. The Papuan statue was a sacred object, and I was not permitted to photograph it, so the store manager rolled Spencer's trolley out of the aisle and into the corridor, close to the door. We looked at Spencer together. "I've got quite attached to him," he reflected. "I'm disappointed we don't have Gillen as well." I asked him how Spencer came to be in the restricted room, and he referred me to another staff member for an explanation.

Seeing that he didn't want to talk about Spencer, I set about photographing the statue. I circled him to catch different angles of his face, then moved the trolley slightly to make room to capture the whole figure in one frame. Spencer rolled toward me, escaping my gaze. I pushed him back. He rolled toward me again. I put my foot out to steady the trolley long enough to take the photo, but I couldn't get far away enough to fit him in the frame. The curator came to the rescue, placing his finger on the trolley. Spencer was finally stilled, and I got my shot (figure 6.3).

I asked to see the outside of the room where Spencer is usually kept, and I was led down a corridor to what looked like a shed, painted gray with "restricted" on the door. Some photographs of Spencer and Gillen, and photographs they took, hung on the outer walls. Pride of place among them was the expedition shot from 1901–2 (figure 6.1). As I photographed the framed photograph, the curator standing behind me seemed to shift into a reflective mode. "He and Gillen knew those old people so well, they trusted him with their objects. It is right that he is in there with the things he collected."

Since my first archival visit, Spencer has not returned to the restricted room. His place in the main stores between two aisles, below the Papuan statue, has become semipermanent. Outside the restricted room he is more visible. A manager of another museum department I spoke to was "quite surprised to see it in the store, I just saw it two days ago." The future of the statue

FIGURE 6.3. Model of Baldwin Spencer on a trolley (dolly or cart) in the Museums Victoria stores, 2017. Photo by the author.

is now a subject of greater discussion among collection management staff, who dislike ambiguous items. Spencer's large dimensions make him particularly vulnerable. Pressure to decide his fate is increasing. "We're running out of storage space," I was told, "and we need to think carefully."

There are essentially two ways to resolve Spencer's ambiguity: accession or disposal. Disposal would be a second burial, completing the process that began when he was removed from display—equivalent to a first burial—in 2011. An analysis from the perspective of Kevin Hetherington's (2004) theory of disposal discussed in chapter 2 would predict that a second burial might quiet Spencer's ghostly presence. An effective second burial would need to be more than a discreet trip to the dump. I am thinking of a ritual that recognizes the contributions—good and bad—of Spencer and his ghostly double to making colonial, postcolonial, and decolonial knowledge about Indigenous Australians and acknowledges the uncertainties that haunt all contemporary knowledge makers.

An alternative to second burial would be to create a place for Spencer's double in the museum. In some of my conversations with staff, I discussed the possibility of accessioning Spencer. He would become part of the official collection, with a number, a description, and a preservation plan. One of the departments would have to propose this and argue the case at a monthly acquisition meeting. I found myself collecting reasons he should be accessioned and saved from second burial. I was told the history of collections curator might be interested in recording the statue's history, but she was never at her desk when I looked for her. When I brought it up with a manager who could potentially take on the accession, she was doubtful: "It's not an object made by Indigenous people." Still, she left the possibility open. "Something is forming about the meaning of this object," she mused. "We must be applying some level of value because we haven't destroyed it." I was now part of this growing web of significance enveloping Spencer, perhaps creating a legitimate place for him in the decolonial museum.

Conclusion

Haunting Biology can be read as three parallel stories, connected but contradictory. These three threads of my argument travel together through time but never merge, as if a force repels them. The first thread is a history of attempts by scientists to understand the original occupants of the Australian continent. The second is a shorter history of attempts by Indigenous activists and their allies to claw back the self-determination that has been violently denied to First Nations people since British colonization. The third is a story of ghostly presences, spectral tendencies, and outright hauntings that complicate the linear narratives of the first two threads. The protagonists of the first two parallel histories wish to see themselves as moving inexorably toward truer knowledge (on the part of scientists) or truer justice (on the part of Indigenous activists). But the past and the present will not cease to intrude on each other, to the consternation of everyone.

From the earliest days of colonial occupation, Indigenous body parts were collected, preserved, circulated, measured, and compared to other world populations. The preceding chapters present episodes in this centuries-long effort to objectify Indigenous biology using their skulls, hair, blood, physiological measurements, and DNA. New samples, new scientific disciplines, and new methods of preservation and analysis led to new theories. Some theories eventually sank under the weight of their misconceptions, including the division of human races by hair form (chapter 3), the archaic Caucasian theory (chapter 4), and the belief that blood groups were a marker of race (chapter 4). By contrast, genomics is on the ascendency, accumulating ever more explanatory power despite its negative historical associations with assimilation, eugenics, and genocide. As told in chapter 1, this book was motivated by the recent flourishing of Indigenous genomics, from precision medicine to direct-to-consumer genetic genealogy to ancient DNA research.

The twentieth-century progress of "science as usual" (Wylie 1997) was punctuated in Australia by the rise of the Indigenous rights movement. The story of successive attempts by Indigenous activists and their allies to decolonize research is the second narrative layer of this book: a story of change and transformation. The profound influence of a new generation of Indigenous people like Marcia Langton on the Australian Institute of Aboriginal Studies (AIAS) was discussed in chapter 2. The central rationale of the AIAS shifted from *scientific knowledge* to *Aboriginal benefit*, a shift that first impacted the disciplines of archaeology and anthropology. As the principal of the AIAS, Peter Ucko, put it, "By 1974 [physical] anthropologists and archaeologists in universities had begun to run for cover" (1983, 15). While other researchers who collected and stored blood samples were initially less affected by these changes, in the 1990s the Human Genome Diversity Project—dubbed the "vampire project" by Indigenous activists—brought these seemingly innocuous samples into the purview of Indigenous critiques.

In chapter 3 I told a similar story of ethical change and transformation from the point of view of ancient DNA (aDNA) research. During the development of aDNA research in (mostly European) laboratories in the 1980s and 1990s, ethics was considered relevant only to research on living people. Research on deceased people, it was thought, was merely a matter of regulation. Samples of DNA extracted from bones of long-deceased people were exposed to questions of authority—did the researchers have the right permissions from museums and national governments to take samples and move them across borders?—but not questions of human ethics. The story of the hair sample that became "the first Aboriginal genome" shows how, in the past decade or so, even prominent researchers working in Europe—that wellspring of colonialism—have been forced to abandon the idea that samples collected from Indigenous ancestors can be considered independent of contemporary Indigenous people.

Chapter 6 discussed the dynamics of political change in relation to museums, tracing the emergence of postcolonial and then decolonial approaches to telling Indigenous stories and managing Indigenous objects. In each of these institutions and disciplines, Indigenous activists and practitioners fought for change over years and decades, with many successes to show for it. In Australia and elsewhere, Indigenous people are slowly but steadily gaining ever more recognition.

The third narrative layer of the book is one of continuity rather than progress or change. Each chapter contains haunting elements that cast echoes into the future. Let me recall one example from each of the chapters.

Colin Mackenzie's ghost haunts Romaine Moreton seven decades after his death, and the bones he collected remain stranded in a storage facility on the fringes of Australia's capital city.

Alfred C. Haddon's 1923 hair-collection encounter leads to the sequencing of the "first Aboriginal genome" eighty-eight years later. That story is told in the journal *Science* with a stock image of "an Aboriginal man" that draws on a century-long tradition of racial portraiture to meld together sample, race, and phenotype (Rasmussen et al. 2011).

The themes of the late nineteenth-century portrait of Jungun the "albino Aborigine" (figure 4.1) are reworked in the picture of three-year-old Lorna (figure 4.2) that A. A. Abbie selected as the frontispiece of his book promoting the archaic Caucasian theory (Abbie [1969] 1976).

C. Stanton Hicks's 1931 musings on the physiological abilities of desert sleepers are echoed in a 2016 genetic analysis of Indigenous Australians' most notable evolutionary quirks (Malaspinas et al. 2016).

An ironic model of the iconic collector Baldwin Spencer is decollected as part of a decolonial turn in museology but persists in the dark alongside the secret/sacred objects he collected.

In each case, a legacy of previous modes of knowledge production is uncannily present. Within each story of white collectors and scientists are signs of an Indigenous spectral agency: ancestors who refuse to be quiet while blood and bones remain displaced.

These three threads woven through the book—scientific research, decolonization, and haunting—are my best answer to the question I posed in the introduction: *How are we to understand Indigenous biological difference in the twenty-first century?* The normative answer to this question in the contemporary Australian settler colony is a melding of scientific progress and racial justice: knowledge of Indigenous biological differences *could* bring health benefits to Indigenous people *if* these efforts are under their control. The National Centre for Indigenous Genomics, the world's first Indigenous-governed genome facility, is perhaps the best example. My contention is that, in the case of Indigenous biological difference, even the most skilled amalgam of science and justice will be haunted.

As explained in chapter 1, the "haunting" of the title is intended as both an adjective and a verb. From an adjectival perspective, the methods, theories, scientific publications, and institutions featured in this book are certainly haunted. These haunted objects, however, are the result of active subjects: those presences that haunt. The verb form of *Haunting Biology* describes the agency of haunting presences, but it is also an imperative for contemporary actors to seek them out and learn to live with them. To provide useful accounts of how the history of biological difference matters in the present—and whether it can or should matter differently—we must haunt Indigenous biology by granting its ghosts a voice.

This is not an easy path. My own discipline of Australian anthropology has largely disavowed its biological past (Gray 2007). By seeking to reclaim this past, albeit in a mode of extreme ambivalence and certainly not celebration, I risk being seen as a troublemaker, parading the discipline's infamy rather than its achievements and future potential. Similarly, I do not take pleasure in spoiling the narrative of decolonial science with my insistent ghosts. Explaining away the ghosts, or simply refusing to hear them in the first place, would make things much easier. The teleology of perfect knowledge and perfect justice could be allowed to merge into an ethical, rigorous Indigenous-led science. Unless the ghosts that line the path to an Indigenous-controlled genomics (or any other form of science that claims to be liberatory) are given a hearing, however, we are in constant danger of repeating the past. It is the responsibility of all those engaged in making biological knowledge about Indigenous people in the present to acquaint themselves with these haunting possibilities. As the Wik people of the Cape York Peninsula advised anthropologist Benjamin Smith (2008, 96), we should not "chase 'em away" but keep them close. The result, as Avery Gordon puts it, "will not be a more tidy world, but one that might be less damaging" (2008, 19).

Kevin Hetherington's (2004) theory of haunting, described in chapter 2, provides one interpretation of my imperative to recall disciplinary ghosts. He theorized haunting as an effect of failed disposal, drawing on anthropological and sociological accounts of first and second burial. Many cultures, including many Indigenous groups, practice two-stage burial (Clarke 2003; Glaskin 2006; Glaskin et al. 2008). A first burial is temporary, providing time to reflect and come to terms with the loss, while a second burial is permanent. Things (objects, people) haunt if they get stuck between the first and second stages of burial (Hetherington 2004). In chapter 2 I asked whether bones, frozen blood samples, and even whole disciplines may be suspended between first and second burial, haunting us. This entire book, however, can also be seen as a project of second burial. I exhume a cast of dead white men—Colin Mackenzie, Alfred C. Haddon, C. Stanton Hicks, A. A. Abbie, Baldwin Spencer—

in order to examine the knowledge they created and its haunting legacies. Through this inquiry into the historical production of biological knowledge about Indigenous people, my fictive ancestors may receive a second burial. This doesn't mean that their ghosts will be forever quiet but that we might be better able to hear what they have to say.

In interrogating the reasons I am attuned to ghosts and can't imagine life without them, my own history must be accounted for. I know my familial intimacy with legacies of violence and transgenerational trauma influences my relationship with ghosts. Over 90 percent of Polish Jews were murdered in the Holocaust, the largest single national group of victims, including almost all my grandparents' friends, family, and acquaintances. A whole world ended. It cannot be restored. All that is left is haunting traces and fading memories. Perhaps because of this history, I am ineluctably drawn to the ambiguous, the ambivalent, and the strange, especially when these are eschewed or denied by dominant narratives. I am especially attuned to the historical antecedents of what we think of as brand new. I believe that we can overcome the past, but I am wary of declarations that we have succeeded. The ghostly methodology I employ in this book is, for me, a way of appraising decolonial moves in society such as Indigenous genomics. To assess how genuinely novel they are, we must listen to their ghosts.

What are these haunting traces trying to tell us? Above all, ghosts raise questions, often uncomfortable ones. The temporal and spatial ruptures they produce invite us to think differently. As cultural theorist Jeffrey Weinstock puts it, "Phantoms *haunt*; their appearances signal epistemological uncertainty and the potential emergence of a different story and a competing history" (2004, 7). Ghosts puncture linear narratives, whether these are narratives of scientific or societal progress. Following Isabelle Stengers (2005) and Marisol de la Cadena (2010), ghosts are cosmopolitical actors, opening up possibilities for a political field that acknowledges ontological disagreements between different worlds.

In weaving these narrative layers together—scientific discovery, antiracist change, and ghostly presences—I have told stories of attempts to move beyond a past that can never be completely left behind. Biological knowledge about Indigenous people has been wielded to destroy countless worlds. Whether twenty-first-century biological knowledge can be wielded differently depends on how we listen and respond to the ghosts we live with.

Appendix 1

Note: People are listed in chronological order by date of birth and then alphabetically for those with the same year of birth.

TRUGANINI (ca. 1812–76), known at the time of her death as the "last Tasmanian"

F. J. GILLEN (1855–1912), Alice Springs post and telegraph station master, special magistrate, and Sub-Protector of Aborigines, coauthor of *The Native Tribes of Central Australia*

ALFRED C. HADDON (1855–1940), reader in ethnology, University of Cambridge; led 1898 Cambridge Anthropological Expedition to Torres Straits

BALDWIN SPENCER (1860–1929), anthropologist, professor of zoology, University of Melbourne; honorary director, National Museum of Victoria; coauthor of *The Native Tribes of Central Australia*

WILLIAM COLIN MACKENZIE (1877–1938), orthopedic surgeon; director of Australian Institute of Anatomy

JOHN B. CLELAND (1878–1971), professor of pathology, University of Adelaide; member of the Board for Anthropological Research

C. STANTON HICKS (1892–1976), professor of physiology, University of Adelaide; member of the Board for Anthropological Research

NORMAN B. TINDALE (1900–1993), anthropologist, South Australian Museum; member of the Board for Anthropological Research; member of the Harvard-Adelaide Universities Anthropological Expedition

XAVIER HERBERT (1901–84), author of *Capricornia* and *Poor Fellow My Country*

P. R. STEPHENSEN (1901–65), publisher, author, activist, founder of Jindyworobak movement

MARGARET LILARDIA TUCKER (1904–96), Indigenous activist, Victorian Aborigines League

A. A. ABBIE (1905–76), professor of anatomy and histology, University of Adelaide; member of the Board for Anthropological Research; author of *The Original Australians*

P. F. SCHOLANDER (1905–80), professor of physiology, Scripps Institution of Oceanography; researched cold tolerance in the 1950s

JOSEPH B. BIRDSELL (1908–94), biological anthropologist, professor of anthropology, University of California, Los Angeles; member of the Harvard-Adelaide Universities Anthropological Expedition

R. L. KIRK (1921–2010), geneticist, John Curtin School of Medical Research, Australian National University; chair of Human Biology Advisory Committee, Australian Institute of Aboriginal Studies

ALAN THORNE (1939–2012), professor of archaeology, Australian National University; chair of Human Biology Advisory Committee, Australian Institute of Aboriginal Studies

SUE SERJEANTSON (1946–), professor of genetics, John Curtin School of Medical Research, Australian National University; deputy vice-chancellor, Australian National University

MICHAEL DODSON (1950–), professor of law and director of National Centre for Indigenous Studies, Australian National University; Aboriginal and Torres Strait Islander social justice commissioner; inaugural member of the Indigenous Governance Board, National Centre for Indigenous Genomics

SIMON EASTEAL (ca. 1950–), professor of genetics, John Curtin School of Medical Research; and inaugural director, National Centre for Indigenous Genomics, Australian National University

MICK GOODA (ca. 1950–), inaugural chair of the Indigenous Governance Board, National Centre for Indigenous Genomics; Aboriginal and Torres Strait Islander social justice commissioner

MARCIA LANGTON (1951–), anthropologist, geographer, activist; professor of Indigenous studies, University of Melbourne; associate provost, University of Melbourne

IAN ANDERSON (1965–), doctor, health researcher; professor of Indigenous health, University of Melbourne; deputy secretary of Indigenous Affairs, Department of Prime Minister and Cabinet; deputy vice-chancellor, Australian National University

ALAN COOPER (1966–), evolutionary geneticist; professor of ancient biomolecules, Oxford University; professor of genetics, University of Adelaide; dismissed in 2019

ESKE WILLERSLEV (1971–), evolutionary geneticist; professor of evolution, Copenhagen University; professor in ecology and evolution, University of Cambridge

MISTY JENKINS (1978–), immunologist; laboratory head, Walter and Eliza Hall Institute for Medical Research; inaugural member of the Indigenous Governance Board, National Centre for Indigenous Genomics

Appendix 2

1788	The First Fleet arrives in Botany Bay; Great Britain establishes the Colony of New South Wales as a penal colony
1835	William Buckley returns to Melbourne after thirty-two years living with the Wadawurrung people
1848	Ludwig Leichhardt goes missing in the western desert
1865	White settlers massacre Indigenous people in Lagrange Bay, Western Australia
1876	Truganini dies in Hobart, Tasmania
1876	Henry Morton Stanley reportedly contacts the white tribe of Gambaragara, Uganda
1889	Alexander McPhee finds Jungun in Joanna Springs, Western Australia
1894	W. L. H. Duckworth publishes his measurements of twenty-eight Aboriginal skulls (Duckworth 1894)
1898	Alfred C. Haddon leads the Cambridge Anthropological Expedition to Torres Straits
1899	Baldwin Spencer and F. J. Gillen publish *The Native Tribes of Central Australia* (Spencer and Gillen 1899); Spencer is appointed honorary director of the National Museum of Victoria (now Museums Victoria)
1901	Baldwin Spencer and F. J. Gillen begin the 1901–2 expedition to central Australia
1901	ABO blood groups are discovered by American biologist Karl Landsteiner
1901	The Commonwealth of Australia is established from six existing colonies; the Immigration Restriction Act is one of the first laws passed

1909	Alfred C. Haddon publishes *The Races of Man and Their Distribution* (Haddon 1909)
1923	Alfred C. Haddon collects a lock of hair from a "young Aboriginal man" at Golden Ridge, Western Australia
1925	Herbert Basedow publishes *The Australian Aboriginal* (Basedow 1925)
1926	The Board for Anthropological Research auspices its first expedition
1930	The Australian Institute of Anatomy opens under the leadership of William Colin Mackenzie
1931	C. Stanton Hicks joins the annual Board for Anthropological Research expedition and speculates on torpor in desert sleepers
1935	Alfred C. Haddon, Julian Huxley, and A. M. Carr-Saunders publish *We Europeans*, critiquing the race concept (Haddon et al. 1935)
1937	A. O. Neville, Western Australian commissioner for native affairs, advocates for the total absorption of the Aboriginal population into the white population (Commonwealth of Australia 1937)
1938	Norman B. Tindale and Joseph B. Birdsell begin the joint Harvard-Adelaide Universities Anthropological Expedition for the study of race mixture in Australia
1938	William Colin Mackenzie dies
1938	Xavier Herbert's novel *Capricornia* is published by P. R. Stephensen
1939	World War II begins
1950	The first UNESCO Statement on Race is released (UNESCO and Its Programme 1950)
1953	Article describing the structure of DNA is published by Francis Crick and James D. Watson (Watson and Crick 1953)
1958	P. F. Scholander and colleagues publish findings on "insulative cooling" among Aboriginal people in central Australia (Scholander et al. 1958)
1961	The Australian Institute of Aboriginal Studies is founded in Canberra
1964	The International Biological Program begins
1967	R. L. Kirk establishes his genetics laboratory at the Australian National University
1967	A national referendum is passed to allow the Commonwealth government to pass legislation regarding Indigenous people (formerly the purview of states)

1969	David Jose and colleagues publish a damning health survey of children on Queensland missions (Jose et al. 1969)
1969	The first documented case of albinism in an Aboriginal person is published in the *Medical Journal of Australia* (Walker 1969)
1969	A. A. Abbie publishes *The Original Australians*, including the archaic Caucasian hypothesis (Abbie [1969] 1976)
1972	Richard Lewontin publishes an article showing that most genetic variation occurs within, not between, population groups (Lewontin 1972)
1972	Peter Ucko is appointed as principal of the Australian Institute of Aboriginal Studies
1976	The Aboriginal Land Rights Act (Northern Territory) is passed by the Commonwealth government
1976	Truganini's remains are repatriated to the Tasmanian Aboriginal community
1976	Roy L. Simmons reports that thirty-five years of blood group research in Indigenous populations produced no conclusive results
1977	Margaret Tucker publishes *If Everyone Cared: Autobiography of Margaret Tucker*, the first book to detail the effects of the Stolen Generations
1981	The Commonwealth Department of Aboriginal Affairs proposes a three-part definition of Indigenous status: self-identification, ancestry, and community acceptance
1983	The first Indigenous doctor graduates from the University of Western Australia medical school
1984	The Australian Institute of Anatomy closes; ancestral remains are transferred to the National Museum of Australia
1985	Museums Victoria repatriates ancestral remains collected by George Murray Black to the Koori community
1987	The Royal Commission into Aboriginal Deaths in Custody is established by the Commonwealth government
1987	The Human Biology Advisory Committee of the Australian Institute of Aboriginal Studies ends; R. L. Kirk retires from the Australian National University
1991	National Health and Medical Research Council publishes guidelines for research in Aboriginal and Torres Strait Islander Communities
1991	The Council for Aboriginal Reconciliation is established by the Commonwealth government

1992	The Australian National University repatriates Mungo Lady to traditional owners
1993	The Native Title Act is passed by the Commonwealth government in response to the High Court's recognition of the land rights of the Meriam people in the Torres Strait
1994	Global Indigenous opposition to the Human Genome Diversity Project peaks
1997	The report of the "Stolen Children" National Inquiry entitled *Bringing Them Home* is tabled in federal Parliament (Human Rights and Equal Opportunity Commission 1997)
2000	The Human Genome Project completes the working draft of the human genome
2000	The new Melbourne Museum opens; the Bunjilaka permanent exhibit includes a model of Spencer in a glass case
2008	Australian prime minister Kevin Rudd formally apologizes to the Stolen Generations
2009	Romaine Moreton is haunted by the ghost of Colin Mackenzie at the National Film and Sound Archive, Canberra
2010	Blood samples taken by Therese Markow for genetic research in the 1990s are returned by Arizona State University to the Havasupai people
2011	Eske Willerslev and colleagues publish the "first Aboriginal genome," sequenced from the lock of hair collected by Haddon in 1923 (Rasmussen et al. 2011)
2011	The Summer Internship for Indigenous Peoples in Genomics (SING) is established in the United States to train Indigenous peoples in genomics
2011	Melbourne Museum opens a new "First Peoples" exhibition; the Spencer exhibit is deinstalled
2013	The National Centre for Indigenous Genomics is established at the Australian National University
2015	Eske Willerslev and colleagues publish genetic analysis of the Ancient One/Kennewick Man (Rasmussen et al. 2015)
2015	Blood samples taken by Napoleon Chagnon for genetic research in the 1960s are returned by the US National Institutes of Health to the Yanomami people in Brazil
2016	Eske Willerslev and colleagues publish their analysis of eighty-three genomes from Aboriginal people around Australia, including speculation on adaptations to desert cold (Malaspinas et al. 2016)

2019	Conservative politician Mark Latham proposes DNA testing be used to establish eligibility for Indigenous benefits
2019	The National Centre for Indigenous Genomics repatriates desiccated blood samples of deceased donors to Galiwin'ku community
2019	The Australian chapter of Summer Internship for Indigenous Peoples in Genomics (SING) is established
2020	AncestryDNA releases an update that provides an "Aboriginal and Torres Strait Islander Ancestry Estimate"
2020	The Native BioData Consortium is established in South Dakota by Indigenous geneticists and ethicists

Notes

1   At this point, the Out of Africa hypothesis—the now-dominant theory that *Homo sapiens* first evolved in Africa and then spread to the rest of the world—was still some years away. That hypothesis was first developed in the 1980s; an article analyzing mitochondrial DNA in 1987, including placental samples from Aboriginal women in Darwin and Alice Springs provided by Kirk, led to its wide acceptance (Cann, Stoneking, and Wilson 1987). In the past decade, it has been shown many times that world populations have admixture with "archaic" hominins such as Neanderthals and Denisovans, complicating the picture (Stringer 2012).

2   John Maynard (2007) outlines the important history of Aboriginal activism prior to its more public presence in the 1960s.

3   The profound health inequalities suffered by Indigenous Australians are well known but bear repeating. Mortality rates are twice that of the non-indigenous population; life expectancy is eight to nine years less; diabetes occurs at 3.5 times and kidney failure at 6.8 times the rate in the non-indigenous population; and all the social determinants of health (e.g., education, employment, housing) are far worse in the Indigenous population compared to the general Australian population (Australian Indigenous HealthInfoNet 2019).

4   Genetics is the study of individual genes, while genomics is the study of the entire genome, that is, twenty-three pairs of chromosomes in humans. In the twenty-first century, "genomics" has replaced "genetics" as the general term for the study of genetic determinants and associations of health and disease, as the methods used involve the production and analysis of genome-wide data.

5   For important reviews of "postcolonial science and technology studies" that capture some of this work, see W. Anderson and Adams 2007; McNeil 2005; and Seth 2009, 2017.

6 "Personalized" or "precision" medicine aims to use genomic information to predict, diagnose, and treat disease more effectively than current methods. It is based on the rationale that genomic information allows greater stratification to identify who is more likely to benefit from, for example, breast cancer screening, or exactly what dose of which medication is most likely to work in a particular person. There are some areas where precision medicine is of clear benefit, such as the treatment of some cancers, and other areas where the benefit is yet to be established, such as in targeted health promotion.

7 An example where these links are particularly stark is forensic DNA databases in the United States that are overwhelmingly made up of samples from African Americans, making them more likely to be falsely linked to a crime (D. Roberts 2011).

8 The current evolutionary anthropology laboratory at Cambridge is named after Duckworth and is part of the story told in chapter 3. The skulls Duckworth measured are still stored there.

9 These issues are explored in more depth by philosophers of biology; see, for example, Godfrey-Smith 2003; and P. Griffiths and Stotz 2013.

10 This is also illustrated in the emerging field of Indigenous epigenetics. Epigenetics is seen as a progressive science that shifts scientific attention from inherited to acquired/development characteristics, but it can be used in ways just as deterministic as genetics (Kowal and Warin 2018; Warin, Kowal, and Meloni 2020; Warin et al. 2022).

CHAPTER 1. LIVING WITH GHOSTS

1 The subheading "DNA Testing Plan for Aboriginal People" is taken from the headline of the news article by Esther Han (2019).

2 One Nation leader Pauline Hanson introduced what was known as the "It's OK to be white" motion into the Senate in October 2018. It was only narrowly defeated after initially being supported by the major conservative party (Norman 2018).

3 The party ended up with less than 7 percent of the vote and two seats, a similar outcome to the previous time they ran for office in New South Wales in 1999.

4 At the time this story broke, there were two companies (one based in the United States, one based in Australia) that offered a genetic test for Australian Indigenous ancestry based on short tandem repeat data. These tests are designed for forensic uses and are widely considered to be inaccurate when used for ancestry purposes. The services were never widely publicized, and both have since ceased operation. See Booth 2018; and Kowal and Jenkins 2016. However, in May 2020, as the COVID-19 pandemic dominated the global headlines, genetic ancestry industry leader Ancestry.com released an update to its algorithm that included an "Aboriginal and Torres Strait Islander ancestry estimate" (Ancestry Marketing Team, Australia 2020). The social effects of this are yet to be determined, and so far Ancestry.com has not actively advertised this capability.

5　Of course, Western notions of heredity and inheritance also have a history; see Keller 2010; and Müller-Wille and Rheinberger 2012.

6　Hauntology is related to Derrida's other concepts of the trace, *revenant*, and différance. These Derridean concepts influence many in the humanities and social sciences, including science and technology studies (e.g., Haraway 2008; Law 2004).

7　As Sigmund Freud put it, "The process of repression is not to be regarded as an event that takes place *once*, the results of which are permanent, as when some living thing has been killed and is from that time onwards dead; repression demands a persistent expenditure of force" ([1953] 2001, 151).

8　Important work on North American settler colonialism and ghosts includes Bergland 2000; and C. Boyd and Thrush 2011.

9　The Boyer Lectures are annual lectures commissioned by the Australian Broadcasting Corporation modeled on the BBC's Reith Lectures.

10　The terminology of "homely" and "unhomely" draws from Freud's ([1919] 1925) concept of the uncanny as *unheimlich*.

11　The first chair in anthropology in Australia, created at the University of Sydney in 1926, was taken up by A. R. Radcliffe-Brown, trained in Cambridge by Alfred C. Haddon (discussed in chapter 3) and psychologist W. H. R. Rivers, highly influenced by Émile Durkheim and considered a founder of social anthropology (see W. Anderson 2019).

12　This concept is inspired by Charis Thompson's (2002) concept of strategic naturalization.

13　Henrietta Lacks was an African American woman who died of cervical cancer in 1951 in Johns Hopkins Hospital in Baltimore. A sample of cancer cells removed after her death was transformed into the first immortal cell culture, called the HeLa cell line, which became a key laboratory tool around the world. Her family only learned of this twenty-four years after her death and has fought to gain recognition and control over the cells and the genomic information they contain (Landecker 2000; Skloot 2010).

CHAPTER 2. BLOOD, BONES, AND THE GHOSTS OF THE ANCESTORS

1　This architectural classification comes from Daley 2014. Funding for the building, constructed during the Depression, was supplemented by William Colin Mackenzie himself, enabling the faunal embellishments (Kaus 2008).

2　The Board for Anthropological Research is discussed in chapter 5. Filmed footage of the expedition is kept at the NSFA but the material collected from these expeditions is held at the South Australian Museum and was never held at the Institute of Anatomy.

3　All quotes from Moreton are from Moreton's narration in the film (Thornton 2013). Halford founded the first Australian medical school, at the University of Melbourne, in 1862.

4　For a related inquiry into the ghosts of racial science in plant biology through a feminist science and technology studies (STS) lens, see Subramaniam 2014. As also mentioned in the previous chapter, encounters with ghosts are everyday experiences in many Aboriginal societies, in both their "traditional" and contemporary iterations (Clarke 2007; Benjamin Smith 2008).

5 Hertz's analysis, first published in French in 1907, was informed by anthropology, including Baldwin Spencer and F. J. Gillen's *The Native Tribes of Central Australia* ([1899] 1968), discussed in chapter 6.

6 Note that in cases where bones are thousands or tens of thousands of years old, the biological or cultural continuity to contemporary Indigenous peoples has often been in question. As mentioned in the previous chapter, the most famous case of this kind is Kennewick Man (Burke et al. 2008; Reardon and TallBear 2012; TallBear 2013).

7 Body parts such as locks of hair may be prized as mementos of dead loved ones or children long grown within Western cultures, however. See Hallam and Hockey 2001.

8 Mackenzie's best-known book in orthopedics came later (1918). He simultaneously worked on his four-volume comparative anatomy, coauthored with W. J. Owen, published in 1918 and 1919.

9 Until 1929 it was officially known as the National Museum of Australian Zoology (Commonwealth of Australia 1924).

10 Plans for the institute included adjoining zoological gardens for native animals that were sacrificed to Depression-era budget cuts. However, a similar vision was realized in Victoria, where the government granted him land outside Melbourne for his field research and he later founded the Sir Colin Mackenzie Sanctuary. The popular tourist and school trip destination now known as Healesville Sanctuary offers visitors close encounters with iconic Australian animals.

11 David Kaus (2008) from the National Museum of Australia believes Mackenzie began collecting human remains around 1920. Along with Aboriginal remains, his collection included body parts of World War I soldiers donated by the Hunterian Museum of the Royal College of Surgeons in 1935 (Daley 2014).

12 The institute received Aboriginal human remains from others; for example, twenty skulls were received from Herbert Basedow, who is discussed in chapter 4 (see Kaus 2008). Other collections of Aboriginal skeletal material housed at the institute included the Ramsay-Smith and Nankivell collections. To my knowledge, the other major Aboriginal collections donated to the institute, the Milne and Horne-Bowie collections, were of ethnographic objects only (*Canberra Times*, March 12, 1938).

13 This included eight Aboriginal children from the Wreck Bay settlement school who visited Canberra in 1964, funded by the Department of the Interior. The account of the visit in the *Canberra Times* includes images of them gazing intently at skulls (the specific exhibit is unclear), "engrossed by the specimens at the Institute of Anatomy" (*Canberra Times* 1964).

14 The letter was countered a week later by one B. F. Dorning (1972) of the Canberra suburb of Narrabundah, who defended the exhibit as portraying neutral facts of biological difference with no assumptions of inferiority.

15 Parts of the following paragraphs are based on Kowal and Radin 2015.

16 Yamaguchi's resulting monograph has been widely cited in the physical anthropological literature and as recently as 2018 (Google Scholar search, September 6, 2021).

17 Gandevia later founded the Australian Society of the History of Medicine (known from 2006 as the Australian and New Zealand Society of the History of Medicine) (Heagney 2006).

18 Cawte was an avid and early supporter of Indigenous community-controlled health services. In 1977 he founded and edited the *Aboriginal Health Worker Journal*—later known as the *Aboriginal and Islander Health Worker Journal*—a unique venue for Aboriginal health workers, activists, and progressive non-indigenous doctors to share knowledge and experiences (see Cawte 1977). The most recent journal issue was published in 2016.

19 Stephanie Moser (1995) discusses the influence of Ucko on "Aboriginalising" Australian archaeology. Ucko exerted a similar influence across the disciplines present at the AIAS.

20 The royal commission examined the reasons for high rates of mortality for Aboriginal and Torres Strait Islander people in police custody. Its 339 recommendations are still discussed in the context of continuing high rates of incarceration (Johnston 1991).

21 Minutes of Human Biology Advisory Committee (HBAC) meeting, September 10, 1973, and August 19, 1975, AIATSIS Collection, Canberra, ACT.

22 Minutes of HBAC meeting, August 11, 1977, AIATSIS Collection.

23 Minutes of HBAC meeting, September 18, 1978, AIATSIS Collection.

24 Minutes of HBAC meeting, July 10, 1987, AIATSIS Collection. In 1987 all the committees were disbanded after a review of the institute by R. J. Walsh. Geneticist Neville White continued on as the sole "Health and Human Biology" representative on the central AIAS research committee.

25 Minutes of HBAC meeting, October 9, 1973, AIATSIS Collection. Mungo Lady was discovered in 1969 and Mungo Man in 1974. Although Thorne himself was a paleoanthropologist, as chair of the committee he oversaw the rejection of osteology as a fundable field of research. He was later at the center of the controversial repatriation of Mungo Lady in 1992 before succumbing to Alzheimer's disease in 2012 at the age of seventy-three.

26 Minutes of HBAC meeting, February 10, 1975, 6, AIATSIS Collection.

27 Horton, an osteologist turned archaeologist turned publisher, is best known today for compiling a map of Indigenous Australian nations (updated from Norman Tindale's earlier map; Tindale 1974) that is among the most recognizable images of Indigenous Australia today, gracing the walls of classrooms, offices, and homes across the country (Horton 1996).

28 Letter from Dr. Ucko to the Hon. D. N. Everingham, minister for health, Parliament House, October 3, 1975, AIATSIS Collection.

29 Minutes of HBAC meeting, September 14, 1976, 5, AIATSIS Collection.

30 The Tasmanians (who were considered racially distinct from mainland Australian Aboriginals) were famous as a case of impending extinction at least since

Darwin's 1836 visit to Tasmania on the *Beagle*. By the 1860s they had become a major focus of international speculation on the causes of racial extinction.

31 Letter from D. R. Gregg, director of the Tasmanian Museum and Art Gallery, to Peter Ucko, June 12, 1974, AIATSIS Collection.

32 Letter from Gregg to Ucko, June 12, 1974.

33 Minutes of HBAC meeting, September 23, 1974, 3–4, AIATSIS Collection. In a memo to the principal, Peter Ucko, Alan Thorne made it clear he saw this as a historic moment: "As an osteologist I am fully aware of the 'thin end of the wedge' implications of the demand for burial and/or return of the remains. . . . However, Truganini is a very special case—last of 'race,' known individual, the Bishop's promise [Bishop Atkinson's promise to not allow her remains to be displayed], the govt involvement in the disturbance and exhumation, the placing on display etc. I would be amazed if Aborigines were to accept the Tas. Chief Sec's notion that she 'must be preserved for possible future scientific study.' The present demand shows clearly that they want her buried once and for all. My personal attitude is to do just that." Memo from A. Thorne to P. Ucko, July 21, 1974, AIATSIS Collection.

34 The Tasmanian Aboriginal community has continued to seek repatriation of other parts and derivatives of Truganini's body and her possessions held in museums overseas, including hair and skin samples from the Royal College of Surgeons (returned in 2002) and her necklace and bracelet from the University of Exeter (returned in 1995). The Tasmanian Aboriginal Centre (TAC) continues to seek the return of busts of Truganini from the British Museum.

35 For an overview of the history of archaeology in Australia, see J. Mulvaney 2011.

36 This assumes that new equivalent substrates cannot be collected and that substrates are specific to disciplines, which is questionable but is a simplification I am adopting for the sake of the argument here.

37 Samples of Aboriginal blood and blood products (including cell lines) are also held by researchers outside Australia, who use them on the ethical authority of their own institutional review boards that do not apply the standards required by Australian committees. See Radin and Kowal 2015.

38 Primarily the collection of Norman Tindale and Joseph Birdsell's hair samples from the 1938–39 Harvard-Adelaide expedition, held by the South Australian Museum, but possibly other large collections collected by R. J. Walsh, the Australian representative on the central IBP-HA committee (University of New South Wales) and Roy T. Simmons (Commonwealth Serum Laboratories, now a private company). The potential use of such samples for provenancing follows from the fact that blood sample collections in Australia generally have very good provenance, while many skeletal specimens do not.

39 The National Museum of Australia had finally opened in 1980 after nearly eighty years of discussion and proposals, although its permanent building was not completed until 2001 (Robin 2003). The opening of the museum was effectively a death warrant for the Institute of Anatomy, demonstrating its irrelevance.

40 Libby Robin (2003, 8) describes the same fate for the labels of A. R. Radcliffe-Brown's ethnological collections stored in the institute basement.

41 Note that it is unlikely that the cooperation of Indigenous people in blood collection in early to mid-twentieth-century research approaches what we think of today as informed consent (see Radin and Kowal 2015), let alone the standard of "free, prior and informed consent" outlined in the UN Declaration on the Rights of Indigenous Peoples (United Nations 2008).

42 Questions of intellectual property in Indigenous human genetic resources were also discussed in the Asia-Pacific region (Mead and Ratuva 2007).

43 Interview with Sue Serjeantson, April 23, 2012. She recalls in the interview that the article was in the *Bulletin*, a weekly Australian magazine with a wide audience. There was no such article in the *Bulletin*, but her mistake could reflect the depth of her reaction to the vampire cartoon.

44 Kirk and Thorne had coedited the important collection *The Origin of the Australians* (1976), which represents the peak of collective scholarship for the Human Biology Advisory Committee.

45 This account of the closure of Kirk's collection is taken from Kowal and Radin 2015. In that article we use Radin's (2013) term "latent life" to refer to the samples before the ontological shift and "incomplete death" to describe them after the "absent presence" of connections among samples, donors, and Indigenous communities has been recognized.

46 In 2018 the NCIG was requested by the Kimberley Aboriginal Land and Culture Centre to take samples from unprovenanced human remains that had been exposed by an eroding riverbank in Fitzroy Crossing. The NCIG enlisted help from ancient DNA scientist Bastien Llamas from the University of Adelaide, who took samples before the remains were reburied. The community can now take time to decide whether to proceed with DNA provenancing (Bamford 2018).

47 An important riposte to the wholly positive media coverage was Professor Kim TallBear's critique of the repatriation on the *Media Indigena* podcast (TallBear and Callison 2019). She specifically objected to Easteal's claim that repatriation was the ultimate form of reconciliation.

48 The possibility of less developed nations, minorities, and Indigenous people harnessing genomics for their own benefit is an emerging area of the social study of genomics. See, for example, Benjamin 2009; Bliss 2013; de Vries and Pepper 2012; Egorova 2013; Garcia Deister 2018; Hinterberger and Porter 2015; and Schwartz-Marín and Restrepo 2013.

CHAPTER 3. A CENTURY IN THE LIFE OF AN ABORIGINAL HAIR SAMPLE

1 The mining town was created in 1910 (Hudson Institute of Mineralogy, n.d.).

2 By 1937 the station was no longer in use ("Travel in Comfort" 1937).

3 He also gives a clue to which direction the man might have come from: "There is a native walk between the south coast and gold-fields which is used by 300 or 400 people, who, from time to time, come down from the interior to enjoy the sympathy of train passengers. We have checked this to some extent, but we cannot altogether stop it" (Commonwealth of Australia 1937, 28). Note that

Neville's comments were aimed at criticizing the administration of "natives" in South Australia and praising his own efforts in Western Australia.

4   Roy MacLeod and Philip Rehbock describe further that "several speakers alerted the world to the great and peculiar interest of the Australian aborigines, whose apparently inevitable decline and disappearance demanded urgent attention" (2000, 215). Edgeworth David, first president of the newly formed Australian National Research Council (later the Australian Academy of Science), told those assembled that "with the help of science we can save our Australian Aborigines" (quoted in MacLeod and Rehbock 2000, 217).

5   Antiabortion activists would also object to the idea that they are protecting an abstract idea of humanity—from their perspective they are protecting the "vulnerable group" of unborn children.

6   Section 4 of the current guidelines for human research, entitled "Ethical considerations specific to participants" contains chapters on (listed in order): "women who are pregnant and the human fetus," "children and young people," "people in dependent or unequal relationships," "people highly dependent on medical care who may be unable to give consent," "people with a cognitive impairment, an intellectual disability, or a mental illness," "people who may be involved in illegal activities," "Aboriginal and Torres Strait Islander peoples," and "people in other countries" (NHMRC 2018b).

7   George Stocking (1996) attributes the use of "fieldwork" and "fieldsite" to Haddon.

8   Thomas H. Huxley, Haddon's mentor, drew on Bory de Saint-Vincent's classification in his essay "On the Methods and Results of Ethnology" ([1865] 1897). Other influential nineteenth- and early twentieth-century analyses include Topinard 1885 and Martin 1914. For a review of all previous frameworks for studying hair, see Trotter 1938. Regarding other aspects of hair analysis, Eugen Fischer's hair color gauge (Haarfarbentafel) is perhaps the best known.

9   Haddon's earlier monograph, The Study of Man (1898), included his classification of hair but subordinated it to head form. Frederic Wood Jones, a founding member of the Board for Anthropological Research in Adelaide, was still using Haddon's 1909 classification in 1943 ("Race Theories" 1943).

10   It is worth noting that antiracist and eugenicist views were by no means in opposition at that time. Carr-Saunders and Huxley were prominent eugenicists.

11   Another criticism that was most likely true was that parts of the book were ghostwritten by Jewish scientists Charles Singer and Charles Seligman (who had been on the Cambridge Anthropological Expedition to Torres Straits with Haddon), who did not want their names associated with the book for fear of its dismissal as propaganda (Barkan 1992; Hart 2013).

12   For example, his collection of ten thousand photographs was organized and presented to Cambridge on his eightieth birthday (Quiggin 1942, 148).

13   At that time, the serological markers in use were the ABO, Rh, MN, Duffy, and Diego blood groups.

14   Laura Peers, for example, describes how researchers make inquiries to the Pitt Rivers Museum to use hair samples for a range of research projects, from "mer-

cury levels to nutritional analysis to DNA studies" (2003, 82). For an overview and analysis of hair samples from Aboriginal and Torres Strait Islander people currently held in museums, see Faithfull 2023.

15 An earlier paper had published the first mtDNA extraction from a bighorn sheep hair sample (Bonnichsen et al. 2001). Incidentally, the lead author is the lead scientist who fought an eight-year court battle for the right to study Kennewick Man. Alan Cooper left Oxford in controversial circumstances in 2005 and moved to Adelaide to set up the Australian Centre for Ancient DNA. I was part of the Aboriginal Heritage Project that Cooper started in 2011 in partnership with the South Australian Museum to seek permission from families to sequence DNA from hair samples collected in the late 1930s by Norman B. Tindale and Joseph B. Birdsell (Tobler et al. 2017). Cooper was fired from the University of Adelaide in 2019 after multiple allegations of bullying and academic misconduct. Ray Tobler, Australia's first Indigenous aDNA scientist, continued to lead the project.

16 The temporal definition of an "archaeological" sample is unclear, but this usually seems to apply to any sample used by an ancient DNA scientist that is from a deceased person.

17 Staffan Müller-Wille (2021) identifies seventeenth-century antecedents in botanical textbooks and in paintings.

18 Thomas H. Huxley (Haddon's mentor) developed one such method whereby a subject was photographed naked in a standard position against a plain background and a measuring rod. Unsurprisingly, those whom Huxley asked to collect images for him often encountered resistance from potential subjects who did not want to shed their clothes, and his final collection consisted mostly of prisoners (in the Straits Settlements and South Africa) and a group of Aboriginal people from South Australia. Huxley was denied access to other Aboriginal groups he sought to photograph as missionaries and government officials thought they would not consent to nudity and it would undermine the civilizing mission (Edwards 1990; Lydon 2005).

19 I thank John Morton for finding this link for me.

20 Even more recently, racial science has echoed again through twenty-first-century population genetics through the phenomena of "ethnically specific reference genomes." Countries including China, Korea, Vietnam, Denmark, and Sweden have selected one or a small number of individuals considered "representative" of the national genetic pool and, using long-read genome sequencing, have produced reference genomes that are seen as more "accurate" than the "universal" reference genome for their population group (Kowal and Llamas 2019).

21 On the other hand, some science bloggers were devastated that a precedent of consultation had been established (Khan 2011). Interestingly, as of 2019 the Goldfields Land and Sea Council ceased to be the native title representative body for the region and is now focused on providing land management services for government and private bodies.

22 The same process ensued with the analysis of the remains known as the Anzick Child in 2014. The remains of a two-year-old child were found in 1968 on the

Montana property of the Anzick family. In 2014 Sarah Anzick, who had become a geneticist, took samples of the remains to Copenhagen to extract and analyze DNA in Willerslev's lab. Only after the research was completed did the scientists consult with Montana tribes, who eventually reburied the remains (Bardill 2018; Rasmussen et al. 2014).

23 "Adopted member of the Crow tribe, Montana (Apsaalooke), got the name ChiitdeeXia'ssee (meaning well known scout) (2014)." Eske Willerslev's CV, University of Copenhagen, n.d., accessed March 31, 2023, https://forskning.ku.dk/soeg/result/?pure=da%2Fpersons%2Feske-willerslev(21d2e042-0513-44fe-8acd-56b0d00a603e)%2Fcv.html.

24 There are resonances here with Thompson's case of stem cell research. She describes how ethical regulation "modified but did not disrupt" the passage of science as usual (2013, 48).

CHAPTER 4. RACE AND NATION

1 McPhee did not leave a first-person account of finding Jungun apart from a short letter to a Melbourne newspaper relating the stories he was told that were thought to describe the fate of missing explorer Ludwig Leichhardt, and an account of returning Jungun to his family (McPhee 1890, 1891). Details of the Jungun-McPhee story in this chapter derive from extensive newspaper reports and the account given in Darrell Lewis 2013.

2 "Traditional" ownership is a form of ownership developed in the Native Title Act (1993) that is tied to the continued maintenance of laws and customs relating to a place by a recognizable Indigenous group. This concept means that native title is unattainable for the Indigenous groups who have been most impacted by colonization (Bartlett 2019).

3 From the late twentieth century to the present, one line of battle has been dubbed the "history wars," whereby historians, politicians, and the public debate whether public history should emphasize colonial violence (called "black-armband" history by its critics) or downplay it (called "whitewashing" by its critics) (Macintyre and Clark 2003).

4 An example is the attempts by migrants from India to evade early twentieth-century anti-Asian immigration restrictions to the United States by arguing they were Aryan and thus racially Caucasian (Hess 1969).

5 As noted later in the chapter, Tindale and Birdsell did not endorse the archaic Caucasian theory, instead positing their own "tri-hybrid" theory that Indigenous people were the product of three distinct migrations of three different "races."

6 Aboriginal and Torres Strait Islander people traditionally had a single name. Once in contact with missionaries or the cattle industry, Indigenous people often were given a Western first name with their traditional name as a surname, or they took the surname of a place or white person in the vicinity (e.g., a station owner). In many parts of the country today, Indigenous people have an Indigenous name in addition to their official Western name.

7 Stanley had become world famous after finding the missing missionary David Livingstone in 1871. He later spent the 1880s engaged by the Belgium government to establish a colonial hold on the Congo River Basin.

8 These themes were reprised and extended in the so-called Lemurian literature of the 1890s. These novels centered on themes of lost civilizations—often light-skinned tribes living in desert oases watered by an inland sea—remnants of the submerged continent Lemuria that once joined Africa, South Asia, and Australia (J. Healy 1978).

9 Captivity narratives are a well-established genre of colonial literature from the seventeenth century to the late nineteenth century (Darian-Smith, Poignant, and Schaffer 1993).

10 Contemporaneous reports that he spoke the "Nangamont" language indicate he was from the Nyangumarta language group. This group later became well known for their association with union organizer Don McLeod, who was instrumental in the 1946 mass strike of Aboriginal stock workers in the Pilbara region. The strike eventually led to legislation for equal wages for Aboriginal people in the pastoral industry and the establishment of multiple Aboriginal pastoral stations.

11 Bunga and Yuarrick, who worked with McPhee on the station and who accompanied him on his journey to find Jungun, were generally referred to as "McPhee's boys" in media accounts, illustrating the racist attitudes toward Indigenous people, who were seen as the property of their employers and did not require the dignity of names.

12 The performance career of Jungun in Perth, Melbourne, and Sydney is part of a global phenomenon of displaying Indigenous people and people with unusual bodies and disabilities throughout the industrialized world. On Indigenous display and performance, see Casey 2011, 2012; Parsons 2002; Qureshi 2011; and Thrush 2016.

13 This was the Elder Scientific Exploring Expedition, 1890–91 (Lindsay 1893).

14 Sadiah Qureshi (2011) has shown how nineteenth-century ethnologists and anthropologists used "displayed peoples" as crucial sources of data for the science of racial difference, particularly in the United States, Germany, and France.

15 The term, coined by American sociologist Edward Alsworth Ross, was used by commentators in Australia and the United States to express concern about nonwhite immigration and falling white birth rates (Lake and Reynolds 2008, 42, 99, 350).

16 A famous act in the American Barnum and Bailey circus purporting to be "Unzie the Australian Aboriginal Albino" was actually a white New Zealander (Nickell 2005).

17 The most prominent is Under the Same Sun, started by Canadian businessman Peter Ash in 2008 and now employing over twenty people in their Tanzanian office, over half of whom have albinism. Under the Same Sun, accessed March 30, 2023, https://www.underthesamesun.com.

18 Walker died in Darwin in 2007.

19 Of course, I had just been discussing Abbie with Mulvaney, who had also known him. However, Walker seemed to inhabit a world much closer to mine than Mulvaney did.

20 The Australian-born Elliot Smith, an anatomist, Egyptologist, and anthropologist, was crucial in the establishment of the first chair of anthropology in Australia in 1926. To the disappointment of the Adelaide scientists, it was given to the University of Sydney and irrevocably moved the discipline away from physical anthropology and toward sociocultural anthropology (Gray 2007; P. Jones 1987; Peterson 1990).

21 Ronald and Catherine Berndt's *The World of the First Australians* was also a huge success, first published in 1964, with a fifth edition in 1988 (see Berndt and Berndt 1988).

22 The discussion here focuses on mainland Australian origins. Torres Strait Islanders were seen as racially "Melanesian" or "Papuan." Tasmanians were almost uniformly regarded as a different race from mainlanders and usually classified as "Negrito," although much scientific uncertainty remained given that the so-called last of the so-called full-blood Tasmanians, Truganini, had died in 1876 (see chapter 2). Note that the debate over Australian origins never ceased; see B. Griffiths 2018.

23 On Simmons's collaborations in India, see Mukharji 2020.

24 On the rise and fall of Birdsell's tri-hybrid theory, see Prentis 1995.

25 The text itself notes that although albinism "should recur regularly in any people, [it] has never been reliably reported in Aborigines" (Abbie [1969] 1976, 27). Abbie finds this troubling given the "general Aboriginal trend towards pigmentary uncertainty."

26 "Vandyke" (also spelled "van dyke") is a dark brown color named for seventeenth-century Flemish painter Anthony van Dyck.

27 These are benign bruise-like spots, commonly on the lower back or buttocks of darker-skinned babies. The medical term is "congenital dermal melanocytosis," and in most cases they fade completely within a few years.

28 The phrase "in a manner of speaking" was added after the manuscript was first typed, indicating Hicks felt a need to at least qualify his view on Aboriginal people as direct descendants of "European nomad hunters" (1974, 11) who had migrated to Australia perhaps twenty thousand years ago.

29 Although the doomed race theory was based on the science of the time, in reality it was a farcical naturalization of the drastic reduction of the Indigenous population from the immediate effects of colonization: introduced diseases, frontier warfare, and dispossession from food and water resources (McGregor 1997).

30 Historian Russell McGregor (2011, 10) is careful to point out that the scientists who advised that biological absorption was possible, principally Tindale and Cleland, did not themselves advocate that the Aboriginal presence in Australia would be "forgotten" but that Indigenous identity and culture would continue within an admixed Indigenous population. It is also notable that Tindale does not mention his and Birdsell's controversial tri-hybrid theory in his 1941 report, perhaps as it would have muddied the policy prescriptions the report contained.

31 Note that the apparent racial similarity of Aboriginal people and Europeans was mobilized by the Aboriginal rights movement. A classic text in the history of Aboriginal activism, John Patten and William Ferguson's *Aborigines Claim Citizen Rights!* (1938), argued that white Australians should have sympathy for Aboriginal rights because it has been scientifically "prove[n] that the Australian Aboriginal is somewhat similar in blood to yourselves" (quoted in McGregor 1996, 14). It is also important to note that the shift from biological absorption to assimilation did not mean that color prejudice disappeared—the stigma of dark skin and the social preference for whiteness continued to greatly affect Indigenous people. Mixed-race children continued to be institutionalized in many jurisdictions up until the 1970s, but this was justified on "welfare" rather than "racial" grounds.

32 Some important works include Ahmed 2004; Bell 2014; Boucher, Carey, and Ellinghaus 2009; Byrne 1996; C. Elder 2007, 2009; Gooder and Jacobs 2000; M. Griffiths 2012; T. Griffiths 1996; Hage 1998, 2003; C. Healy 2008; Howitt 2001; A. Moran 2005; Moreton-Robinson 2003; Muecke 2004; Mulcock 2007; Potter 2019; Povinelli 2002; Probyn 2002; Riggs and Augoustinos 2004; Russell 2001b; Rutherford 2000; Slater 2018; E. Smith 2014; Trigger 2008; and Veracini 2008.

33 There is a parallel here with the belief in "lost white tribes" of Africa. "If white tribes had their own history in Africa, it followed that Europeans . . . were not settling, but *resettling*, lands that had been conquered by fair-skin invaders centuries before" (Robinson 2016, 8).

34 Another set of tensions related to the "maternal protection" trope concerns the role of white Australian women in Australian nationalism and eugenics in this period (J. Carey 2009; Lake 1998; Paisley 2000).

35 There is no corroborating evidence for Gustafson's account of the conversation between McPhee and Jungun. It is likely McPhee was driven by curiosity and hope of financial gain rather than any lofty racial ideals. After accompanying Jungun in the return trip to his family, McPhee returned to station work until he enlisted in World War I, fought at Gallipoli, and succumbed to meningitis in Egypt.

36 This category of newly identified is applied to people who have identified as nonindigenous on a previous census. As the census is usually filled out by the "head" of a household, there is a complex relationship between identification on the census and personal identification. For example, adolescents and adult children living with their parents may have a different personal identification than the one recorded in the census.

37 Note that Ancestry.com updated their product in April 2020 to provide a specific "Indigenous Ancestry Estimate," separating out Indigenous Australian ancestry from "Melanesia."

CHAPTER 5. INDIGENOUS PHYSIOLOGY

1 Writing from the perspective of new materialism, Arun Saldahna cogently links the denial of race as an ontological fact to "a wider anxiety in the social sciences about matter" (2006, 9).

2 On Wood Jones, see R. Jones 2013, 2020; and R. Jones and Anderson 2015.

3 H. C. Earle conducted the research in China, and Benedict repeated it on Chinese Americans. Other research was conducted on Tamils and Mayans. For a review, see Elsie Wilson 1945.

4 Hicks (1974, 9), among many others, designated Indigenous people as "paleolithic." In his analysis of a late twentieth-century example of racialized metabolic science, Anthony Hatch (2016) examines the centrality of racialized conceptions of African Americans in research on "metabolic syndrome."

5 The current spellings of "Arunda" and "Anmatjera" are Arrernte and Anmatjerre, respectively. Ilpirra is a misnomer for Anmatjerre people introduced by Baldwin Spencer and F. G. Gillen ([1899] 1968). It is an Arrernte word for Warlpiri people (Gibson 2020).

6 The person Hicks calls "Peter" was probably Mickey Akwerre Dow Dow (Gibson 2020).

7 Some animals use these mechanisms seasonally or daily (obligative hibernation), and others only if the conditions require it (facultative hibernators).

8 Interestingly, and unfortunately predictably, the US Army Research Office and US Army Medical Research and Material Command funded research into the ethics of hibernation research that discussed the ethics of animal experimentation but not the ethics of defense applications (Jinka and Duffy 2013).

9 He is known, among other things, for his research on the "master switch" that transforms the metabolism of free divers (Hagen 2018).

10 Although Hicks's memoir describes this as occurring "four years after the war," the research publications say the visits occurred in July to August 1957 and December 1957–January 1958 (Hammel et al. 1959). Hicks also fails to mention that they were supported by A. A. Abbie, professor of anatomy and history and associate dean of the faculty at time, suggesting a less than perfect relationship between the two.

11 The other two oft-mentioned "racial" groups are pre-1970s Korean women free divers and the Yaghan people of Tierra del Fuego. In contrast to Scholander's papers, the work of other researchers of Aboriginal metabolism—Hicks, Sydney physiologist H. S. Halcro Wardlaw, and a single study by Alaskan physiologist Peter Morrison (opportunistically carried out during a Guggenheim fellowship in 1954–55)—have barely been cited (Morrison 1965; Wardlaw, Davies, and Joseph 1934; Wardlaw and Horsley 1928; Wardlaw and Lawrence 1932). This is due in part to where they were published and the peripheral interests this represents. Hicks and Wardlaw contributed to the *Australian Journal of Experimental Biology and Medical Science*, the journal of the Medical Sciences Club of South Australia from 1924 to 1986. Scholander's group published in the *Journal of Applied Physiology*, published by the American Physiological Society since 1948 and still going strong.

12 W. V. Macfarlane, another New Zealander, who was a professor of animal physiology at the University of Queensland, the Australian National University, and, from 1964, the University of Adelaide and founder of the Australian Physiological Society, was funded in the early 1970s by the US Army Medical Research Devel-

opment Command to investigate "desert survival and the function of Aboriginal nomads in the summer desert" (Macfarlane 1969).

13 More recently, scholars and journalists have expressed concerns about Chinese genome research and the Uighur minority that are very likely to be true (Munsterhjelm 2019).

14 Birdsell (1993), based on fieldwork in the 1930s and 1950s, was also cited in the supplementary materials.

15 The Extended Data Table is not part of the printed article in the hard-copy journal but is linked on the web version and is the final page of the article PDF.

16 These markers are known by a unique label called a Reference SNP cluster ID (rsID).

CHAPTER 6. SPENCER'S DOUBLE

This chapter is adapted from Kowal 2019.

1   The details about Spencer and Gillen and others mentioned in this chapter derive from the definitive biography of Spencer (D. Mulvaney and Calaby 1985). See also Morphy 1996; and D. Mulvaney, Morphy, and Petch 1997. On expedition photography, see J. Ryan 1997.

2   Letter from Frazer to Spencer, June 4, 1900, quoted in D. Mulvaney and Calaby 1985, 189. Henrika Kuklick (2006) has masterfully explored the impact of *The Native Tribes of Central Australia* on European scholarship and Australian policy.

3   On repatriation in Australia, see Fforde, Hubert, and Turnbull 2002; McKeown, Fforde, and Keeler 2020; Roginski 2015; Turnbull 2017; and Turnbull and Pickering 2010.

4   Australian National University, Museums Victoria, South Australian Museum, Northern Territory Library, Australian Capital Equity, Barr Smith Library, and Australian Research Council, *Spencer and Gillen: A Journey through Aboriginal Australia*, accessed March 8, 2020, http://spencerandgillen.net/.

5   I am aware that pursuing theories of the double to understand Spencer's double is complicated by the fact that the relationships I primarily attempt to explain are those between non-indigenous people and Spencer's double, not between Spencer himself and his double. However, I contend the theories are still useful to understand Spencer's double as a double of non-indigenous people in the sense that he stands in for colonial science and negative aspects of non-indigenous identities more broadly. Note that Rank and Freud, among many European theorists of the time, were influenced by Spencer's ethnography.

6   Important works on reconciliation and historical consciousness in Australia include Ahmed 2005; Attwood 2005; Johnson 2011; A. Moran 2009; Moses 2011; and Regan 2010.

7   On embarrassment and the global history of biological anthropology, see Lindee and Santos 2012. Key literature on the history of scientific research on Indigenous Australians includes W. Anderson 2002, 2014; Douglas and Ballard 2008; R. Jones and Anderson 2015; Peterson, Allen, and Hamby 2008; Robin 2003; and Turnbull 2017.

8   For example, Spencer features in Frank Stevens's (1972) three-volume study.

9   But note that Howard Morphy (1997) has argued the now-infamous phrase "naked, howling savages" was included at the behest of Sir James Frazer and is not representative of Spencer's views of Indigenous people.

10 On the new museology in the Asia-Pacific region, see C. Healy and Witcomb 2006.

11 For example, Gurminder Bhambra (2014) has argued that postcolonial studies and decolonial scholarship are not in opposition to each other but rather reflect two different communities of scholars with different major geographic referents: India for postcolonialism, and Latin America for decoloniality.

12 The novelty of calls to decolonize the museum is illustrated by the fact that the author of the touchstone 2012 monograph for decolonizing museums, Amy Lonetree, does not use the word "decolonize" once in an earlier edited collection although the word "postcolonial" appears many times (see Cobb and Lonetree 2008).

13 He later completed a PhD in anthropology and returned to the museum in his current role.

14 "Koorie" (alternative spelling Koori) is a term for Indigenous people from Victoria.

15 "Indigenous cultures" brochure, ca. 1998, Museums Victoria archives, Melbourne.

16 "Props and Dressing Brief," Bunjilaka, Melbourne Museum, November 15, 1999, Museums Victoria archives.

17 This section's title was taken from the title of a 1996 book on collecting in Australia (also the name of a famous 1980s band) (T. Griffiths 1996).

18 The label for the goannas shows how they were intended as another layer of postcolonial pedagogy. The label was entitled "Who Discovered the Goannas?" It told the audience: "The name *Varanus spencerii* suggests that Spencer discovered this lizard. In fact, he acquired the first specimen for registration as a new species. The specimen was actually collected by an Aboriginal man. To this day he remains anonymous." Photocopy of Label 53, ca. 1999, Museums Victoria archives.

19 The idea was not lost completely. It was taken up in another part of the exhibition called "Dialogue," which consisted of a short film staging a conversation between Spencer and Irrapmwe in which Irrapmwe chastises Spencer for not appreciating his status as a professor in his own culture, for writing derogatory things about Indigenous people, and for displaying sacred objects in the museum.

20 "Props and Dressing Brief."

21 Excerpt from text of "Two Laws," version February 21, 2000, electronic file, Museums Victoria archives.

22 This website was launched the following year; see note 4.

23 For the remainder of the chapter, I refer to the statue as "Spencer" and with the corresponding pronoun, following the naming practices of some museum staff (he was also called "Baldy," short for Baldwin). While acknowledging that this risks anthropomorphizing a representation of a person, the technically incorrect terminology helps to explore my central question of what the model means to museum staff.

24 Personal communication, February 23, 2017.

25 On the history of repatriation, see Fforde, Hubert, and Turnbull 2002; Fine-Dare 2002; and Turnbull and Pickering 2010. For an early example of a secret-sacred collection policy, see South Australian Museum, Board, and South Australian Museum 1986.

26 Philip Batty, personal communication, May 11, 2016.

27 For example, possum droppings were found in a Bunjilaka display in June 2010.

28 Bliss Jensen, "Phased Closure of Jumbanna," electronic document, June 2011, Museums Victoria archives.

29 For context on the institutional mechanics of museum exhibitions, including the management of props, see Lord and Piacente 2014.

30 "Exhibition Props Information Sheet," electronic document, Exhibition Collection Management, May 21, 2015, Museums Victoria archives.

31 In the Bunjilaka exhibit, the list of props included a facsimile of a list of rules for residents of Lake Tyers Mission, a quoll skin, and a teddy bear.

32 "Exhibition Props Information Sheet."

33 The Spencer model was made by a production company from an off-the-shelf seated mannequin and a bentwood chair. The mannequin's head and hands were removed and replaced by fiberglass casts of Spencer's head and hands. The casts were produced from clay sculptures created by in-house sculptor Peter "Smiley" Williams from photographs of Spencer. The mannequin's joints were fixed with fiberglass bandages, and the costume department dressed it with starched clothing. The dressed model and chair were then sprayed with urethane to create a 1.5-millimeter-thick exoskeleton. To finish the model, undercuts and fabric folds were filled with resin, and the entire structure was painted with a sand-textured paint and darker highlights forcing shadows in the folds. Interestingly, the production of the statue illustrates the history of prop creation: if it were produced now, it would simply be 3D printed. John Kerr, creative director of Stage One Productions, email to author, September 15, 2017.

34 Quotes in this paragraph and the next are taken from personal communications with museum staff, February 23, 2017, and March 28, 2017.

35 On the indigenized museum, see Simpson 2006, 174.

36 Note that what I explain here as a shift from postcolonial to decolonial could also be told through the lens of whiteness studies, the academic study of white privilege that boomed in the 1990s but has shrunk in influence, partly due to critiques that being self-reflexive about white privilege is itself a form of white privilege. Being silent is sometimes proposed as a better strategy for white people. For an Australian example, see Aveling 2013.

37 Tony Birch, personal communication, November 1, 2017.

38 This terminology was suggested by Tony Birch, personal communication, November 1, 2017.

39 Restricted rooms contain sacred objects that are supposed to be viewed only by initiated men of the relevant language group.

40 Quotes in the following paragraphs are from personal communications with museum staff, September 13, 2017.

References

Abbie, A. A. 1951. "The Australian Aborigine." *Oceania* 22 (2): 91–100. DOI: 10.1002/j.1834-4461.1951.tb00551.x.

Abbie, A. A. 1965. "Address by Professor A. A. Abbie, Convener of the Advisory Panel on Human Biology at the Australian Institute of Aboriginal Studies General Meeting 15–16 October 1964, Canberra." *Australian Journal of Science* 2 (12): 305–16.

Abbie, A. A. (1969) 1976. *The Original Australians.* Adelaide: Rigby.

Adelaide Observer. 1876. "Notes on Science." October 21, 1876, 17.

Advertiser. 1954. "Aero-Medical Laboratory at University." July 3, 1954, 1.

Ahmed, Sara. 2004. "Declarations of Whiteness: The Non-performativity of Anti-racism." *Borderlands* 3 (2). http://www.borderlands.net.au/vol3no2_2004/ahmed_declarations.htm.

Ahmed, Sara. 2005. "The Politics of Bad Feeling." *Australian Critical Race and Whiteness Studies Association Journal* 1 (1): 72–85.

AIATSIS Collection, Australian Institute of Aboriginal and Torres Strait Islander Studies, Canberra, ACT.

Alimardanian, Mahnaz. 2014. "Burnt Woman of the Mission: Gender and Horror in an Aboriginal Settlement in Northern New South Wales." In *Monster Anthropology in Australasia and Beyond,* edited by Yasmine Musharbash and Geir Henning Presterudstuen, 93–108. New York: Palgrave Macmillan.

Allen, Lindy. 2014. "The Never Ending Story: The Repatriation of Ancestral Remains from Museums." *Melbourne Historical Journal* 42 (2): 22–28.

Ancestry. n.d. "Melanesian Ethnicity." Accessed October 22, 2019. https://www.ancestry.com/dna/ethnicity/melanesia.

Ancestry Marketing Team, Australia. 2020. "Ancestry® Updates Ethnicity Results to Include 'Aboriginal and Torres Strait Islander' Region." Accessed March 18, 2023. https://blogs.ancestry.com.au/ancestry/2020/03/31/ancestry-updates-ethnicity-results-to-include-aboriginal-and-torres-strait-islander-region/.

Anderson, Helen. 1994. "Keep an Open Mind about Genetics Project: Professor." *Canberra Times,* January 26, 1994, 3. http://nla.gov.au/nla.news-article126924851.

Anderson, Warwick. 2000. "The Possession of Kuru: Medical Science and Biocolonial Exchange." *Comparative Studies in Society and History* 42:713–44. DOI: 10.1017/S0010417500003297.

Anderson, Warwick. 2002. *The Cultivation of Whiteness: Science, Health and Racial Destiny in Australia*. Melbourne: Melbourne University Press.

Anderson, Warwick. 2008. *The Collectors of Lost Souls: Turning Kuru Scientists into Whitemen*. Baltimore, MD: Johns Hopkins University Press.

Anderson, Warwick. 2012. "Objectivity and Its Discontents." *Social Studies of Science* 43 (4): 557–76.

Anderson, Warwick. 2014. "Hermannsburg, 1929: Turning Aboriginal 'Primitives' into Modern Psychological Subjects." *Journal of the History of the Behavioral Sciences* 50 (2): 127–47. DOI: 10.1002/jhbs.21649.

Anderson, Warwick. 2015. "The Frozen Archive, or Defrosting Derrida." *Journal of Cultural Economy* 8 (3): 379–87. DOI: 10.1080/17530350.2014.890637.

Anderson, Warwick. 2019. "Knowing Natives: Instituting Social Anthropology in Australia after the Great War." In *Expert Nation: Universities, War, and 1920s and 1930s Australia*, edited by Kate Darian-Smith and James Waghorne, 249–60. Melbourne: Melbourne University Press.

Anderson, Warwick, and Vincanne Adams. 2007. "Pramoedya's Chickens: Postcolonial Studies of Technoscience." In *The Handbook of Science and Technology Studies*, edited by Edward J. Hackett, Olga Amsterdamska, Michael Lynch, and Judy Wajcman, 181–204. Cambridge, MA: MIT Press.

Andrews, Matthew T. 2007. "Advances in Molecular Biology of Hibernation in Mammals." *BioEssays* 29 (5): 431–40. DOI: 10.1002/bies.20560.

Andrews, Matthew T. 2019. "Molecular Interactions Underpinning the Phenotype of Hibernation in Mammals." *Journal of Experimental Biology* 222 (2): jeb160606. DOI: 10.1242/jeb.160606.

Annas, George, and Michael Grodin, eds. 1995. *The Nazi Doctors and the Nuremberg Code: Human Rights in Human Experimentation*. New York: Oxford University Press.

Aronson, Jay D. 2012. "Humanitarian DNA Identification in Post-apartheid South Africa." In *Genetics and the Unsettled Past: The Collision of DNA, Race, and History*, edited by Keith Wailoo, Alondra Nelson, and Catherine Lee, 295–312. New Brunswick, NJ: Rutgers University Press.

Asad, Talal. 1973. *Anthropology and the Colonial Encounter*. London: Ithaca.

Attwood, Bain. 2005. "Unsettling Pasts: Reconciliation and History in Settler Australia." *Postcolonial Studies* 8 (3): 243–59. DOI: 10.1080/13688790500231012.

Attwood, Bain. 2013. "Difficult Histories: The Museum of New Zealand Te Papa Tongarewa and the Treaty of Waitangi Exhibit." *Public Historian* 35 (3): 46–71. DOI: 10.1525/tph.2013.35.3.46.

Austin, Tony. 1990. "Cecil Cook, Scientific Thought and 'Half-Castes' in the Northern Territory, 1927–1939." *Aboriginal History* 14 (1/2): 104–22. DOI: 10.3316/ielapa.037371461366980.

Australian Bureau of Statistics. 1999. *The Health and Welfare of Australia's Aboriginal and Torres Strait Islander Peoples*. Canberra: Australian Government Publishing Service.

Australian Bureau of Statistics. 2016. *Census of Population and Housing: Understanding the Increase in Aboriginal and Torres Strait Islander Counts*. ABS. Accessed April 2, 2023. https://www.abs.gov.au/statistics/people/aboriginal-and-torres-strait-islander-peoples /understanding-change-counts-aboriginal-and-torres-strait-islander-australians -census/latest-release.

Australian Indigenous HealthInfoNet. 2019. *Overview of Aboriginal and Torres Strait Islander Health Status, 2018*. Perth, WA: Australian Indigenous HealthInfoNet.

Australian Institute of Aboriginal Studies. 1965. "Research Sponsored by the Institute: Human Biology." *A.I.A.S. Newsletter* 2 (2): 2–3.

Australian Law Reform Commission. 2003. *Essentially Yours: The Protection of Human Genetic Information in Australia—Section 36: Kinship and Identity*. Canberra: Australian Government Publishing Service.

Australian National University. 2014. "National Centre to Close the Gap." February 19, 2014. https://www.anu.edu.au/news/all-news/national-centre-to-close-the-gap.

Aveling, Nado. 2013. "'Don't Talk about What You Don't Know': On (Not) Conducting Research with/in Indigenous Contexts." *Critical Studies in Education* 54 (2): 203–14. DOI: 10.1080/17508487.2012.724021.

Bakhtin, Mikhail. 1981. "Form of Time and Chronotope in the Novel." In *The Dialogic Imagination: Four Essays*, 84–258. Austin: University of Texas Press.

Bamford, Matt. 2018. "Human Skull Sparks DNA Hunt to Identify Dozens of Unmarked Remains in Remote Australia." *ABC News*, August 20, 2018. https://www.abc.net.au /news/2018-08-20/human-skull-sparks-dna-hunt-to-identify-unmarked-remains /10132860.

Bangham, Jenny. 2014. "Blood Groups and Human Groups: Collecting and Calibrating Genetic Data after World War Two." *Studies in History and Philosophy of Science Part C: Studies in History and Philosophy of Biological and Biomedical Sciences* 47, pt. A (0): 74–86. DOI: 10.1016/j.shpsc.2014.05.008.

Bangham, Jenny. 2020. *Blood Relations: Transfusion and the Making of Human Genetics*. Chicago: University of Chicago Press.

Bangham, Jenny, and Soraya de Chadarevian. 2014. "Human Heredity after 1945: Moving Populations Centre Stage." *Studies in History and Philosophy of Science Part C: Studies in History and Philosophy of Biological and Biomedical Sciences* 47, pt. A (0): 45–49. DOI: 10.1016/j.shpsc.2014.05.005.

Bardill, Jessica. 2018. "Ancestors and Identities: DNA, Genealogy, and Stories." In *The Palgrave Handbook of Biology and Society*, edited by Maurizio Meloni, John Cromby, Des Fitzgerald, and Stephanie Lloyd, 831–49. London: Palgrave Macmillan.

Barkan, Elazar. 1992. *The Retreat of Scientific Racism: Changing Concepts of Race in Britain and the United States between the Two World Wars*. Cambridge: Cambridge University Press.

Barringer, T. J., and Tom Flynn. 1998. *Colonialism and the Object: Empire, Material Culture, and the Museum*. Abingdon, UK: Routledge.

Bartlett, Richard H. 2020. *Native Title in Australia*. 4th ed. Chatsworth, NSW: LexisNexis.

Basedow, Herbert. 1925. *The Australian Aboriginal*. Adelaide: F. W. Preece and Sons.

Bates, Daisy. 1966. *The Passing of the Aborigines: A Lifetime Spent among the Natives of Australia*. 2nd ed. London: John Murray.

Beaton, Angela, Barry Smith, Valmaine Toki, Kim Southey, and Maui Hudson. 2015. "Engaging Maori in Biobanking and Genetic Research: Legal, Ethical and Policy Challenges." *International Indigenous Policy Journal* 6 (3). DOI: 10.18584/iipj.2015.6.3.1.

Beckett, Jeremy. 2014. *Encounters with Indigeneity: Writing about Aboriginal and Torres Strait Islander Peoples.* Canberra: Aboriginal Studies Press, 2014.

Behrendt, Larissa. 2003. *Achieving Social Justice: Indigenous Rights and Australia's Future.* Canberra: Federation Press.

Bell, Avril. 2014. *Relating Indigenous and Settler Identities: Beyond Domination.* New York: Palgrave Macmillan.

Benedict, Francis G. 1912. "An Experiment on a Fasting Man." *Science* 35 (909): 865. DOI: 10.1126/science.35.909.865.

Benjamin, Ruha. 2009. "A Lab of Their Own: Genomic Sovereignty as Postcolonial Science Policy." *Policy and Society* 28 (4): 341–55. DOI: 10.1016/j.polsoc.2009.09.007.

Bennett, Tony. 1995. *The Birth of the Museum: History, Theory, Politics.* Abingdon, UK: Routledge.

Bennett, Tony. 2004. *Pasts beyond Memory: Evolution, Museums, Colonialism.* New York: Routledge.

Berg, Jim. 2010. "This Is My Journey." In *Power and the Passion: Our People Return Home*, edited by Shannon Faulkhead and Jim Berg, 3–30. Melbourne: Koorie Heritage Trust.

Bergland, Renée. 2000. *The National Uncanny: Indian Ghosts and American Subjects.* Hanover, NH: University of New England Press.

Berndt, Ronald M., and Catherine H. Berndt. 1988. *The World of the First Australians: Aboriginal Traditional Life: Past and Present.* 5th ed. Canberra: Aboriginal Studies Press.

Bhambra, Gurminder K. 2014. "Postcolonial and Decolonial Dialogues." *Postcolonial Studies* 17 (2): 115–21. DOI: 10.1080/13688790.2014.966414.

Birch, Tony. 1996. "The Recognition of Indigenous Rights in Museum Victoria." Museums Victoria archives, Melbourne.

Birdsell, Joseph B. 1972. "Physical Anthropology: *The Original Australians.* A. A. Abbie." *American Anthropologist* 74 (1–2): 149–52. DOI: 10.1525/aa.1972.74.1-2.02a01300.

Birdsell, Joseph B. 1979. "Physical Anthropology in Australia Today." *Annual Review of Anthropology* 8 (1): 417–30. DOI: 10.1146/annurev.an.08.100179.002221.

Birdsell, Joseph B. 1993. *Microevolutionary Patterns in Aboriginal Australia: A Gradient Analysis of Clines.* Oxford: Oxford University Press.

Birman, Wendy, and G. C. Bolton. 2006. "Wittenoom, Frederick Francis (Frank) (1855–1939)." *Australian Dictionary of Biography*, National Centre of Biography, Australian National University. Accessed April 1, 2023. https://adb.anu.edu.au/biography/wittenoom-frederick-francis-frank-9292/text16185. First published in print 1990, vol. 12; first published online 2006.

Bjornberg, Osten. 1960. "Total Albinos among the Cuna Indians." *Journal of the History of Medicine and Allied Sciences* 15 (3): 265–67. DOI: 10.1093/jhmas/XV.3.265.

Blackstone, Eric, Mike Morrison, and Mark B. Roth. 2005. "H2S Induces a Suspended Animation–Like State in Mice." *Science* 308 (5721): 518. DOI: 10.1126/science.1108581.

Blanco, Marina B., Kathrin H. Dausmann, Sheena L. Faherty, and Anne D. Yoder. 2018. "Tropical Heterothermy Is 'Cool': The Expression of Daily Torpor and Hibernation in Primates." *Evolutionary Anthropology* 27 (4): 147–61. DOI: 10.1002/evan.21588.

Bliss, Catherine. 2012. *Race Decoded: The Genomic Fight for Social Justice.* Stanford, CA: Stanford University Press.

Bliss, Catherine. 2013. "The Marketization of Identity Politics." *Sociology* 47 (5): 1011–25. DOI: 10.1177/0038038513495604.

Blumberg, Baruch S. 1976. "Australia Antigen and the Biology of Hepatitis B." Nobel Lecture, December 13, 1976.

Bolt, Andrew. 2000. "A Museum of Spin." *Herald Sun*, November 20, 2000.

Bonnichsen, Robson, Larry Hodges, Walter Ream, Katharine G. Field, Donna L. Kirner, Karen Selsor, and R. E. Taylor. 2001. "Methods for the Study of Ancient Hair: Radio-carbon Dates and Gene Sequences from Individual Hairs." *Journal of Archaeological Science* 28 (7): 775–85. DOI: 10.1006/jasc.2000.0624.

Bootcov, Michelle. 2024. "Hepatitis: The Transformation of Viral Diagnostics in the Late 20th Century." PhD diss., University of New South Wales.

Booth, Andrea. 2016. "Thousands of DNA Samples May Reconnect Families Torn Apart by Assimilation Policies." *NITV News*, May 12, 2016. https://www.sbs.com.au/nitv/article/thousands-of-dna-samples-may-reconnect-families-torn-apart-by-assimilation-policies/x2qfkjbiq.

Booth, Andrea. 2018. "Indigeneity and DNA Ancestry Tests." *Saturday Paper*, October 20, 2018. https://www.thesaturdaypaper.com.au/news/indigenous-affairs/2018/10/20/indigeneity-and-dna-ancestry-tests/15399540007021.

Borofsky, Robert. 2005. *Yanomami: The Fierce Controversy and What We Might Learn from It.* Berkeley: University of California Press.

Bory de Saint-Vincent, Jean-Baptiste-Geneviève-Marcellin. 1827. *L'Homme (homo): Essai zoologique sur le genre humain.* Paris: Rey et Gravier.

Boucher, Leigh, Jane Carey, and Katherine Ellinghaus, eds. 2009. *Re-orienting Whiteness.* New York: Palgrave Macmillan.

Boyd, Colleen, and Coll Thrush, eds. 2011. *Phantom Past, Indigenous Presence: Native Ghosts in North American Culture and History.* Lincoln: University of Nebraska Press.

Boyd, J. D. 1956. "Dr. W. L H. Duckworth." *Nature* 177:505–6. DOI: 10.1038/177505b0.

Boym, S. 2001. *The Future of Nostalgia.* New York: Basic Books.

Bradley, Michael. 2019. *Coniston.* Perth: University of Western Australia Publishing.

Briscoe, Gordon. 1978. "What Do Aborigines Want from Research?" *Research Newsletter* (Department of Aboriginal Affairs), no. 6, 29–30.

Brocco, Giorgio. 2016. "Albinism, Stigma, Subjectivity and Global-Local Discourses in Tanzania." *Anthropology and Medicine* 23 (3): 229–43. DOI: 10.1080/13648470.2016.1184009.

Broome, Richard. 2002. *Aboriginal Australians: Black Responses to White Dominance, 1788–2001.* Crows Nest, NSW: Allen and Unwin.

Broome, Richard, Ian Hoskins, Kathy De La Rue, Shauna Bostock-Smith, Shirley Fitzgerald, Karen O'Brien, and Alison Wishart. 2014. "Exhibition Reviews." *History Australia* 11 (3): 207–23.

Brown, Kenneth S. 1954. "*Race Crossing in Man* (Eugenics Lab. Mem. XXXVI)." *American Journal of Human Genetics* 6 (1): 195–96.

Bryceson, Deborah Fahy, Jesper Bosse Jønsson, and Richard Sherrington. 2010. "Miners' Magic: Artisanal Mining, the Albino Fetish and Murder in Tanzania." *Journal of Modern African Studies* 48 (3): 353–82. DOI: 10.1017/S0022278X10000303.

Bulletin. 1929. "The Plagues of Egypt." September 18, 1929, 25.

Bunjilaka Aboriginal Cultural Centre. n.d. "About Us." Museums Victoria. Accessed April 7, 2018. https://museumsvictoria.com.au/bunjilaka/about-us/.

Burke, Heather D., Claire E. Smith, Dorothy Lippert, Joe E. Watkins, and Larry Zimmerman. 2008. *Kennewick Man: Perspectives on the Ancient One.* Walnut Creek, CA: Left Coast.

Byrne, Denis. 1996. "Deep Nation: Australia's Acquisition of an Indigenous Past." *Aboriginal History* 20:82–107.

Calloway, Ewen. 2011. "Aboriginal Genome Analysis Comes to Grips with Ethics." *Nature* 477 (7366): 522–23.

Canberra Times. 1964. "Aborigines Spend Day in Canberra." September 3, 1964, 10.

Canberra Times. 1969. "An Albino Aborigine in Northern Territory." November 29, 1969, 3.

Cann, Rebecca L., Mark Stoneking, and Allan C. Wilson. 1987. "Mitochondrial DNA and Human Evolution." *Nature* 325:31–36. DOI: 10.1038/325031a0.

Carey, Hannah V., and Fariba M. Assadi-Porter. 2017. "The Hibernator Microbiome: Host-Bacterial Interactions in an Extreme Nutritional Symbiosis." *Annual Review of Nutrition* 37:477–500. DOI: 10.1146/annurev-nutr-071816-064740.

Carey, Jane. 2009. "White Anxieties and the Articulation of Race: The Women's Movement and the Making of White Australia, 1910s–1930s." In *Creating White Australia,* edited by Jane Carey and Claire McLisky, 195–213. Sydney: Sydney University Press.

Carlson, Bronwyn. 2016. *The Politics of Identity: Who Counts as Aboriginal Today?* Canberra: Aboriginal Studies Press.

Carter, Paul. 1987. *The Road to Botany Bay: An Essay in Spatial History.* Sydney: Faber and Faber.

Casey, Maryrose. 2011. "Cross-Cultural Encounters: Aboriginal Performers and European Audiences in the Late 1800s and Early 1900s." *Double Dialogues,* no. 14, 1–10. https://www.doubledialogues.com/article/cross-cultural-encounters-aboriginal-performers-and-european-audiences-in-the-late-1800s-and-early-1900s/.

Casey, Maryrose. 2012. *Telling Stories: Aboriginal Australian and Torres Strait Islander Performance.* Melbourne: Australian Scholarly Publishing.

Cavalli-Sforza, Luigi Luca, and Francesco Cavalli-Sforza. 1995. *The Great Human Diasporas: The History of Diversity and Evolution.* Reading, MA: Addison-Wesley.

Cawte, John. 1974. *Medicine Is the Law: Studies in Psychiatric Anthropology of Australian Tribal Societies.* Honolulu: University Press of Hawai'i.

Cawte, John. 1977. Editorial. *Aboriginal and Islander Health Worker Journal* 1 (1): 2.

Cawte, John. 1993. *The Universe of the Warramirri: Art, Medicine, and Religion in Arnhem Land.* Kensington: New South Wales University Press.

Cawte, John. 1996. *Healers of Arnhem Land.* Sydney: University of New South Wales Press.

Central Australian Aboriginal Congress. 1994. "The Vampire Project: An Aboriginal Perspective on Genome Diversity Research." *Search* 25 (3): 88–90.

Centre for GeoGenetics. 2011. "Aboriginals Get New History." University of Copenhagen. Accessed December 10, 2013. https://www.heritagedaily.com/2011/09/aboriginals-get-new-history/10335.

Cerri, Matteo. 2017. "The Central Control of Energy Expenditure: Exploiting Torpor for Medical Applications." *Annual Review of Physiology* 79:167–86. DOI: 10.1146/annurev-physiol-022516-034133.

Cerri, Matteo, Marco Mastrotto, Domenico Tupone, Davide Martelli, Marco Luppi, Emanuele Perez, Giovanni Zamboni, and Roberto Amici. 2013. "The Inhibition of Neurons in the Central Nervous Pathways for Thermoregulatory Cold Defense Induces a Suspended Animation State in the Rat." *Journal of Neuroscience* 33 (7): 2984. DOI: 10.1523/JNEUROSCI.3596-12.2013.

Chadarevian, Soraya de. 2002. *Designs for Life: Molecular Biology after World War II*. Cambridge: Cambridge University Press.

Chesterman, John, and Brian Galligan. 1997. *Citizens without Rights: Aborigines and Australian Citizenship*. Cambridge: Cambridge University Press.

Choukèr, A., Jürgen Bereiter-Hahn, D. Singer, and G. Heldmaier. 2019. "Hibernating Astronauts—Science or Fiction?" *Pflügers Archiv* 461 (6): 819–28. DOI: 10.1007/s00424-018-2244-7.

Clarke, Philip A. 2003. *Where the Ancestors Walked: Australia as an Aboriginal Landscape*. Sydney: Allen and Unwin.

Clarke, Philip A. 2007. "Indigenous Spirit and Ghost Folklore of 'Settled' Australia." *Folklore* 118 (2): 141–61. DOI: 10.1080/00155870701337346.

Claw, Katrina G., Matthew Z. Anderson, Rene L. Begay, Krystal S. Tsosie, Keolu Fox, Nanibaa' A. Garrison, and Summer Internship for Indigenous Peoples in Genomics Consortium. 2018. "A Framework for Enhancing Ethical Genomic Research with Indigenous Communities." *Nature Communications* 9 (1): 2957. DOI: 10.1038/s41467-018-05188-3.

Clifford, James. 1997. "Museums as Contact Zones." In *Routes: Travel and Translation in the Late Twentieth Century*, 188–219. Cambridge, MA: Harvard University Press.

Clifford, James, and George E. Marcus. 1986. *Writing Culture: The Poetics and Politics of Ethnography*. Berkeley: University of California Press.

CNN. 2000. "President Clinton, British Prime Minister Tony Blair Deliver Remarks on Human Genome Milestone." June 26, 2000. Transcript. http://www.cnn.com/TRANSCRIPTS/0006/26/bn.01.html.

Cobb, Amanda J., and Amy Lonetree. 2008. *The National Museum of the American Indian: Critical Conversations*. Lincoln: University of Nebraska Press.

Collard, Mark, Sally Wasef, Shaun Adams, Kirsty Wright, R. John Mitchell, Joanne L. Wright, Gabriel Wrobel, et al. 2019. "Giving It a Burl: Towards the Integration of Genetics, Isotope Chemistry, and Osteoarchaeology in Cape York, Tropical North Queensland, Australia." *World Archaeology* 51 (4): 602–19. DOI: 10.1080/00438243.2019.1686418.

Collette, John. 1987. "Hermann Klaatsch's Views on the Significance of the Australian Aborigines." *Aboriginal History* 11 (1/2): 98–100.

Collins, K. J., and J. S. Weiner. 1977. *Human Adaptability: A History and Compendium of Research in the International Biological Programme*. London: Taylor and Francis.

Colwell, Chip. 2017. "Kennewick Man: Build Bridges to Prevent a Repeat of Ill Will." *Seattle Times*, March 3, 2017. https://www.seattletimes.com/opinion/kennewick-man -build-bridges-to-prevent-a-repeat-of-ill-will/.

Commonwealth of Australia. 1924. *Zoological Museum Agreement, No. 49*. Canberra: Commonwealth of Australia.

Commonwealth of Australia. 1937. *Aboriginal Welfare: Initial Conference of Commonwealth and State Aboriginal Authorities Held at Canberra, 21st to 23rd April, 1937*. Canberra: Commonwealth Government Printer.

Conroy, Glenn, Jane Phillips-Conroy, Roy Peterson, Robert Sussman, and Steven Molnar. 1992. "Obituary: Mildred Trotter, Ph.D. (Feb. 2, 1899–Aug. 23, 1991)." *American Journal of Physical Anthropology* 87 (3): 373–74.

Cook, C. E. 1970. "Notable Changes in the Incidence of Disease in Northern Territory Aborigines." In *Diprotodon to Detribalization: Studies of Change among Australian Aborigines*, edited by Arnold R. Pilling and Richard A. Waterman, 116–30. East Lansing: Michigan State University Press.

Couzin-Frankel, Jennifer. 2010a. "The Legacy Plan." *Science* 329 (5988): 135–37.

Couzin-Frankel, Jennifer. 2010b. "Researchers to Return Blood Samples to the Yanomamo." *Science* 328 (5983): 1218.

Cowlishaw, Gillian. 1988. *Black, White or Brindle: Race in Rural Australia*. Cambridge: Cambridge University Press.

Cowlishaw, Gillian. 1999. *Rednecks, Eggheads and Blackfellas: A Study of Racial Power and Intimacy in Australia*. St. Leonards, NSW: Allen and Unwin.

Cowlishaw, Gillian. 2004. *Blackfellas, Whitefellas and the Hidden Injuries of Race*. Oxford: Blackwell.

Cowlishaw, Gillian. 2015. "Friend or Foe? Anthropology's Encounter with Aborigines." *Inside Story*, August 19, 2015. https://insidestory.org.au/friend-or-foe-anthropologys -encounter-with-aborigines/.

Crawford, Heather. 2015. "Identity and Experience of Discrimination among Aboriginal and Torres Strait Islanders." Centre for Aboriginal Economic Policy Research Seminar Series, October 7, 2015.

Daanen, Hein A. M., and Wouter D. Van Marken Lichtenbelt. 2016. "Human Whole Body Cold Adaptation." *Temperature* 3 (1): 104–18. DOI: 10.1080/23328940.2015.1135688.

Daily News. 1887. "An Aboriginal Albino." September 23, 1887, 3.

Daley, Paul. 2014. "Restless Indigenous Remains." *Meanjin* 73 (1): 1–16.

Dammann, Carl. 1873–76. *Anthropologisch-Ethnologisches Album in Photographien*. Berlin: Wiegardt.

Darian-Smith, Kate, Roslyn Poignant, and Kay Schaffer, eds. 1993. *Captured Lives: Australian Captivity Narratives*. London: Sir Robert Menzies Centre for Australian Studies, Institute of Commonwealth Studies, University of London.

Daston, Lorraine. 2004. "Type Specimens and Scientific Memory." *Critical Inquiry* 31 (1): 153–82. DOI: 10.1086/427306.

Davis, Fiona. 2009. "Calculating Colour: Whiteness, Anthropological Research and the Cummeragunja Aboriginal Reserve, May and June 1938." In *Creating White Australia*, edited by Jane Carey and Claire McLisky, 79–92. Sydney: Sydney University Press.

Dayton, Leigh, and Stuart Rintoul. 2011. "Genes Map Aborigines' Arrival in Australia." *Australian*, September 23, 2011. https://www.theaustralian.com.au/nation/health -science/genes-map-aborigines-arrival-in-australia/news-story/0342e2c656c33d8a6d0 f96c71f6b7716.

de la Cadena, Marisol. 2010. "Indigenous Cosmopolitics in the Andes: Conceptual Reflections beyond 'Politics.'" *Cultural Anthropology* 25 (2): 334–70. DOI: 10.1111/j.1548-1360.2010.01061.x.

Delroy, Anne. 2001. "REVIEWS: Exhibitions." *Australian Historical Studies* 32 (116): 147–50.

Derrida, Jacques. 1994. *Specters of Marx: The State of the Debt, the Work of Mourning, and the New International*. New York: Routledge.

Devitt, Jeannie, and Anthony McMasters. 1998a. *Living on Medicine: A Cultural Study of End-Stage Renal Disease among Aboriginal People*. Alice Springs, NT: IAD Press.

Devitt, Jeannie, and Anthony McMasters. 1998b. *On the Machine: Aboriginal Stories about Kidney Troubles*. Alice Springs, NT: IAD Press.

de Vries, Jantina, and Michael Pepper. 2012. "Genomic Sovereignty and the African Promise: Mining the African Genome for the Benefit of Africa." *Journal of Medical Ethics* 38 (8): 474–78. DOI: 10.1136/medethics-2011-100448.

Dick, M., and F. Watson. 1980. "Prevalent Low Serum Thyroxine-Binding Globulin Level in Western Australian Aborigines: Its Effect on Thyroid Function Tests." *Medical Journal of Australia* 1 (3): 115–18.

Dodson, Michael. 2000. "Human Genetics: Control of Research and Sharing of Benefits." *Australian Aboriginal Studies* 1–2:56–64.

Dodson, Michael, and R. Williamson. 1999. "Indigenous Peoples and the Morality of the Human Genome Diversity Project." *Journal of Medical Ethics* 25 (2): 204–8. DOI: 10.1136/ jme.25.2.204.

Dorning, B. F. 1972. "The Rating of Skulls." *Canberra Times*, February 17, 1972.

Douglas, Bronwen, and Chris Ballard, eds. 2008. *Foreign Bodies: Oceania and the Science of Race, 1750–1940*. Canberra: Australian National University Press.

Drummond, Katie. 2009. "Pentagon: Zombie Pigs First, Then Hibernating Soldiers." *Wired*, April 12, 2009. https://www.wired.com/2009/12/pentagon-zombie-pigs-first -then-hibernating-gis/.

Duckworth, W. L. H. 1894. "A Critical Study of the Collection of Crania of Aboriginal Australians in the Cambridge University Museum." *Journal of the Anthropological Institute of Great Britain and Ireland* 23:284–314.

Dunklee, Brady, Jenny Reardon, and Kara Wentworth. 2006. "Race and Crisis." In "Is Race 'Real'?" (web forum), Social Science Research Council, June 7, 2006. http:// raceandgenomics.ssrc.org/Reardon/.

Duster, Troy. 1990. *Backdoor to Eugenics*. New York: Routledge.

E. G. R. T. 1936. "*We Europeans: A Survey of 'Racial' Problems*. By Julian Huxley, Alfred C. Haddon and A. M. Carr-Saunders. Jonathan Cape, 1935. pp. 299. 8s 6d." *Antiquity* 10 (37): 112–13. DOI: 10.1017/S0003598X00011303.

Edwards, Elizabeth. 1990. "Photographic 'Types': The Pursuit of Method." *Visual Anthropology* 3 (2–3): 235–58. DOI: 10.1080/08949468.1990.9966534.

Edwards, Elizabeth, and Chris Morton. 2005. "Introduction." In *Photography, Anthropology and History: Expanding the Frame*, edited by Chris Morton and Elizabeth Edwards, 1–24. Farnham, UK: Ashgate.

Egorova, Yulia. 2013. "The Substance That Empowers? DNA in South Asia." *Contemporary South Asia* 21 (3): 291–303.

Elder, Bruce. 1992. *Blood on the Wattle: Massacres and Maltreatment of Aboriginal Australians since 1788*. Brookvale, NSW: National Book Distributors.

Elder, Catriona. 2007. *Being Australian: Narratives of National Identity*. Crows Nest, NSW: Allen and Unwin Academic.

Elder, Catriona. 2009. *Dreams and Nightmares of a White Australia: Representing Aboriginal Assimilation in the Mid-Twentieth Century*. Bern: Peter Lang.

Elkin, A. P. 1944. *Citizenship for the Aborigines: A National Aboriginal Policy*. Sydney: Australasian Publishing Company.

Elkin, A. P. 1946. *Aboriginal Men of High Degree*. Sydney: Australasian Publishing Company.

Elkin, A. P. 1974. *The Australian Aborigines*. 5th ed. Sydney: Angus and Robertson.

Elmslie, Ronald, and Susan Nance. 2006. "Abbie, Andrew Arthur (1905–1976)." *Australian Dictionary of Biography*, National Centre of Biography, Australian National University. Accessed April 2, 2023. https://adb.anu.edu.au/biography/abbie-andrew-arthur-9300 /text16317. First published in print 1993, vol. 13; first published online 2006.

Endicott, Phillip, M. Thomas, P. Gilbert, Chris Stringer, Carles Lalueza-Fox, Eske Willerslev, Anders J. Hansen, and Alan Cooper. 2003. "The Genetic Origins of the Andaman Islanders." *American Journal of Human Genetics* 72 (1): 178–84. DOI: 10.1086/345487.

Fabian, Ann. 2010. *The Skull Collectors: Race, Science, and America's Unburied Dead*. Chicago: University of Chicago Press.

Fabian, Johannes. 1983. *Time and the Other: How Anthropology Makes Its Object*. New York: Columbia University Press.

Faithfull, Anne. 2023. "Hair Samples from Aboriginal and Torres Strait Islander Peoples in Museum Collections." PhD diss., Deakin University.

Farish, Matthew. 2013. "The Lab and the Land: Overcoming the Arctic in Cold War Alaska." *Isis* 104 (1): 1–29. DOI: 10.1086/669881.

Fforde, Cressida. 2004. *Collecting the Dead: Archaeology and the Reburial Issue*. London: Duckworth.

Fforde, Cressida, Lawrence Bamblett, Ray Lovett, Scott Gorringe, and Bill Fogarty. 2013. "Discourse, Deficit and Identity: Aboriginality, the Race Paradigm and the Language of Representation in Contemporary Australia." *Media International Australia* 149 (1): 162–73. DOI: 10.1177/1329878X1314900117.

Fforde, Cressida, Jane Hubert, and Paul Turnbull, eds. 2002. *The Dead and Their Possessions: Repatriation in Principle, Policy and Practice*. Abingdon, UK: Routledge.

Fine-Dare, Kathleen S. 2002. *Grave Injustice: The American Indian Repatriation Movement and NAGPRA*. Lincoln: University of Nebraska Press.

Fisher, Daniel. 2019. "To Sing with Another's Voice." *American Ethnologist* 46 (1): 34–46. DOI: 10.1111/amet.12732.

Flower, William Henry, and Richard Lydekker. 1891. *An Introduction to the Study of Mammals Living and Extinct*. London: A. and C. Black.

Forrest, Kay. 1996. *The Challenge and the Chance: The Colonisation and Settlement of North West Australia, 1861–1914*. Aboriginal Studies Series 9. Victoria Park, WA: Hesperian.

Freud, Sigmund. (1919) 1925. "The 'Uncanny.'" In *The Standard Edition of the Complete Psychological Works of Sigmund Freud*, edited by James Strachey, translated by Alix Strachey and James Strachey, 17:217–56. London: Hogarth.

Freud, Sigmund. (1953) 2001. "Repression (1915)." In *The Standard Edition of the Complete Psychological Works of Sigmund Freud*, edited by James Strachey, translated by C. M. Baines and James Strachey, 14:146–57. London: Vintage.

Frost, Samantha. 2016. *Biocultural Creatures: Toward a New Theory of the Human*. Durham, NC: Duke University Press.

Frost, Samantha. 2018. "Ten Theses on the Subject of Biology and Politics." In *The Palgrave Handbook of Biology and Society*, edited by Maurizio Meloni, Des Fitzgerald, John Cromby, and Stephanie Lloyd, 897–924. London: Palgrave Macmillan.

Gandevia, Bryan. 1967. "The Prevalence of Signs of Chronic Respiratory Disease in Pintubi and Walbiri Aborigines at Papunya, Central Australia, and Warburton, Western Australia." *Medical Journal of Australia* 2 (6): 237–42. DOI: 10.5694/j.1326-5377.1967.tb97759.x.

Garcia Deister, Vivette. 2018. "In Sickness and in Myth: Genetic Avatars of Indigenous Alterity and the Mexican Nation." In *Beyond Alterity: Destabilizing the Indigenous Other in Mexico*, edited by Paula Lopez Caballero and Ariadna Acevedo-Rodrigo, 263–83. Tucson: University of Arizona Press.

Garrison, Nanibaa' A., Māui Hudson, Leah L. Ballantyne, Ibrahim Garba, Andrew Martinez, Maile Taualii, Laura Arbour, Nadine R. Caron, and Stephanie Carroll Rainie. 2019. "Genomic Research through an Indigenous Lens: Understanding the Expectations." *Annual Review of Genomics and Human Genetics* 20 (1): 495–517. DOI: 10.1146/annurev-genom-083118-015434.

Geiser, Fritz, Shannon E. Currie, Kelly A. O'Shea, and Sara M. Hiebert. 2014. "Torpor and Hypothermia: Reversed Hysteresis of Metabolic Rate and Body Temperature." *American Journal of Physiology—Regulatory, Integrative and Comparative Physiology* 307 (11): R1324–29. DOI: 10.1152/ajpregu.00214.2014.

Gelder, Ken, ed. 1994. *The Oxford Book of Australian Ghost Stories*. Melbourne: Oxford University Press.

Gelder, Ken, and Jane Jacobs. 1998. *Uncanny Australia: Sacredness and Identity in a Postcolonial Nation*. Carlton, VIC: Melbourne University Press.

Genomics Aotearoa. n.d. "About Genomics Aotearoa." Accessed December 11, 2017. https://www.genomics-aotearoa.org.nz/about.

Gerritsen, Rupert. 1994. *And Their Ghosts May Be Heard*. South Fremantle, WA: Fremantle Arts Centre Press.

Gerritsen, Rupert. 2006. "The Evidence for Cohabitation between Indigenous Australians and Marooned Dutch Mariners and VOC Passengers." In *The Dutch Down Under: 1606–2006*, edited by Nonja Peters, 38–55. Sydney: Wolters Kluwer.

Gibbons, Ann. 2011. "Aboriginal Genome Shows Two-Wave Settlement of Asia." *Science* 333 (6050): 1689–91.

Gibson, Jason. 2020. *Ceremony Men: Making Ethnography and the Return of the Strehlow Collection*. Albany: State University of New York Press.

Gilbert, Kevin. 1973. *Because a White Man'll Never Do It*. Sydney: Angus and Robertson.

Gilbert, M. Thomas P., Andrew S. Wilson, Michael Bunce, Anders J. Hansen, Eske Willerslev, Beth Shapiro, Thomas F. G. Higham, et al. 2004. "Ancient Mitochondrial DNA from Hair." *Current Biology* 14 (12): R463–64. DOI: 10.1016/j.cub.2004.06.008.

Glaskin, Katie. 2006. "Death and the Person: Reflections on Mortuary Rituals, Transformation and Ontology in an Aboriginal Society." *Paideuma* 52:107–26.

Glaskin, Katie, Myrna Tonkinson, Yasmine Musharbash, and Victoria Burbank, eds. 2008. *Mortality, Mourning and Mortuary Practices in Indigenous Australia*. London: Ashgate.

Godfrey-Smith, Peter. 2003. *Philosophy of Biology*. Princeton, NJ: Princeton University Press.

Goffman, Erving. 1959. *The Presentation of Self in Everyday Life*. New York: Anchor Books.

Gooder, Haydie, and Jane Jacobs. 2000. "'On the Border of the Unsayable': The Apology in Postcolonizing Australia." *Interventions* 2 (2): 229–47.

Gordon, Avery. 2008. *Ghostly Matters: Haunting and the Sociological Imagination*. 2nd ed. Minneapolis: University of Minnesota Press.

Gray, Geoffrey G. 2007. *A Cautious Silence: The Politics of Australian Anthropology*. Canberra: Aboriginal Studies Press.

Green Left Weekly. 1994. "Concerns at 'Vampire' Project." February 2, 1994. https://www.greenleft.org.au/content/concerns-vampire-project.

Gribbin, Caitlyn. 2014. "Genetic Mutation Helps Aboriginal People Survive Tough Climate, Research Finds." *ABC News*, January 29, 2014. https://mobile.abc.net.au/news/2014-01-29/genetic-modification-helps-aboriginal-people-survive-hot-climat/5225742.

Griffiths, Billy. 2018. *Deep Time Dreaming: Uncovering Ancient Australia*. Melbourne: Black Inc.

Griffiths, Michael R. 2012. "The White Gaze and Its Artifacts: Governmental Belonging and Non-Indigenous Evaluation in a (Post)-Settler Colony." *Postcolonial Studies* 15 (4): 415–35. DOI: 10.1080/13688790.2013.777993.

Griffiths, Paul, and Karola Stotz. 2013. *Genetics and Philosophy: An Introduction*. Cambridge: Cambridge University Press.

Griffiths, Tom. 1996. *Hunters and Collectors: The Antiquarian Imagination in Australia*. Studies in Australian History. Cambridge: Cambridge University Press.

Grosfoguel, Ramón. 2007. "The Epistemic Decolonial Turn." *Cultural Studies* 21 (2–3): 211–23. DOI: 10.1080/09502380601162514.

Gustafson, Zadel Barnes. 1893. "Jungun, the Albino: An American View." *West Australian*, January 18, 1893, 3.

Haddon, Alfred C. 1898. *The Study of Man*. Progressive Science Series. London: John Murray.

Haddon, Alfred C. (1901) 1932. *Head-Hunters: Black, White, and Brown*. Abridged ed. Thinker's Library 26. London: Watts.

Haddon, Alfred C. 1909. *The Races of Man and Their Distribution*. New York: F. A. Stokes.

Haddon, Alfred C. 1924. *The Races of Man and Their Distribution*. Rev. ed. Cambridge: Cambridge University Press.

Haebich, Anna. 1992. *For Their Own Good: Aborigines and Government in the Southwest of Western Australia, 1900–1940*. Nedlands: University of Western Australia Publishing.

Haebich, Anna. 2000. *Broken Circles: Fragmenting Indigenous Families, 1800–2000*. Freemantle, WA: Freemantle Arts Centre Press.

Hage, Ghassan. 1998. *White Nation: Fantasies of White Supremacy in a Multicultural Society*. Annandale, NSW: Pluto.

Hage, Ghassan. 2003. *Against Paranoid Nationalism: Searching for Hope in a Shrinking Society*. Annandale, NSW: Pluto.

Hagen, Joel B. 2018. "The Diving Reflex and Asphyxia: Working across Species in Physiological Ecology." *History and Philosophy of the Life Sciences* 40 (1): 1–19. DOI: 10.1007/s40656-018-0188-z.

Haggard, H. Rider. 1885. *King Solomon's Mines*. London: Cassell.

Haggard, H. Rider. 1887. *Allan Quartermain*. London: Longmans, Green, and Co.

Hallam, Elizabeth, and Jenny Hockey. 2001. *Death, Memory and Material Culture*. Oxford: Berg.

Hamilton, Cindy. 2000. "The Human Genome Diversity Project and the New Biological Imperialism." *Santa Clara Law Review* 41 (2). https://digitalcommons.law.scu.edu/lawreview/vol41/iss2/8/.

Hamilton, Jennifer A. 2012. "The Case of the Genetic Ancestor." In *Genetics and the Unsettled Past: The Collision of DNA, Race, and History*, edited by Keith Wailoo, Alondra Nelson, and Catherine Lee, 266–78. New Brunswick, NJ: Rutgers University Press.

Hammel, H. T., R. W. Elsner, D. H. Le Messurier, H. T. Andersen, and F. A. Milan. 1959. "Thermal and Metabolic Responses of the Australian Aborigine Exposed to Moderate Cold in Summer." *Journal of Applied Physiology* 14 (4): 605–15. DOI: 10.1152/jappl.1959.14.4.605.

Han, Esther. 2019. "'Everybody Hates a Welfare Rorter': Latham Spruiks DNA Testing Plan for Aboriginal People." *Sydney Morning Herald*, March 11, 2019. https://www.smh.com.au/politics/nsw/everybody-hates-a-welfare-rorter-latham-spruiks-dna-testing-plan-for-aboriginal-people-20190311-p513au.html.

Haraway, Donna. 1997. *Modest_Witness@Second_Millennium: FemaleMan_Meets_OncoMouse*. New York: Routledge.

Haraway, Donna. 2008. *When Species Meet*. Minneapolis: University of Minnesota Press.

Haraway, Donna. 2016. *Staying with the Trouble: Making Kin in the Chthulucene*. Experimental Futures: Technological Lives, Scientific Arts, Anthropological Voices. Durham, NC: Duke University Press, 2016.

Harding, Sandra. 1986. *The Science Question in Feminism*. Ithaca, NY: Cornell University Press.

Harding, Sandra. 2016. "Latin American Decolonial Social Studies of Scientific Knowledge: Alliances and Tensions." *Science, Technology and Human Values* 41 (6): 188–219. DOI: 10.1177/0162243916656465.

Harmon, Amy. 2010. "Indian Tribe Wins Fight to Limit Research of Its DNA." *New York Times*, April 21, 2010, A1. https://www.nytimes.com/2010/04/22/us/22dna.html.

Harry, Debra, Stephanie Howard, and Brett Lee Shelton. 2000. "Indigenous Peoples, Genes and Genetics: What Indigenous Peoples Should Know about Biocolonialism." Indigenous Peoples Council on Biocolonialism, May 2000. http://www.ipcb.org/pdf_files/ipgg.pdf.

Hart, Bradley. 2013. "Science, Politics, and Prejudice: The Dynamics and Significance of British Anthropology's Failure to Confront Nazi Racial Ideology." *European History Quarterly* 43 (2): 301–25. DOI: 10.1177/0265691413477069.

Hatch, Anthony Ryan. 2016. *Blood Sugar: Racial Pharmacology and Food Justice in Black America*. Minneapolis: University of Minnesota Press.

Heagney, Brenda. 2006. "Bryan Harle Gandevia." *Health and History* 8 (2): 186–91.

Healy, Chris. 1995. "Revisiting Histories and Mythologies." Museums Victoria archives, Melbourne.

Healy, Chris. 1997. *From the Ruins of Colonialism: History as Social Memory*. Melbourne: Cambridge University Press.

Healy, Chris. 2008. *Forgetting Aborigines*. Sydney: University of New South Wales Press.

Healy, Chris, and Andrea Witcomb. 2006. "Experiments in Culture: An Introduction." In *South Pacific Museums: Experiments in Culture*, edited by Chris Healy and Andrea Witcomb, 1–5. Clayton, VIC: Monash University ePress.

Healy, J. J. 1978. "The Lemurian Nineties." *Australian Literary Studies* 8 (3): 307–16.

Herbert, Xavier. (1938) 1972. *Capricornia*. Sydney: Angus and Robertson.

Hertz, Robert. 1960. *Death and the Right Hand*. Translated by Rodney and Claudia Needham. London: Cohen and West.

Hess, Gary. 1969. "The 'Hindu' in America: Immigration and Naturalization Policies and India, 1917–1946." *Pacific Historical Review* 38 (1): 59–79. DOI: 10.2307/3636886.

Hetherington, Kevin. 2004. "Secondhandedness: Consumption, Disposal, and Absent Presence." *Environment and Planning D: Society and Space* 22 (1): 157–73. DOI: 10.1068/d315t.

Hicks, C. Stanton. 1926a. "On the Innervation and Secretory Path of the Thyroid Gland." *Journal of Physiology* 62 (2): 198–202.

Hicks, C. Stanton. 1926b. "Studies in Tryphtophane Feeding I." *Australian Journal of Experimental Biology and Medical Science* 3 (4): 193–202.

Hicks, C. Stanton. 1963. "Climatic Adaptation and Drug Habituation of the Central Australian Aborigine." *Perspectives in Biology and Medicine* 7 (1): 39–57. DOI: 10.1353/pbm.1963.0028.

Hicks, C. Stanton. 1974. "Just in Time: A Physiologist among the Nomad Tribes of Central Australia, 1929–1939." Sir Cedric Stanton Hicks Papers, Rare Books and Special Collections, Barr Smith Library, University of Adelaide.

Hicks, C. Stanton, and R. F. Matters. 1933. "The Standard Metabolism of the Australian Aborigines." *Australian Journal of Experimental Biology and Medical Science* 11:177–83.

Hicks, C. Stanton, H. O. Moore, and Ernest Eldridge. 1934. "The Respiratory Exchange of the Australian Aborigine." *Australian Journal of Experimental Biology and Medical Science* 12 (2): 79–89. DOI: 10.1038/icb.1934.11.

Higuchi, Russell, Barbara Bowman, Mary Freiberger, Oliver A. Ryder, and Allan C. Wilson. 1984. "DNA Sequences from the Quagga, an Extinct Member of the Horse Family." *Nature* 312 (5991): 282–84. DOI: 10.1038/312282a0.

Hinterberger, Amy, and Natalie Porter. 2015. "Genomic and Viral Sovereignty: Tethering the Materials of Global Biomedicine." *Public Culture* 27 (2) (76): 361–86. DOI: 10.1215/08992363-2841904.

Hollinger, David. 2003. "Amalgamation and Hypodescent: The Question of Ethnoracial Mixture in the History of the United States." *American Historical Review* 108 (5): 1363–90. DOI: 10.1086/ahr/108.5.1363.

Hook, Gary Raumati. 2009. "'Warrior Genes' and the Disease of Being Maori." *MAI Review* 2009 (2): 1–11.

Horton, David. 1996. *Aboriginal Australia*. Canberra: Australian Institute for Aboriginal and Torres Strait Islander Studies.

Howard, Alan. 1990. "Cultural Paradigms, History, and the Search for Identity in Oceania." In *Cultural Identity and Ethnicity in the Pacific*, edited by Jocelyn Linnekin and Lin Poyer, 259–80. Honolulu: University of Hawai'i Press.

Howitt, Richie. 2001. "Frontiers, Borders, Edges: Liminal Challenges to the Hegemony of Exclusion." *Australian Geographical Studies* 39 (2): 233–45. DOI: 10.1111/1467-8470.00142.

Hsu, Jeremy. 2018. "Human Powers of Hibernation May Be Dormant in Genetic Code." *NBC News*, October 21, 2018. https://www.nbcnews.com/mach/science/human-powers -hibernation-may-be-dormant-genetic-code-ncna922326.

Hudson, Maui, Khyla Russell, Lynley Uerata, Moe Milne, Phillip Wilcox, Ramari Viola Port, Barry Smith, Valmaine Toki, and Angela Beaton. 2016. "Te Mata Ira—Faces of the Gene: Developing a Cultural Foundation for Biobanking and Genomic Research Involving Maori." *AlterNative: An International Journal of Indigenous Peoples* 12 (4): 341–55. DOI: 10.20507/AlterNative.2016.12.4.1.

Hudson, Maui, Kim Southey, Lynley Uerata, Angela Beaton, Moe Milne, Khyla Russell, Barry Smith, et al. 2016. "Key Informant Views on Biobanking and Genomic Research with Maori." *New Zealand Medical Journal (Online)* 129 (1447): 29–42. https://journal .nzma.org.nz/journal-articles/key-informant-views-on-biobanking-and-genomic -research-with-maori.

Hudson Institute of Mineralogy. n.d. "Golden Ridge Gold Mine (Waterfall), Kalgoorlie-Boulder, Kalgoorlie-Boulder Shire, Western Australia, Australia." Mindat.org. Accessed March 12, 2019. http://www.mindat.org/loc-271942.html.

Human Rights and Equal Opportunity Commission. 1996. *Aboriginal and Torres Strait Islander Social Justice Commissioner, Fourth Report*. Sydney: Human Rights and Equal Opportunity Commission.

Human Rights and Equal Opportunity Commission. 1997. *Bringing Them Home: Report of the National Inquiry into the Separation of Aboriginal and Torres Strait Islander Children from Their Families*. Canberra: Human Rights and Equal Opportunity Commission.

Huxley, Julian, Alfred C. Haddon, and Alexander M. Carr-Saunders. 1935. *We Europeans: A Survey of "Racial" Problems*. London: Jonathan Cape.

Huxley, Thomas H. (1865) 1897. "On the Methods and Results of Ethnology." In *Man's Place in Nature and Other Anthropological Essays*, 209–52. New York: D. Appleton and Company.

Huxley, Thomas H. 1870. "On the Geographical Distribution of the Chief Modifications of Mankind." *Journal of the Ethnological Society of London* 2 (4): 404–12. DOI: 10.2307/3014371.

Institute of Medicine and National Research Council. 1996. *The Arctic Aeromedical Laboratory's Thyroid Function Study: A Radiological Risk and Ethical Analysis*. Washington, DC: National Academies Press.

Ivens, Walter. 1932. Review of *Headhunters, Black, White, and Brown*, by Alfred C. Haddon. *Man* 32:147.

Janke, Terri. 1998. *Our Culture, Our Future: Report on Australian Indigenous Cultural and Intellectual Property Rights*. Canberra: Aboriginal and Torres Strait Islander Commission.

Jinka, Tulasi R., and Lawrence K. Duffy. 2013. "Ethical Considerations in Hibernation Research." *Lab Animal* 42 (7): 248–52. DOI: 10.1038/laban.253.

Johnson, Miranda. 2011. "Reconciliation, Indigeneity, and Postcolonial Nationhood in Settler States." *Postcolonial Studies* 14 (2): 187–201. DOI: 10.1080/13688790.2011.563457.

Johnston, Elliott. 1991. *Royal Commission into Aboriginal Deaths in Custody*. Canberra: Australian Government Publishing Services.

Jones, Elizabeth D., and Elsbeth Bösl. 2021. "Ancient Human DNA: A History of Hype (Then and Now)." *Journal of Social Archaeology* 21 (2): 236–55. DOI: 10.1177/1469605321990115.

Jones, Philip. 1987. "South Australian Anthropological History: The Board for Anthropological Research and Its Early Expeditions." *Records of the South Australian Museum* 20:71–92.

Jones, Philip. 2008. "The 'Idea behind the Artefact': Norman Tindale's Early Years as a Salvage Ethnographer." In *Makers and Making of Indigenous Australian Museum Collections*, edited by Nicolas Peterson, Lindy Allen, and Louise Hamby, 315–46. Carlton, VIC: Melbourne University Press.

Jones, Ross L. 2013. "Macaws, Elephants and Mahouts: Frederic Wood Jones, the Rockefeller Foundation and the Human Biology Project." *Australian Historical Studies* 44 (2): 189–205. DOI: 10.1080/1031461X.2013.791706.

Jones, Ross L. 2020. *Anatomists of Empire: Race, Evolution and the Discovery of Human Biology in the British World*. North Melbourne: Australian Scholarly Publishing.

Jones, Ross L., and Warwick Anderson. 2015. "Wandering Anatomists and Itinerant Anthropologists: The Antipodean Sciences of Race in Britain between the Wars." *British Journal for the History of Science* 48 (1): 1–16. DOI: 10.1017/S0007087413000939.

Jonsen, Albert. 1998. *The Birth of Bioethics*. New York: Oxford University Press.

Jose, David G., M. H. R. Self, and N. D. Stallman. 1969. "A Survey of Children and Adolescents on Queensland Aboriginal Settlements, 1967." *Journal of Paediatrics and Child Health* 5 (2): 71–88. DOI: 10.1111/j.1440-1754.1969.tb02812.x.

Kahn, Jonathan. 2013. *Race in a Bottle: The Story of BiDil and Racialized Medicine in a Postgenomic Age*. New York: Columbia University Press.

Kahn, Jonathan, Alondra Nelson, Joseph Graves, Sarah Abel, Ruha Benjamin, Sarah Blacker, Catherine Bliss, et al. 2018. "How Not to Talk about Race and Genetics." *BuzzFeed News*, March 30, 2018. https://www.buzzfeednews.com/article/bfopinion/race-genetics-david-reich.

Kakaliouras, Ann M. 2012. "An Anthropology of Repatriation." *Current Anthropology* 53 (S5): S210–21. DOI: 10.1086/662331.

Kakaliouras, Ann M. 2019. "The Repatriation of the Palaeoamericans: Kennewick Man/the Ancient One and the End of a Non-Indian Ancient North America." *BJHS Themes* 4:79–98. DOI: 10.1017/bjt.2019.9.

Karp, Ivan, and Steven Lavine. 1991. *Exhibiting Cultures: The Poetics and Politics of Museum Display*. Washington, DC: Smithsonian Institution Press.

Kauanui, J. Kehaulani. 2008. *Hawaiian Blood: Colonialism and the Politics of Sovereignty and Indigeneity*. Durham, NC: Duke University Press.

Kaus, David. 2008. *A Different Time: The Exhibition Photographs of Herbert Basedow, 1903–1928*. Canberra: National Museum of Australia.

Keen, Ian. 2006. "Ancestors, Magic, and Exchange in Yolngu Doctrines: Extensions of the Person in Time and Space." *Journal of the Royal Anthropological Institute* 12 (3): 515–30. DOI: 10.1111/j.1467-9655.2006.00350.x.

Keller, Evelyn Fox. 2010. *The Mirage of a Space between Nature and Nurture*. Durham, NC: Duke University Press.

Kent, Michael. 2013. "The Importance of Being Uros: Indigenous Identity Politics in the Genomic Age." *Social Studies of Science* 43 (4): 534–56. DOI: 10.1177/0306312712468520.

Khan, Razib. 2011. "All Your Genes Belong to the Tribal Council!" *Discover*, September 28, 2011. https://www.discovermagazine.com/health/all-your-genes-belong-to-the-tribal-council.

Kidd, Rosalind. 1997. *The Way We Civilise: Aboriginal Affairs, the Untold Story*. Brisbane: University of Queensland Press.

Kirk, R. L. 1966. "Population Genetic Studies in Australia and New Guinea." In *The Biology of Human Adaptability*, edited by Paul Baker and J. S. Weiner, 395–430. Oxford: Clarendon.

Kirk, R. L. 1973. "Genetic Studies of Cape York Populations." In *The Human Biology of Aborigines in Cape York*, edited by Robert Kirk, 25–36. Canberra: Australian Institute of Aboriginal Studies.

Kirk, R. L. 1985. "History of Physical Anthropology in Australia." *International Association of Human Biologists, Occasional Papers* 1 (5): 1–34.

Kirk, R. L. 2001. "Population Genetic Studies." In *The John Curtin School of Medical Research: The First Fifty Years, 1948–1998*, edited by Frank Fenner and David Curtis, 294–98. Gundaroo, NSW: Brolga.

Kirk, R. L. n.d. "Patterns in Blood: A Memoir." Unpublished manuscript.

Kirk, R. L., and Alan G. Thorne. 1976. "Introduction." In *The Origin of the Australians*, edited by Robert Louis Kirk and Alan G. Thorne, 1–8. Canberra: Australian Institute of Aboriginal Studies.

Knapp, Michael, and Michael Hofreiter. 2010. "Next Generation Sequencing of Ancient DNA: Requirements, Strategies and Perspectives." *Genes* 1 (2): 227–43. DOI: 10.3390/genes1020227.

Kolopenuk, Jessica. 2014. "Wiindigo Incarnate: Consuming 'Native American DNA.'" *GeneWatch* 27 (2): 18–20.

Kowal, Emma. 2006. "Moving towards the Mean: Dilemmas of Assimilation and Improvement." In *Moving Anthropology: Critical Indigenous Studies*, edited by Tess Lea, Emma Kowal, and Gillian Cowlishaw, 65–78. Darwin, NT: Charles Darwin University Press.

Kowal, Emma. 2008. "The Politics of the Gap: Indigenous Australians, Liberal Multiculturalism and the End of the Self-Determination Era." *American Anthropologist* 11 (3): 338–48.

Kowal, Emma. 2012a. *ANU Indigenous Biospecimen Collection Background Paper*. Canberra: Australian National University.

Kowal, Emma. 2012b. "Genetic Research in Indigenous Health: Significant Progress, Substantial Challenges." *Medical Journal of Australia* 197 (1): 19–20.

Kowal, Emma. 2015. *Trapped in the Gap: Doing Good in Indigenous Australia.* New York: Berghahn.

Kowal, Emma. 2017. "Descent, Classification and Indigeneity in Australia." In *Mixed Race Identities in Australia, New Zealand and the Pacific Islands*, edited by Kirsten McGavin and Farida Fozda, 19–35. Abingdon, UK: Routledge.

Kowal, Emma. 2019. "Spencer's Double: The Decolonial Afterlife of a Postcolonial Museum Prop." In "How Collections End," edited by Boris Jardine, Emma Kowal, and Jenny Bangham. Special issue, *BJHS Themes* 4:55–77.

Kowal, Emma, and Ian Anderson. 2012. *Genetic Research in Aboriginal and Torres Strait Islander Communities: Continuing the Conversation.* Melbourne: Lowitja Institute.

Kowal, Emma, Simon Easteal, and Mick Gooda. 2016. "Indigenous Genomics." *Australasian Science*, July/August 2016, 18–20.

Kowal, Emma, Ashley Greenwood, and Rebekah E. McWhirter. 2015. "All in the Blood: A Review of Aboriginal Australians' Cultural Beliefs about Blood and Implications for Biospecimen Research." *Journal of Empirical Research on Human Research Ethics* 10 (4): 347–59. DOI: 10.1177/1556264615604521.

Kowal, Emma, and Misty Jenkins. 2016. "DNA Nation Raises Tough Questions for Indigenous Australians." *The Conversation*, May 25, 2016. https://theconversation.com/dna -nation-raises-tough-questions-for-indigenous-australians-59877.

Kowal, Emma, and Bastien Llamas. 2019. "Race in a Genome: Long Read Sequencing, Ethnicity-Specific Reference Genomes and the Shifting Horizon of Race." *Journal of Anthropological Sciences* 97:91–106. DOI: 10.4436/JASS.97004.

Kowal, Emma, Bastien Llamas, and Sarah Tishkoff. 2017. "Consent: Data-Sharing for Indigenous Peoples." *Nature* 546:474–74. DOI: 10.1038/546474a.

Kowal, Emma, and Yin Paradies. 2017. "Indigeneity and the Refusal of Whiteness." *Postcolonial Studies* 20 (1): 101–17. DOI: 10.1080/13688790.2017.1334287.

Kowal, Emma, and Joanna Radin. 2015. "Indigenous Biospecimen Collections and the Cryopolitics of Frozen Life." *Journal of Sociology* 51 (1): 63–80. DOI: 10.1177/1440783314562316.

Kowal, Emma, Joanna Radin, and Jenny Reardon. 2013. "Indigenous Body Parts, Mutating Temporalities, and the Half-Lives of Postcolonial Technoscience." *Social Studies of Science* 43 (4): 465–83. DOI: 10.1177/0306312713490843.

Kowal, Emma, Lobna Rouhani, and Ian Anderson. 2011. *Genetic Research in Aboriginal and Torres Strait Islander Communities: Beginning the Conversation.* Melbourne: Lowitja Institute.

Kowal, Emma, and Megan Warin. 2018. "Anthropology, Indigeneity, and the Epigenome." *American Anthropologist* 120 (4): 822–25. DOI: 10.1111/aman.13141.

Kristeva, Julia. 1991. *Strangers to Ourselves.* Translated by Leon Roudiez. New York: Columbia University Press.

Kuklick, Henrika. 2006. "'Humanity in the Chrysalis Stage': Indigenous Australians in the Anthropological Imagination, 1899–1926." *British Journal for the History of Science* 39 (143): 535–68. DOI: 10.1017/S0007087406008405.

Kuper, Adam. 1998. *The Invention of Primitive Society: Transformations of an Illusion.* Abingdon, UK: Routledge.

Lake, Marilyn. 1998. "Feminism and the Gendered Policies of Antiracism, Australia 1927–57: From Maternal Protectionism to Leftist Assimilationism." *Australian Historical Studies* 29 (110): 91–108.

Lake, Marilyn, and Henry Reynolds. 2008. *Drawing the Global Colour Line: White Men's Countries and the International Challenge for Racial Equality.* Cambridge: Cambridge University Press.

Lambert, Jacqueline Ann. 2011. "A History of the Australian Institute of Aboriginal Studies, 1959–1989: An Analysis of How Aboriginal and Torres Strait Islander People Achieved Control of a National Research Institute." PhD diss., Australian National University.

Landecker, Hannah. 2000. "Immortality, In Vitro: A History of the HeLa Cell Line." In *Biotechnology and Culture: Bodies, Anxieties and Ethics,* edited by Paul Brodwin, 53–74. Bloomington: Indiana University Press.

Landecker, Hannah. 2005. "Living Differently in Time: Plasticity, Temporality and Cellular Biotechnologies." *Culture Machine* 7. https://culturemachine.net/biopolitics/living-differently-in-time/.

Landecker, Hannah. 2007. *Culturing Life: How Cells Became Technologies.* Cambridge, MA: Harvard University Press.

Langford, R. 1983. "Our Heritage—Your Playground." *Australian Archaeology* 16 (1): 1–6.

Langton, Marcia. 1981. "Anthropologists Must Change." *Identity* 4 (4): 11.

Langton, Marcia. 1993. *"Well, I Heard It on the Radio and I Saw It on the Television": An Essay for the Australian Film Commission on the Politics and Aesthetics of Filmmaking by and about Aboriginal People and Things.* Sydney: Australian Film Commission.

Lanzarotta, Tess. 2020. "Ethics in Retrospect: Biomedical Research, Colonial Violence, and Iñupiat Sovereignty in the Alaskan Arctic." *Social Studies of Science* 50 (5): 778–801. DOI: 10.1177/0306312720943678.

Latimore, Jack. 2019. "Mark Latham Got What He Wanted out of His Absurd Proposal to DNA Test Aboriginal People." *Guardian,* March 16, 2019. https://www.theguardian.com/commentisfree/2019/mar/16/mark-latham-got-what-he-wanted-out-of-his-absurd-proposal-to-dna-test-aboriginal-people.

Latour, Bruno. 1993. *We Have Never Been Modern.* Cambridge, MA: Harvard University Press.

Latour, Bruno. 2004. "Why Has Critique Run Out of Steam? From Matters of Fact to Matters of Concern." *Critical Inquiry* 30 (2): 224–48. DOI: 10.1086/421123.

Law, John. 2004. *After Method: Mess in Social Science Research.* Abingdon, UK: Routledge.

Lawrence, Marie. 1967. "Dr J. C. Trevor." *Nature* 216:523. DOI: 10.1038/216523b0.

Lee, Cheng Chi. 2008. "Is Human Hibernation Possible?" *Annual Review of Medicine* 59 (1): 177–86. DOI: 10.1146/annurev.med.59.061506.110403.

"Leonard Darwin Scholarship of the Eugenics Society." 1936. *Nature* 138:756. DOI: 10.1038/138756a0.

Lewin, Roger. 1984. "Extinction Threatens Australian Anthropology: Moves by Aborigines to Impound and Rebury Skeletal Remains in Universities and Museums Could End Physical Anthropology in Australia." *Science* 225 (4660): 393–94. DOI: 10.1126/science.225.4660.393.

Lewis, Darrell. 2006. "The Fate of Leichhardt." *Historical Records of Australian Science* 17 (1): 1–30. DOI: 10.1071/HR05010.

Lewis, Darrell. 2013. *Where Is Dr Leichhardt? The Greatest Mystery in Australian History.* Clayton, VIC: Monash University Publishing.

Lewis, Dyani. 2020. "Australian Biobank Repatriates Hundreds of 'Legacy' Indigenous Blood Samples." *Nature* 577 (7788): 11–12. DOI: 10.1038/d41586-019-03906-5.

Lewontin, Richard. 1972. "The Apportionment of Human Diversity." *Evolutionary Biology* 6:391–98. DOI: 10.1007/978-1-4684-9063-3_14.

Lewontin, Richard. 1974. *The Genetic Basis of Evolutionary Change.* New York: Columbia University Press.

Liddle, J., and B. Shaw. [ca. 1983]. *Some Research Guidelines.* Alice Springs, NT: Central Australian Aboriginal Congress.

Lindee, M. Susan. 1994. *Suffering Made Real: American Science and the Survivors at Hiroshima.* Chicago: University of Chicago Press.

Lindee, M. Susan, and Ricardo Ventura Santos. 2012. "The Biological Anthropology of Living Human Populations: World Histories, National Styles, and International Networks: An Introduction to Supplement 5." *Current Anthropology* 53 (S5): S3–S16. DOI: 10.1086/663335.

Lindsay, David. 1893. *Journal of the Elder Exploring Expedition.* Adelaide: South Australian Parliament.

Linnaeus, Carolus. (1735) 1964. *Systema Naturae.* Nieuwkoop, Holland: De Graaf.

Llamas, Bastien, Eske Willerslev, and Ludovic Orlando. 2017. "Human Evolution: A Tale from Ancient Genomes." *Philosophical Transactions of the Royal Society of London: Series B, Biological Sciences* 372 (1713). DOI: 10.1098/rstb.2015.0484.

Lonetree, Amy. 2012. *Decolonizing Museums: Representing Native America in National and Tribal Museums.* Chapel Hill: University of North Carolina Press.

Lord, Barry, and Maria Piacente, eds. 2014. *Manual of Museum Exhibitions.* 2nd ed. Lanham, MD: Rowman and Littlefield.

Lydon, Jane. 2005. *Eye Contact: Photographing Indigenous Australians.* Durham, NC: Duke University Press.

Lyons, Kristina, Juno Salazar Parreñas, Noah Tamarkin, Banu Subramaniam, Lesley Green, and Tania Pérez-Bustos. 2017. "Engagements with Decolonization and Decoloniality in and at the Interfaces of STS." *Catalyst: Feminism, Theory, Technoscience* 3 (1). DOI: 10.28968/cftt.v3i1.231.

MacCallum, Monica. 2006. "MacKenzie, Sir William Colin (1877–1938)." In *Australian Dictionary of Biography*, National Centre of Biography, Australian National University. Accessed April 1, 2023. http://adb.anu.edu.au/biography/mackenzie-sir-william-colin-7392/text12831. First published in print 1986, vol. 10; first published online 2006.

MacDonald, Helen. 2010. *Possessing the Dead: The Artful Science of Anatomy.* Melbourne: Melbourne University Press.

Macdonald, Sharon. 2009. *Difficult Heritage: Negotiating the Nazi Past in Nuremberg and Beyond.* Abingdon, UK: Routledge.

Macfarlane, W. V. 1969. "Desert Survival and the Function of Aboriginal Nomads in the Summer Desert." File 2/51, "U.S. Army Medical Research Command—Application for grant 1969 for research on water and electrolyte metabolism of desert aborigines and New Guinea Melanesians, and related reports and correspondence, 1969-1974."

W. V. Macfarlane Papers, University of Adelaide Special Collections, BSL MSS 0006, Adelaide, South Australia.

Macintyre, S., and A. Clark. 2003. *The History Wars*. Carlton, VIC: Melbourne University Press.

Mackenzie, William Colin. 1910. *The Treatment of Infantile Paralysis: A Study on Muscular Action and Muscle Regeneration*. Melbourne: Stillwell.

Mackenzie, William Colin. 1918. *The Action of Muscles: Including Muscle Rest and Muscle Re-education*. Edited by Charles Mackay. London: Lewis.

Mackenzie, William Colin, and W. J. Owen. 1918–19. *The Comparative Anatomy of Australian Mammals*. Melbourne: Jenkin, Buxton.

MacLeod, Roy, and Philip F. Rehbock. 2000. "Developing a Sense of the Pacific: The 1923 Pan-Pacific Science Congress in Australia." *Pacific Science* 54 (3): 209–25.

Maio, Marcos Chor, and Ricardo Ventura Santos. 2015. "Antiracism and the Uses of Science in the Post–World War II: An Analysis of UNESCO's First Statements on Race (1950 and 1951)." *Vibrant: Virtual Brazilian Anthropology* 12 (2): 1–26. DOI: 10.1590/1809-43412015v12n2p001.

Maitland Daily Mercury. 1924. "Remarkable Aborigine." March 10, 1924, 4. http://nla.gov.au/nla.news-article127626102.

Malaspinas, Anna-Sapfo, Michael C. Westaway, Craig Muller, Vitor C. Sousa, Oscar Lao, Isabel Alves, Anders Bergström, et al. 2016. "A Genomic History of Aboriginal Australia." *Nature* 538 (7624): 207–14. DOI: 10.1038/nature18299.

Maldonado-Torres, Nelson. 2011. "Thinking through the Decolonial Turn: Post-continental Interventions in Theory, Philosophy, and Critique—an Introduction." *Transmodernity* 1 (2): 1–15.

Marett, Allan. 2000. "Ghostly Voices: Some Observations on Song-Creation, Ceremony and Being in NW Australia." *Oceania* 71 (1): 18–29. DOI: 10.1002/j.1834-4461.2000.tb02721.x.

Marks, Jonathan. 1996. "The Legacy of Serological Studies in American Physical Anthropology." *History and Philosophy of the Life Sciences* 18 (3): 345–62.

Markus, Andrew. 1994. *Australian Race Relations, 1788–1993*. Sydney: Allen and Unwin.

Marshall, Virginia. 2017. *Overturning Aqua Nullius: Securing Aboriginal Water Rights*. Canberra: Aboriginal Studies Press.

Martin, Rudolf. 1914. *Lehrbuch der Anthropologie*. Jena: Gustav Fischer.

Maynard, John. 2007. *Fight for Liberty and Freedom: The Origins of Australian Aboriginal Activism*. Canberra: Aboriginal Studies Press.

McCarthy, Michael. 2003. "The Holistic Approach to the Maritime Heritage: The Western Australian Case Study after 30 Years." *Journal of the Australasian Institute for Maritime Archaeology* 27:25–34.

McDougall, Russell. 2007. "Herbert, Albert Francis Xavier (1901–1984)." In *Australian Dictionary of Biography*, National Centre of Biography, Australian National University. Accessed April 2, 2023. https://adb.anu.edu.au/biography/herbert-albert-francis-xavier-12623/text22741. First published in print 2007, vol. 17.

McGregor, Russell. 1996. "An Aboriginal Caucasian: Some Uses for Racial Kinship in Early Twentieth Century Australia." *Australian Aboriginal Studies* 1996 (1): 11–20.

McGregor, Russell. 1997. *Imagined Destinies: Aboriginal Australians and the Doomed Race Theory, 1880–1939*. Melbourne: Melbourne University Press.

McGregor, Russell. 2011. *Indifferent Inclusion: Aboriginal People and the Australian Nation*. Canberra: Aboriginal Studies Press.

M'charek, Amade. 2005. *The Human Genome Diversity Project: An Ethnography of Scientific Practice*. Cambridge: Cambridge University Press.

M'charek, Amade. 2014. "Race, Time and Folded Objects: The HeLa Error." *Theory, Culture and Society* 31 (6): 29–56. DOI: 10.1177/0263276413501704.

McKenna, Mark. 2002. *Looking for Blackfellas' Point: An Australian History of Place*. Sydney: University of New South Wales Press.

McKeown, C. Timothy, Cressida Fforde, and Honor Keeler, eds. 2020. *The Routledge Companion to Indigenous Repatriation: Return, Reconcile, Renew*. Abingdon, UK: Routledge.

McNeil, Maureen. 2005. "Introduction: Postcolonial Technoscience." *Science as Culture* 14 (2): 105–12. DOI: 10.1080/09505430500110770.

McNiven, Ian, and Lynette Russell. 2008. "Towards a Postcolonial Archeology of Indigenous Australia." In *Handbook of Archaeological Theories*, edited by R. Alexander Bentley, Herbert D. G. Maschner, and Christopher Chippindale, 423–46. Lanham, MD: AltaMira.

McPhee, Alexander. 1890. Letter to the editor. *Argus*, February 5, 1890, 9.

McPhee, Alexander. 1891. "Discovery of Another Aboriginal Albino: Tidings of a Lost Party of White Men." *Western Mail*, January 31, 1891, 9.

Mead, Aroha Te Pareake, and Steven Ratuva. 2007. *Pacific Genes and Life Patents: Pacific Experiences and Analysis of the Commodification and Ownership of Life*. Tokyo: Call of the Earth Llamado de la Tierra, United Nations University—Institute of Advanced Studies.

Mello, Michelle M., and Leslie E. Wolf. 2010. "The Havasupai Indian Tribe Case—Lessons for Research Involving Stored Biologic Samples." *New England Journal of Medicine* 363 (3): 204–7. DOI: 10.1056/NEJMp1005203.

Mignolo, Walter. 2011. *The Darker Side of Western Modernity: Global Futures, Decolonial Options*. Latin America Otherwise: Languages, Empires, Nations. Durham, NC: Duke University Press.

Millar, Craig D., and David M. Lambert. 2019. "Archaeogenetics and Human Evolution: The Ontogeny of a Biological Discipline." *World Archaeology* 51 (4): 546–59. DOI: 10.1080/00438243.2019.1683466.

Moran, Anthony. 2002. "As Australia Decolonizes: Indigenizing Settler Nationalism and the Challenges of Settler/Indigenous Relations." *Ethnic and Racial Studies* 25 (6): 1013–42. DOI: 10.1080/0141987022000009412.

Moran, Anthony. 2005. *Australia: Nation, Belonging and Globalization*. New York: Routledge.

Moran, Anthony. 2009. "What Settler Australians Talk about When They Talk about Aborigines: Reflections on an In-Depth Interview Study." *Ethnic and Racial Studies* 32 (5): 781–801. DOI: 10.1080/01419870802023936.

Moran, E. T. 1972. "Letters to the Editor: Skulls, in Order of Superiority." *Canberra Times*, February 10, 1972, 2.

Moreton-Robinson, Aileen. 2003. "I Still Call Australia Home: Indigenous Belonging and Place in a White Postcolonizing Society." In *Uprootings/Regroundings: Questions of Home and Migration*, edited by Sara Ahmed, Claudia Castada, Anne-Marie Fortier, and Mimi Sheller, 131–49. Oxford: Berg.

Moreton-Robinson, Aileen, ed. 2004. *Whitening Race: Essays in Social and Cultural Criticism.* Canberra: Aboriginal Studies Press.

Morgan, Lynn. 2009. *Icons of Life: A Cultural History of Human Embryos.* Berkeley: University of California Press.

Morphy, Howard. 1996. "More Than Mere Facts: Repositioning Spencer and Gillen in the History of Anthropology." In *Exploring Central Australia: Society, Environment and the 1894 Expedition*, edited by S. R. Morton and D. J. Mulvaney, 135–49. Chipping North, NSW: Surrey Beatty.

Morphy, Howard. 1997. "Gillen—Man of Science." In *"My Dear Spencer": The Letters of F. J. Gillen to Baldwin Spencer*, edited by Derek John Mulvaney, Howard Morphy, and Alison Petch, 23–51. Melbourne: Hyland House.

Morrison, Peter. 1965. "Body Temperatures in Some Australian Mammals. V. Aboriginals." *Journal of Applied Physiology* 20 (6): 1278–82. DOI: 10.1152/jappl.1965.20.6.1278.

Morton, John. 2004. "'Such a Man Would Find Few Races Hostile': History, Fiction and Anthropological Dialogue in the Melbourne Museum." *Arena Journal*, no. 22, 53–71.

Mosby, Ian. 2013. "Administering Colonial Science: Nutrition Research and Human Biomedical Experimentation in Aboriginal Communities and Residential Schools, 1942–1952." *Histoire sociale/Social history* 46 (91): 145–72. DOI: 10.1353/his.2013.0015.

Moser, Stephanie. 1995. "The 'Aboriginalisation' of Australian Archaeology: The Contribution of the Australian Institute of Aboriginal Studies to the Indigenous Transformation of the Discipline." In *Theory in Archaeology: A World Perspective*, edited by Peter J. Ucko, 150–77. Abingdon, UK: Routledge.

Moses, A. Dirk. 2011. "Official Apologies, Reconciliation, and Settler Colonialism: Australian Indigenous Alterity and Political Agency." *Citizenship Studies* 15 (2): 145–59. DOI: 10.1080/13621025.2011.549698.

Mourant, Arthur E. 1954. *The Distribution of the Human Blood Groups.* Oxford: Blackwell Scientific.

Muecke, Stephen. 2004. *Ancient and Modern: Time, Culture and Indigenous Philosophy.* Sydney: University of New South Wales Press.

Mukharji, Projit Bihari. 2020. "Bloodworlds: A Hematology of the 1952 Indo-Australian Genetical Survey of the Chenchus." *Historical Studies in the Natural Sciences* 50 (5): 525–53. DOI: 10.1525/hsns.2020.50.5.525.

Mulcock, Jane. 2007. "Dreaming the Circle: Indigeneity and the Longing for Belonging in White Australia." In *Transgressions*, edited by Macfarlane Ingereth and Hannah Mark, 63–82. Canberra: Australian National University Press.

Müller-Wille, Staffan. 2021. "Corners, Tables, Lines: Towards a Diagrammatics of Race." *Nuncius* 36 (3): 517–31. DOI: 10.1163/18253911-03603001.

Müller-Wille, Staffan, and Hans-Jörg Rheinberger. 2012. *A Cultural History of Heredity.* Chicago: University of Chicago Press.

Mullins, Steve. 2006. "Haddon, Alfred Cort (1855–1940)." In *Australian Dictionary of Biography*, National Centre of Biography, Australian National University. Accessed April 2, 2023. https://adb.anu.edu.au/biography/haddon-alfred-cort-10386/text18401. First published in print 1996, vol. 14; first published online 2006.

Mulvaney, Derek John. 2011. *Digging Up a Past*. Sydney: University of New South Wales Press.

Mulvaney, Derek John, and J. H. Calaby. 1985. *"So Much That Is New": Baldwin Spencer, 1860–1929, a Biography*. Carlton, VIC: Melbourne University Press.

Mulvaney, Derek John, Howard Morphy, and Alison Petch, eds. 1997. *"My Dear Spencer": The Letters of F. J. Gillen to Baldwin Spencer*. Melbourne: Hyland House.

Munro, Craig. 1992. *Inky Stephensen: Wild Man of Letters*. St. Lucia: University of Queensland Press.

Munsterhjelm, Mark. 2019. "Scientists Are Aiding Apartheid in China." *Just Security*. June 18, 2019. https://www.justsecurity.org/64605/scientists-are-aiding-apartheid-in-china/.

Museums and Galleries of NSW. 2015. "At Home: Genevieve Grieves." February 18, 2015. https://mgnsw.org.au/articles/home-genevieve-grieves/.

Musharbash, Yasmine. 2014. "Introduction: Monsters, Anthropology, and Monster Studies." In *Monster Anthropology in Australasia and Beyond*, edited by Yasmine Musharbash and G. Presterudstuen, 1–24. New York: Palgrave Macmillan.

nadjamarin22. 2007. "Napepe—Yanomami Ask Their Blood Back." YouTube, posted April 24, 2007. 5:35. https://www.youtube.com/watch?v=7608Vu-D_9U.

Nakata, Martin. 2007. *Disciplining the Savages, Savaging the Disciplines*. Canberra: Aboriginal Studies Press.

Nash, Heather. 2006. "Hicks, Sir Cedric Stanton (1892–1976)." In *Australian Dictionary of Biography*, National Centre of Biography, Australian National University. Accessed April 2, 2023. https://adb.anu.edu.au/biography/hicks-sir-cedric-stanton-10499 /text18627. First published in print 1996, vol. 14; first published online 2006.

National Centre for Indigenous Genomics. 2020. "Repatriation: Bringing Home the Manggu* Samples." Australian National University, last modified January 20, 2020. Accessed January 5, 2021. https://ncig.anu.edu.au/repatriation-bringing-home -manggu-samples.

National Film and Sound Archive. n.d. "Indigenous Connections." Accessed October 23, 2015. https://www.nfsa.gov.au/about/what-we-collect/indigenous-connections.

National Health and Medical Research Council (NHMRC). 1991. *Guidelines on Ethical Matters in Aboriginal and Torres Strait Islander Health Research*. Canberra: National Health and Medical Research Council.

National Health and Medical Research Council (NHMRC). 2018a. *Ethical Conduct in Research with Aboriginal and Torres Strait Islander Peoples and Communities: Guidelines for Researchers and Stakeholders*. Canberra: Commonwealth of Australia.

National Health and Medical Research Council (NHMRC). 2018b. *National Statement on Ethical Conduct in Human Research*. Canberra: Commonwealth of Australia.

Neale, Tim, and Eve Vincent, eds. 2016. *Unstable Relations: Indigenous People and Environmentalism*. Perth: University of Western Australia Press.

Nelson, Alondra. 2008. "Bio Science: Genetic Genealogy Testing and the Pursuit of African Ancestry." *Social Studies of Science* 38 (5): 759–83.

Nelson, Alondra. 2012. "Reconciliation Projects: From Kinship to Justice." In *Genetics and the Unsettled Past: The Collision of DNA, Race, and History*, edited by Keith Wailoo, Alondra Nelson, and Catherine Lee, 20–31. New Brunswick, NJ: Rutgers University Press.

Neville, A. O. 1947. *Australia's Coloured Minority: Its Place in the Community.* Sydney: Currawong.

Newcastle Morning Herald. 1932. "An Aboriginal Albino." July 9, 1932, 6.

Nickell, Joe. 2005. *Secrets of the Sideshows.* Lexington: University Press of Kentucky.

Noonuccal, Oodgeroo. 1970. *My People: A Kath Walker Collection.* Milton, QLD: Jacaranda.

Nordeen, Claire A., and Sandra L. Martin. 2019. "Engineering Human Stasis for Long-Duration Spaceflight." *Physiology* 34 (2): 101–11. DOI: 10.1152/physiol.00046.2018.

Norman, Jane. 2018. "Scott Morrison Says It's 'Regrettable' His Senators Backed Pauline Hanson's 'It's OK to Be White' Motion." *ABC News*, October 16, 2018. https://www.abc .net.au/news/2018-10-16/morrison-regrets-senators-backing-anti-white-racism-support /10381038.

North Australian and Northern Territory Government Gazette. 1890. "Miscellaneous Clippings." February 29, 1889, 3.

O'Brien, Lewis. 2007. *And the Clock Struck Thirteen: The Life and Thoughts of Kaurna Elder Uncle Lewis Yerloburka O'Brien as Told to Mary-Anne Gale.* Kent Town, South Australia: Wakefield.

Office of the United Nations High Commissioner for Human Rights. n.d. People with Albinism: Not Ghosts but Human Beings. Accessed October 12, 2019. https://albinism .ohchr.org.

Oreskes, Naomi. 2014. "Introduction." In *Science and Technology in the Global Cold War*, edited by Naomi Oreskes and John Krige, 1–10. Cambridge, MA: MIT Press.

O'Sullivan, Sandy. 2016. "Recasting Identities: Intercultural Understandings of First Peoples in the National Museum Space." In *The Routledge International Handbook of Intercultural Arts Research*, edited by Pamela Burnard, Elizabeth Mackinlay, and Kimberly Powell, 35–45. Abingdon, UK: Routledge.

Ottosson, Ase. 2014. "To Know One's Place: Belonging and Differentiation in Alice Springs Town." *Anthropological Forum* 24 (2): 115–35. DOI: 10.1080/00664677.2014.901212.

Pääbo, S. 1986. "Molecular Genetic Investigations of Ancient Human Remains." *Cold Spring Harbor Symposia on Quantitative Biology* 51:441–46. DOI: 10.1101/ SQB.1986.051.01.053.

Paisley, Fiona. 1997. "No Back Streets in the Bush: 1920s and 1930s Pro-Aboriginal White Women's Activism and the Trans-Australia Railway." *Australian Feminist Studies* 12 (25): 119–37. DOI: 10.1080/08164649.1997.9994845.

Paisley, Fiona. 2000. *Loving Protection? Australian Feminism and Aboriginal Women's Rights, 1919–1939.* Melbourne: Melbourne University Press.

Pan, Mingke. 2018. "Hibernation Induction in Non-hibernating Species." *Bioscience Horizons: The International Journal of Student Research* 11. DOI: 10.1093/biohorizons/ hzy002.

Parry, Bronwyn. 2004. "Technologies of Immortality: The Brain on Ice." *Studies in History and Philosophy of Biological and Biomedical Sciences* 35 (2): 391–413. DOI: 10.1016/j. shpsc.2004.03.012.

Parsons, Michael. 2002. "'Ah That I Could Convey a Proper Idea of This Interesting Wild Play of the Natives': Corroborees and the Rise of Indigenous Australian Cultural Tourism." *Australian Aboriginal Studies* 2:14–26.

Patten, John, and William Ferguson. 1938. *Aborigines Claim Citizen Rights! A Statement of the Case for the Aborigines Progressive Association.* Sydney: Publicist.

Peers, Laura. 2003. "Strands Which Refuse to Be Braided: Hair Samples from Beatrice Blackwood's Ojibwe Collection at the Pitt Rivers Museum." *Journal of Material Culture* 8 (1): 75–96. DOI: 10.1177/1359183503008001763.

Peters-Little, Frances. 1999. *The Community Game: Aboriginal Self-Definition at the Local Level.* Canberra: Australian Institute of Aboriginal and Torres Strait Islander Studies.

Peterson, Nicolas. 1990. "'Studying Man and Man's Nature': The History of the Institutionalisation of Aboriginal Anthropology." *Australian Aboriginal Studies* 2:3–19.

Peterson, Nicolas, Lindy Allen, and Louise Hamby, eds. 2008. *The Makers and Making of Indigenous Australian Museum Collections.* Carlton, VIC: Melbourne University Press, 2008.

Phillips, Ruth B. 2011. *Museum Pieces: Toward the Indigenization of Canadian Museums.* Montreal: McGill-Queen's University Press.

Pilkington, Doris (Nugi Garimara). 1996. *Follow the Rabbit-Proof Fence.* Brisbane: University of Queensland Press.

Pinkney, John. 2005. *Haunted: The Book of Australia's Ghosts.* Rowville, VIC: Five Mile.

Potter, Emily. 2019. *Writing Belonging at the Millennium: Notes from the Field on Settler-Colonial Place.* Bristol: Intellect.

Povinelli, Elizabeth. 2002. *The Cunning of Recognition: Indigenous Alterities and the Making of Australian Multiculturalism.* Durham, NC: Duke University Press.

Prentis, Malcolm D. 1995. "From Lemuria to Kow Swamp: The Rise and Fall of Tri-Hybrid Theories of Aboriginal Origins." *Journal of Australian Studies* 19 (45): 79–91. DOI: 10.1080/14443059509387229.

Probyn, Fiona. 2002. "How Does the Settler Belong?" *Westerly* 47:75–95.

Probyn, Fiona. 2003. "The White Father: Denial, Paternalism and Community." *Cultural Studies Review* 9 (1): 60–76. DOI: 10.5130/csr.v9i1.3584.

Pruner-Bey, Franz. 1864. "On Human Hair as a Race-Character, Examined by the Aid of the Microscope." *Anthropological Review* 2 (4): 1–23. DOI: 10.2307/3025132.

Pybus, Cassandra. 2020. *Truganini: Journey through the Apocalypse.* Crows Nest, NSW: Allen and Unwin.

Qi, Xiaoqiang, Wee Lee Chan, Randy J. Read, Aiwu Zhou, and Robin W. Carrell. 2014. "Temperature-Responsive Release of Thyroxine and Its Environmental Adaptation in Australians." *Proceedings of the Royal Society B: Biological Sciences* 281 (1779). DOI: 10.1098/rspb.2013.2747.

QIMR Berghofer Medical Research Institute. 2019. *Genomic Partnerships: Guidelines for Genomic Research with Aboriginal and Torres Strait Islander Peoples of Queensland.* Herston: QIMR Berghofer Medical Research Institute.

Quiggin, A. H. 1942. *Haddon, the Head Hunter.* Cambridge: Cambridge University Press.

Qureshi, Sadiah. 2011. *Peoples on Parade: Exhibitions, Empire, and Anthropology in Nineteenth-Century Britain.* Chicago: University of Chicago Press.

Rabinow, Paul. 1996. "Severing the Ties: Fragmentation and Dignity in Late Modernity." In *Essays on the Anthropology of Reason*, 129–52. Princeton, NJ: Princeton University Press.

"Race Theories." 1943. *Nature* 151:220. DOI: 10.1038/151220b0.

Radin, Joanna. 2013. "Latent Life: Concepts and Practices of Human Tissue Preservation in the International Biological Program." *Social Studies of Science* 43 (4): 484–508. DOI: 10.1177/0306312713476131.

Radin, Joanna. 2014a. "Collecting Human Subjects: Ethics and the Archive in the History of Science and the Historical Life Sciences." *Curator* 57 (2): 249–58. DOI: 10.1111/cura.12065.

Radin, Joanna. 2014b. "Unfolding Epidemiological Stories: How the WHO Made Frozen Blood into a Flexible Resource for the Future." *Studies in History and Philosophy of Biological and Biomedical Sciences* 47:62–73. DOI: 10.1016/j.shpsc.2014.05.007.

Radin, Joanna 2017. *Life on Ice: A History of New Uses for Cold Blood.* Chicago: University of Chicago Press.

Radin, Joanna, and Emma Kowal. 2015. "Indigenous Blood and Ethical Regimes in the United States and Australia since the 1960s." *American Ethnologist* 42 (4): 749–65. DOI: 10.1111/amet.12168.

Rae-Ellis, Vivienne. 1976. *Trucanini: Queen or Traitor?* Hobart, Tasmania: O.B.M.

Ramsay Smith, William. 1932. "Parent of the Human Race." *Advertiser*, January 9, 1932, 14.

Rank, Otto. (1914) 1989. *The Double: A Psychoanalytical Study.* London: Karnac.

Rasmussen, Morten, Sarah L. Anzick, Michael R. Waters, Pontus Skoglund, Michael DeGiorgio, Thomas W. Stafford Jr., Simon Rasmussen, et al. 2014. "The Genome of a Late Pleistocene Human from a Clovis Burial Site in Western Montana." *Nature* 506 (7487): 225–29.

Rasmussen, Morten, Xiaosen Guo, Yong Wang, Kirk E. Lohmueller, Simon Rasmussen, Anders Albrechtsen, Line Skotte, et al. 2011. "An Aboriginal Australian Genome Reveals Separate Human Dispersals into Asia." *Science* 334 (6052): 94–98. DOI: 10.1126/science.1211177.

Rasmussen, Morten, Yingrui Li, Stinus Lindgreen, Jakob Skou Pedersen, Anders Albrechtsen, Ida Moltke, Mait Metspalu, et al. 2010. "Ancient Human Genome Sequence of an Extinct Palaeo-Eskimo." *Nature* 463 (7282): 757–62. DOI: 10.1038/nature08835.

Rasmussen, Morten, Martin Sikora, Anders Albrechtsen, Thorfinn Sand Korneliussen, J. Víctor Moreno-Mayar, G. David Poznik, Christoph P. E. Zollikofer, et al. 2015. "The Ancestry and Affiliations of Kennewick Man." *Nature* 523 (7561): 455–58. DOI: 10.1038/nature14625.

Read, Peter. 1982. *The Stolen Generations: The Removal of Aboriginal Children in New South Wales, 1883 to 1969.* Occasional paper, New South Wales, Ministry of Aboriginal Affairs, no. 1. Sydney: Government Printer.

Read, Peter. 2003. *Haunted Earth.* Sydney: University of New South Wales Press.

Reardon, Jenny. 2005. *Race to the Finish: Identity and Governance in an Age of Genomics.* Princeton, NJ: Princeton University Press.

Reardon, Jenny. 2008. "Race and Biology: Beyond the Perpetual Return of Crisis." *NTM Zeitschrift für Geschichte der Wissenschaften, Technik und Medizin* 16 (3): 373–78.

Reardon, Jenny, and Kim TallBear. 2012. "Your DNA Is Our History." *Current Anthropology* 53 (5): s233–45.

Redwood, Thomas. 2014. "Skeletons in the Nation's Cupboard: Warwick Thornton on Being an Aboriginal Artist." *Metro Magazine: Media and Education Magazine*, no. 181, 84–87.

Regan, Paulette. 2010. *Unsettling the Settler Within: Indian Residential Schools, Truth Telling, and Reconciliation in Canada*. Vancouver: University of British Columbia Press.

Reich, David. 2018. "How Genetics Is Changing Our Understanding of 'Race.'" *New York Times*, March 23, 2018. https://www.nytimes.com/2018/03/23/opinion/sunday/genetics -race.html.

Reid, Janice. 1983. *Sorcerers and Healing Spirits: Continuity and Change in an Aboriginal Medical System*. Canberra: Australian National University Press.

Reynolds, Henry. 1987. *Frontier: Aborigines, Settlers and Land*. Sydney: Allen and Unwin.

Reynolds, Henry. 2000. *Why Weren't We Told? A Personal Search for the Truth about Our History*. Ringwood, VIC: Penguin.

Reynolds, Henry. 2021. *Truth-Telling: History, Sovereignty and the Uluru Statement*. Sydney: NewSouth.

Riggs, Damien, and Martha Augoustinos, M. 2004. "Projecting Threat: Managing Subjective Investments in Whiteness." *Psychoanalysis, Culture and Society* 9 (2): 219–36. DOI: 10.1057/palgrave.pcs.2100020.

Roberts, Amy, Madeleine Fowler, and Tauto Sansbury. 2014. "A Report on the Exhibition 'Children, Boats and "Hidden Histories": Crayon Drawings by Aboriginal Children at Point Pearce Mission (Burgiyana) (South Australia), 1939.'" *Bulletin of the Australasian Institute for Maritime Archaeology* 38:24–30.

Roberts, Dorothy. 2011. *Fatal Invention: How Science, Politics, and Big Business Re-create Race in the Twenty-First Century*. New York: New Press.

Robin, Libby. 2003. "Collections and the Nation: Science, History and the National Museum of Australia." *Historical Records of Australian Science* 14 (3): 251–89. DOI: 10.1071/HR02013.

Robinson, Michael F. 2016. *The Lost White Tribe: Explorers, Scientists, and the Theory That Changed a Continent*. Oxford: Oxford University Press.

Roginski, Alexandra. 2015. *The Hanged Man and the Body Thief: Finding Lives in a Museum Mystery*. Melbourne: Monash University Press.

Rowley, C. D. 1972. *Outcasts in White Australia*. Ringwood, VIC: Penguin.

Rowse, Tim. 1986. "Aborigines as Historical Actors: Evidence and Inference." *Historical Studies* 22 (87): 176–98. DOI: 10.1080/10314618608595743.

Rowse, Tim. 2017. *Indigenous and Other Australians since 1901*. Sydney: New South Books.

Royal Commission into Institutional Responses to Child Sexual Abuse. 2015. *Report of Case Study No. 17: The Response of the Australian Indigenous Ministries, the Australian and Northern Territory Governments and the Northern Territory Police Force and Prosecuting Authorities to Allegations of Child Sexual Abuse Which Occurred at the Retta Dixon Home*. Sydney: Royal Commission into Institutional Responses to Child Sexual Abuse. https://nla.gov.au/nla.obj-541682400/view.

Royal Geographical Society of Australasia (Victoria). 1890. "Council Meeting, 14th February 1890." *Transactions of the Royal Geographical Society of Australasia (Victoria Branch)* 8 (1): 23.

Rundell, W. G. 1934. Letter to the editor. *West Australian*, January 17, 1934, 11.

Russell, Lynette. 2001a. "Bunjilaka Brooding." *Meanjin* 60 (4): 99–103.

Russell, Lynette. 2001b. *Savage Imaginings: Historical and Contemporary Constructions of Australian Aboriginalities*. Melbourne: Australian Scholarly Publishing.

Rutherford, Jennifer. 2000. *The Gauche Intruder: Freud, Lacan and the White Australian Fantasy*. Carlton, VIC: Melbourne University Press.

Ryan, James R. 1997. *Picturing Empire: Photography and the Visualization of the British Empire*. Chicago: University of Chicago Press.

Ryan, Lyndall. 1977. "The Struggle for Recognition: Part-Aborigines in Bass Strait in the Nineteenth Century." *Aboriginal History* 1 (1/2): 27–51.

Ryan, Lyndall. 2012. *Tasmanian Aborigines: A History since 1803*. Crows Nest, NSW: Allen and Unwin.

Sahota, Puneet Chawla. 2014. "Body Fragmentation: Native American Community Members' Views on Specimen Disposition in Biomedical/Genetics Research." *AJOB Empirical Bioethics* 5 (3): 19–30. DOI: 10.1080/23294515.2014.896833.

Said, Edward. 1978. *Orientalism*. New York: Pantheon.

Saldahna, A. 2006. "Reontologising Race: The Machinic Geography of Phenotype." *Environment and Planning D: Society and Space* 24 (1): 9–24. DOI: 10.1068/d61j.

Santos, Ricardo Ventura, Susan Lindee, and Vanderlei Sebastião de Souza. 2014. "Varieties of the Primitive: Human Biological Diversity Studies in Cold War Brazil (1962–1970)." *American Anthropologist* 116 (4): 723–35. DOI: 10.1111/aman.12150.

Schaffer, Gavin. 2008. *Racial Science and British Society, 1930–62*. London: Palgrave Macmillan.

Schmidt-Nielsen, Knut. 1987. "Per Fredrik Thorkelsson Scholander." In *Biographical Memoirs*, edited by National Academy of Sciences, 56:386–412. Washington, DC: National Academies Press.

Schneider, William H. 1995. "Blood Group Research in Great Britain, France, and the United States between the World Wars." *American Journal of Physical Anthropology* 38 (S21): 87–114. DOI: 10.1002/ajpa.1330380606.

Schneider, William H. 1996. "The History of Research on Blood Group Genetics: Initial Discovery and Diffusion." *History and Philosophy of the Life Sciences* 18 (3): 277–303.

Scholander, P. F., H. T. Hammel, K. Lange Andersen, and Y. Løyning. 1958. "Metabolic Acclimation to Cold in Man." *Journal of Applied Physiology* 12 (1): 1–8. DOI: 10.1152/jappl.1958.12.1.1.

Scholander, P. F., H. T. Hammel, J. S. Hart, D. H. LeMessurier, and J. Steen. 1958. "Cold Adaptation in Australian Aborigines." *Journal of Applied Physiology* 13 (2): 211–18. DOI: 10.1152/jappl.1958.13.2.211.

Schwartz-Marín, Ernesto, and Eduardo Restrepo. 2013. "Biocoloniality, Governance, and the Protection of 'Genetic Identities' in Mexico and Colombia." *Sociology* 47 (5): 993–1010. DOI: 10.1177/0038038513494506.

Serjeantson, S. 1994. "The Human Genome Diversity Project: Fact versus Fiction." *Search* 25 (3): 85–87.

Serres, Michel. 1995. *Conversations on Science, Culture, and Time*. With Bruno Latour. Translated by Roxanne Lapidus. Studies in Literature and Science. Ann Arbor: University of Michigan Press.

Seth, Suman. 2009. "Putting Knowledge in Its Place: Science, Colonialism, and the Postcolonial." *Postcolonial Studies* 12 (4): 373–88. DOI: 10.1080/13688790903350633.

Seth, Suman. 2017. "Colonial History and Postcolonial Science Studies." *Radical History Review* 2017 (127): 63–85. DOI: 10.1215/01636545-3690882.

Silverman, Rachel. 2000. "The Blood Group 'Fad' in Post-war Racial Anthropology." *Kroeber Anthropological Society Papers*, no. 84, 11–27.

Simmons, Roy T. 1976. "The Biological Origin of Australian Aboriginals: An Examination of Blood Group Genes and Gene Frequencies for Possible Evidence in Populations from Australia to Eurasia." In *The Origin of the Australians*, edited by R. L. Kirk and A. G. Thorne, 307–28. Canberra: Australian Institute of Aboriginal Studies.

Simpson, Moira G. 2006. "Revealing and Concealing: Museums, Objects, and the Transmission of Knowledge in Aboriginal Australia." In *New Museum Theory and Practice: An Introduction*, edited by Janet Marstine, 152–77. Malden, MA: Blackwell.

Singer, Dominique. 2006. "Human Hibernation for Space Flight: Utopistic Vision or Realistic Possibility?" *Journal of the British Interplanetary Society* 59:139–43.

Skloot, Rebecca. 2010. *The Immortal Life of Henrietta Lacks*. New York: Crown/Archetype.

Slater, Lisa. 2018. *Anxieties of Belonging in Settler Colonialism: Australia, Race and Place*. Abingdon, UK: Routledge.

Smith, Benjamin Richard. 2008. "'We Don't Want to Chase 'Em Away': Hauntology in Central Cape York Peninsula." In *Mortality, Mourning and Mortuary Practices in Indigenous Australia*, edited by Katie Glaskin, 189–208. Farnham, UK: Ashgate.

Smith, Bernard. 1980. *The Spectre of Truganini*. Sydney: Australian Broadcasting Commission.

Smith, Claire, and Heather Burke. 2007. "A Brief History of Australian Archaeology." In *Digging It Up Down Under: A Practical Guide to Doing Archaeology in Australia*, 1–22. New York: Springer.

Smith, Ellen. 2014. "White Aborigines." *Interventions* 16 (1): 97–116. DOI: 10.1080/1369801X.2013.776241.

Smith, Linda Tuhiwai. 2012. *Decolonizing Methodologies: Research and Indigenous Peoples*. 2nd ed. London: Zed Books.

Smocovitis, Vassiliki Betty. 2012. "Humanizing Evolution: Anthropology, the Evolutionary Synthesis, and the Prehistory of Biological Anthropology, 1927–1962." *Current Anthropology* 53 (S5): S108–25. DOI: 10.1086/662617.

South Australian Museum, Board, and South Australian Museum (issuing organization). 1986. "Statement on the Secret/Sacred Collection." Adelaide: South Australian Museum.

Spencer, Baldwin, and F. J. Gillen. (1899) 1968. *The Native Tribes of Central Australia*. New York: Dover.

Spencer, Baldwin, and F. J. Gillen. 1904. *The Northern Tribes of Central Australia*. London: Macmillan and Co.

Stanner, W. E. H. 1979. "After the Dreaming (1968)." In *White Man Got No Dreaming: Essays, 1938–1973*, edited by W. E. H. Stanner, 198–248. Canberra: Australian National University Press.

Staples, J. F. 2016. "Metabolic Flexibility: Hibernation, Torpor, and Estivation." *Comprehensive Physiology* 6 (2): 737–71. DOI: 10.1002/cphy.c140064.

Stengers, Isabelle. 2005. "The Cosmopolitical Proposal." In *Making Things Public: Atmospheres of Democracy*, edited by Bruno Latour and Peter Weibel, 994–1003. Cambridge, MA: MIT Press.

Stepan, N. L. 1982. *The Idea of Race in Science: Great Britain, 1800–1960*. London: Macmillan.

Stephensen, P. R. 1936. *The Foundations of Culture in Australia: An Essay towards National Self Respect*. Gordon, NSW: W. J. Miles.

Stevens, Frank S. 1972. *Racism, the Australian Experience: A Study of Race Prejudice in Australia*. New York: Taplinger.

Stocking, George W. 1968. *Race, Culture and Evolution: Essays in the History of Anthropology*. New York: Free Press.

Stocking, George W. 1996. *After Tylor: British Social Anthropology, 1888–1951*. Madison: University of Wisconsin Press.

Strathern, Marilyn. 1992. *Reproducing the Future: Essays on Anthropology, Kinship and the New Reproductive Technologies*. Manchester: Manchester University Press.

Strehlow, T. G. H. 1971. *Songs of Central Australia*. Sydney: Angus and Robertson.

Stringer, Chris. 2012. *Lone Survivors: How We Came to Be the Only Humans on Earth*. New York: Griffin.

Subramaniam, Banu. 2014. *Ghost Stories for Darwin: The Science of Variation and the Politics of Diversity*. Urbana: University of Illinois Press.

Subramaniam, Banu. 2019. *Holy Science: The Biopolitics of Hindu Nationalism*. Seattle: University of Washington Press.

Survival for Tribal Peoples. 2010. "Blood Samples Return to Amazon Indians." May 20, 2010. http://www.survivalinternational.org/news/5962.

Swoap, Steven J., Meaghan Rathvon, and Margaret Gutilla. 2007. "AMP Does Not Induce Torpor." *American Journal of Physiology—Regulatory, Integrative and Comparative Physiology* 293 (1): R468–73. DOI: 10.1152/ajpregu.00888.2006.

Table Talk. 1890. "The Waxworks." February 28, 1890, 15. http://nla.gov.au/nla.news-article147281417.

Takeda, K., Y. Mori, S. Sobieszczyk, H. Seo, M. Dick, F. Watson, I. L. Flink, S. Seino, G. I. Bell, and S. Refetoff. 1989. "Sequence of the Variant Thyroxine-Binding Globulin of Australian Aborigines: Only One of Two Amino Acid Replacements Is Responsible for Its Altered Properties." *Journal of Clinical Investigation* 83 (4): 1344–48. DOI: 10.1172/JCI114021.

TallBear, Kim. 2013. *Native American DNA: Tribal Belonging and the False Promise of Genetic Science*. Minneapolis: University of Minnesota Press.

TallBear, Kim, and Candis Callison. 2019. "Ep. 187: Is Repatriation Really 'Reconciliation'?" *Media Indigena* (podcast), hosted by Rick Harp, November 29, 2019. https://mediaindigena.libsyn.com/2019/11.

Tasmanian Aboriginal Centre. 1997. "Free Exchange or a Captive Culture? The Tasmanian Aboriginal Perspective on Museums and Repatriation." Museums Association Seminar, Museums and Repatriation, London, November 4, 1997.

Tauali'i, Maile, Elise Leimomi Davis, Kathryn L. Braun, JoAnn Umilani Tsark, Ngiare Brown, Maui Hudson, and Wylie Burke. 2014. "Native Hawaiian Views on Biobanking." *Journal of Cancer Education* 29 (3): 570–76. DOI: 10.1007/s13187-014-0638-6.

Taylor, Griffith. 1921. "The Evolution and Distribution of Race, Culture, and Language." *Geographical Review* 11 (1): 54–119. DOI: 10.2307/207857.

Taylor, Griffith. 1925. "Aborigines in North-West Australia." *Sydney Morning Herald*, March 27, 1925, 10.

Thomas, David Piers. 2004. *Reading Doctors' Writing: Race, Politics and Power in Indigenous Health Research, 1870–1969*. Canberra: Aboriginal Studies Press.

Thomas, Martin. 2014. "Turning Subjects into Objects and Objects into Subjects: Collecting Human Remains on the 1948 Arnhem Land Expedition." In *Circulating Cultures: Indigenous Music, Dance and Media across Genres in Australia*, edited by Amanda Harris, 129–69. Canberra: Australian National University Press.

Thomas, Nicholas. 1994. *Colonialism's Culture: Anthropology, Travel, and Government*. Princeton, NJ: Princeton University Press.

Thompson, Charis. 2002. "Strategic Naturalizing: Kinship in an Infertility Clinic." In *Relative Values: Reconfiguring Kinship Studies*, edited by Sarah Franklin and Susan McKinnon, 175–202. Durham, NC: Duke University Press.

Thompson, Charis. 2013. *Good Science: The Ethical Choreography of Stem Cell Research*. Cambridge, MA: MIT Press.

Thornton, Warwick, dir. 2009. *Samson and Delilah*. Surry Hills, NSW: Scarlett Pictures.

Thornton, Warwick. 2010. "Warwick Thornton—Interview." Interview by Kenjo McCurtain. *Film in Japan* (blog), September 20, 2010. http://filminjapan.blogspot.com/2010/09/samson-and-delilah-interview-and.html.

Thornton, Warwick. 2012. "Sense of Place." *Art and Australia* 50 (1): 82–83.

Thornton, Warwick, dir. 2013. *The Darkside*. Mitchell, ACT: Ronin Films.

Thrush, Coll. 2016. *Indigenous London: Native Travelers at the Heart of Empire*. New Haven, CT: Yale University Press.

Tierney, Patrick. 2001. *Darkness in El Dorado: How Scientists and Journalists Devastated the Amazon*. New York: W. W. Norton.

Tindale, Norman B. 1941. *Survey of the Half-Caste Problem in South Australia*. Adelaide: Royal Geographical Society, S.A. Branch.

Tindale, Norman B. 1974. *Aboriginal Tribes of Australia: Their Terrain, Environmental Controls, Distribution, Limits, and Proper Names*. Canberra: Australian National University Press.

Tobler, Ray, Adam Rohrlach, Julien Soubrier, Pere Bover, Bastien Llamas, Jonathan Tuke, Nigel Bean, et al. 2017. "Aboriginal Mitogenomes Reveal 50,000 Years of Regionalism in Australia." *Nature* 544 (7649): 180–84. DOI: 10.1038/nature21416.

Toohey, Paul. 2016. "The Seething Streets of Kalgoorlie-Boulder, WA, Where Racism towards Indigenous Boys Has Hit a Flashpoint." *News.com.au*, November 16, 2016. https://www.news.com.au/national/western-australia/special-report-the-seething-streets-of-kalgoorlie/news-story/d47a67bb37f772da4239e83dbb31ae13.

Topinard, Paul. 1885. *Éléments d'anthropologie générale*. Paris: A. Delahaye et É. Lecrosnier.

Tout, Dan. 2017. "Encountering Indigeneity: Xavier Herbert, 'Inky' Stephensen and the Problems of Settler Nationalism." *Cultural Studies Review* 23 (2): 141–61. DOI: 10.5130/csr.v23i2.5823.

Tramposch, William J. 1998. "Te Papa: Reinventing the Museum." *Museum Management and Curatorship* 17 (4): 339–50. DOI: 10.1080/09647779800201704.

Transmission Films. 2013. *The Darkside: Press Kit*. Surry Hills, NSW: Scarlett Pictures.

"Travel in Comfort: Trans-Australian Railway." 1937. State Library Victoria. http://handle.slv.vic.gov.au/10381/107886.

Trevor, J. C. 1953. *Race Crossing in Man: The Analysis of Metrical Characters*. Biology Monographs and Manuals 9. Cambridge: Cambridge University Press.

Trigger, David. 2008. "Place, Belonging and Nativeness in Australia." In *Making Sense of Place: Exploring the Concepts and Expressions of Place through Different Senses*, edited by Frank Vanclay, Matthew Higgins, and Adam Blackshaw, 301–10. Canberra: National Museum of Australia.

Trotter, Mildred. 1938. "A Review of the Classifications of Hair." *American Journal of Physical Anthropology* 24 (1): 105–26. DOI: 10.1002/ajpa.1330240131.

Truswell, Stewart A., Ian Darnton-Hill, and Beverley Wood. 2007. "NSA Lecture in Honour of Dr Frederick (Fred) WA Clements (1904–1995)." *Asia Pacific Journal of Clinical Nutrition* 16 (S3). http://211.76.170.15/server/APJCN/ProcNutSoc/2000+/2007/Clements.pdf.

Tsosie, Krystal S., Joseph M. Yracheta, Jessica Kolopenuk, and Rick W. A. Smith. 2021. "Indigenous Data Sovereignties and Data Sharing in Biological Anthropology." *American Journal of Physical Anthropology* 174 (2): 183–86. DOI: 10.1002/ajpa.24184.

Tuck, Eve, and K. Wayne Yang. 2012. "Decolonization Is Not a Metaphor." *Decolonization: Indigeneity, Education and Society* 1 (1): 1–40.

Tucker, Margaret. 1977. *If Everyone Cared: Autobiography of Margaret Tucker*. Sydney: Ure Smith.

Tupone, Domenico, Christopher J. Madden, and Shaun F. Morrison. 2013. "Central Activation of the A1 Adenosine Receptor (A1AR) Induces a Hypothermic, Torpor-Like State in the Rat." *Journal of Neuroscience* 33 (36): 14512. DOI: 10.1523/JNEUROSCI.1980-13.2013.

Turnbull, Paul. 2017. *Science, Museums and Collecting the Indigenous Dead in Colonial Australia*. Palgrave Studies in Pacific History. Cham, Switzerland: Palgrave Macmillan.

Turnbull, Paul, and Michael Pickering. 2010. *The Long Way Home: The Meaning and Values of Repatriation*. Oxford: Berghahn.

Tylor, Edward B. 1876. "Damman's Race Photographs." *Nature* 13:184–85.

Ucko, Peter J. 1983. "Australian Academic Archaeology: Aboriginal Transformation of Its Aims and Practices." *Australian Archaeology*, no. 16, 11–26.

UNESCO. 1952. The Race Concept: Results of an Inquiry. Paris: UNESCO.

UNESCO and Its Programme. 1950. *The Race Question*. Paris: UNESCO.

United Nations. 2008. United Nations Declaration on the Rights of Indigenous Peoples. Geneva: United Nations.

Veracini, Lorenzo. 2008. "Settler Collective, Founding Violence and Disavowal: The Settler Colonial Situation." *Journal of Intercultural Studies* 29 (4): 363–79. DOI: 10.1080/07256860802372246.

Vergo, Peter. 1989. *The New Museology*. London: Reaktion Books.

Vos, G. H., and R. L. Kirk. 1962. "A 'Naturally-Occurring' Anti-E Which Distinguishes a Variant of the E Antigen in Australian Aborigines." *Vox Sanguinis* 7 (1): 22–32. DOI: 10.1111/j.1423-0410.1962.tb03225.x.

Vos, G. H., R. L. Kirk, and A. G. Steinberg. 1963. "The Distribution of the Gamma Globulin Types Gm(a), Gm(x) and Gm-Like in South and Southeast Asia and Australia." *American Journal of Human Genetics* 15 (1): 44–52.

Vos, G. H., Dell Vos, R. L. Kirk, and Ruth Sanger. 1961. "A Sample of Blood with No Detectable Rh Antigens." *Lancet* 277 (7167): 14–15. DOI: 10.1016/s0140-6736(61)92183-3.

Waldby, Cathy, and Robert Mitchell. 2006. *Tissue Economies: Blood, Organs, and Cell Lines in Late Capitalism.* Science and Cultural Theory. Durham, NC: Duke University Press.

Walker, A. C. 1969. "Albinism in a Full-Blood Aboriginal Child." *Medical Journal of Australia* 2 (22): 1105.

Walsh, R. J., and C. Montgomery. 1947. "A New Human Isoagglutinin Subdividing the MN Blood Group." *Nature* 160 (4067): 504–5.

Wardlaw, H. S. Halcro, H. Whitridge Davies, and M. R. Joseph. 1934. "Energy Metabolism and Insensible Perspiration of Australian Aborigines." *Australian Journal of Experimental Biology and Medical Science* 12 (2): 63–74. DOI: 10.1038/icb.1934.9.

Wardlaw, H. S. Halcro, and C. H. Horsley. 1928. "The Basal Metabolism of Some Australian Aborigines." *Australian Journal of Experimental Biology and Medical Science* 5 (4): 263–72. DOI: 10.1038/icb.1928.22.

Wardlaw, H. S. Halcro, and W. J. Lawrence. 1932. "Further Observations on the Basal Metabolism of Australian Aborigines." *Australian Journal of Experimental Biology and Medical Science* 10 (3): 157–66.

Warin, Megan, Jaya Keaney, Emma Kowal, and Henrietta Byrne. 2022. "Circuits of Time: Enacting Postgenomics in Indigenous Australia." *Body and Society* (February 24). DOI: 10.1177/1357034x211070041.

Warin, Megan, Emma Kowal, and Maurizio Meloni. 2020. "Indigenous Knowledge in a Postgenomic Landscape: The Politics of Epigenetic Hope and Reparation in Australia." *Science, Technology, and Human Values* 45 (1): 87–111. DOI: 10.1177/0162243919831077.

Warner, Lloyd. 1937. *A Black Civilization: A Social Study of an Australian Tribe.* New York: Harper and Brothers.

Washburn, Sherwood. 1951. "The New Physical Anthropology." *Transactions of the New York Academy of Sciences* 13 (7): 298–304. DOI: 10.1111/j.2164-0947.1951.tb01033.x.

Watson, James D., and Francis Crick. 1953. "A Structure for Deoxyribose Nucleic Acid." *Nature* 171:737–38.

Watt, Elizabeth, and Emma Kowal. 2019a. "To Be or Not to Be Indigenous? Understanding the Rise of Australia's Aboriginal and Torres Strait Islander Population since 1971." *Ethnic and Racial Studies* 42 (16): 63–82. DOI: 10.1080/01419870.2018.1546021.

Watt, Elizabeth, and Emma Kowal. 2019b. "What's at Stake? Determining Indigeneity in the Era of DIY DNA." *New Genetics and Society* 38 (2): 142–64. DOI: 10.1080/14636778.2018.1559726.

Watt, Elizabeth, Emma Kowal, and Carmen Cummings. 2020. "Traditional Laws Meet Emerging Biotechnologies: The Impact of Genetic Genealogy on Indigenous Land Title in Australia." *Human Organization* 79 (2): 140–49. DOI:10.17730/1938-3525.79.2.140.

Weinstock, Jeffrey. 2004. "Introduction: The Spectral Turn." In *Spectral America: Phantoms and the National Imagination*, edited by Jeffrey Weinstock, 3–17. Madison: University of Wisconsin Press.

Wellington, Shahni. 2019. "Indigenous Blood Samples Return to Galiwin'ku after 50 Years in Medical Storage." *NITV News*, November 19, 2019. https://www.sbs.com.au /nitv/article/indigenous-blood-samples-return-to-galiwinku-after-50-years-in-medical -storage/kzwfv5vu3.

West Australian. 1890. "West Australian Exploration." December 9, 1890, 4.

West Australian. 1934. "Memories of Jungun." January 17, 1934, 11.

White, Graham H., and Rodney Morice. 1980. "Diagnostic Biochemical Tests in Aboriginals." *Medical Journal of Australia* 1 (S1): 6–8. DOI: 10.5694/j.1326-5377.1980.tb135259.x.

Widders, Terence. 1974. *Open Letter Concerning the Australian Institute of Aboriginal Studies [and the Significance of Its Conference, May, 1974], from T. Widders, P. Thompson, G. Williams, L. Thompson, B. Bellear, L. Watson*. Brickfield Hill, NSW: Eaglehawk and Crow.

Wilde, Oscar. 1891. *The Picture of Dorian Gray*. London: Ward, Lock and Co.

Wilson, Elsie A. 1945. "Basal Metabolism from the Standpoint of Racial Anthropology." *American Journal of Physical Anthropology* 3 (1): 1–19. DOI: 10.1002/ajpa.1330030114.

Wilson, Emily K. 2019. "Women's Experiences in Early Physical Anthropology." *American Journal of Physical Anthropology* 170 (2): 308–18. DOI: 10.1002/ajpa.23912.

Wilson, Emily K. 2022. *Mildred Trotter and the Invisible Histories of Physical and Forensic Anthropology*. New York: Routledge.

Wiminydji and Anthony Rex Peile. 1978. "A Desert Aborigine's View of Health and Nutrition." *Journal of Anthropological Research* 34 (4): 497–523. DOI: 10.1086/jar.34.4.3629647.

Winter, Barbara. 2005. *The Australia First Movement and the Publicist, 1936–1942*. Carindale, QLD: Glass House Books.

Wiwchar, D. 2004. "Nuu-Chah-Nulth Blood Returns to West Coast." *Ha-Shilth-Sa* 31 (25): 1–4.

Wolf, Eric. 1982. *Europe and the People without History*. Berkeley: University of California Press.

Wolfe, Patrick. 1999. *Settler Colonialism and the Transformation of Anthropology: The Politics and Poetics of an Ethnographic Event*. New York: Cassell.

Wolfe, Wendy A. 2007. *Encounters with the Paranormal: Contemporary Indigenous Narratives Merge with Ancient Mythology*. York, WA: Hannahs.

Worms, Ernest. 1998. *Australian Aboriginal Religions*. Translated by Helmut Petri. Richmond, VIC: Spectrum.

Worthington, E. B. 1975. "Preparations." In *The Evolution of IBP*, edited by E. B. Worthington, 51–62. Cambridge: Cambridge University Press.

Wright, Joanne L., Sally Wasef, Tim H. Heupink, Michael C. Westaway, Simon Rasmussen, Colin Pardoe, Gudju Gudju Fourmile, et al. 2018. "Ancient Nuclear Genomes Enable Repatriation of Indigenous Human Remains." *Science Advances* 4 (12). DOI: 10.1126/sciadv.aau5064.

Wylie, Alison. 1997. "Good Science, Bad Science, or Science as Usual? Feminist Critiques of Science." In *Women in Human Evolution*, edited by Lori D. Hager, 29–55. Abingdon, UK: Routledge.

Wyndham, C. H., and J. F. Morrison. 1958. "Adjustment to Cold of Bushmen in the Kalahari Desert." *Journal of Applied Physiology* 13 (2): 219–25. DOI: 10.1152/jappl.1958.13.2.219.

Xu, Yichi, Chunxuan Shao, Vadim B. Fedorov, Anna V. Goropashnaya, Brian M. Barnes, and Jun Yan. 2013. "Molecular Signatures of Mammalian Hibernation: Comparisons with Alternative Phenotypes." *BMC Genomics* 14 (1): 567. DOI: 10.1186/1471-2164-14-567.

Yamaguchi, Bin. 1967. *A Comparative Osteological Study of the Ainu and the Australian Aborigines.* Australian Institute of Aboriginal Studies, Occasional Papers 10. Canberra: Australian Institute of Aboriginal Studies.

Zhang, Jianfa, Krista Kaasik, Michael R. Blackburn, and Cheng Chi Lee. 2006. "Constant Darkness Is a Circadian Metabolic Signal in Mammals." *Nature* 439 (7074): 340–43. DOI: 10.1038/nature04368.

Zimmer, Carl. 2016. "Eske Willerslev Is Rewriting History with DNA." *New York Times*, May 16, 2016. http://www.nytimes.com/2016/05/17/science/eske-willerslev-ancient-dna-scientist.html.

Zogbaum, Heidi. 2010. *Changing Skin Colour in Australia: Herbert Basedow and the Black Caucasian.* North Melbourne, VIC: Australian Scholarly Publishing.

Index

Berg, Jim, 145
Bevan, Llewelyn, 97
"Big Biology," 134
bioethics, 27, 73, 88
biological absorption, 8, 93, 106–9, 192n30,
    193n31; failure of, 30, 116; miscegenation
    seen as solution, 107, 108, *113*, 115. *See also*
    "extinction," of Indigenous Australians
biological difference: afterlives of research,
    2, 6, 16; as both fundamental and excep-
    tional, 135; as colonial imposition, 18;
    and conspiracy theories, 122–23, 136–41;
    contemporary views of, 5–6; hair samples
    used to measure, 70; legacies of earlier
    paradigms, 7–8; periodic crises of, 10,
    121–22; possibility of, 14, 16, 19, 25, 120; as
    socially or environmentally determined, 9;
    spectacular forms of, 119; used as weapon
    of domination, 15–16, 120–21; vs. variation
    within populations, 14
"biological fitness," 93, 99, 107
biological knowledge, non-indigenous pro-
    duction of, 4–5, 47, 145; "good" and "bad"
    science, 9, 19, 26, 72–73, 80, 89; haunting
    of, 16, 37, 170–71; uses for, 8–9
"biological processes," social science view
    of, 121
biomimicry research, 2, 30, 122, 130
biosphere, 46
Birch, Tony, 151, 158, 162
Birdsell, Bee, 108
Birdsell, Joseph B., 93, 105, 108, 119, 186n38,
    190n5
birrimbirr (benign aspect of spirits), *23*
Black, George Murray, 43, 145
blood group research, 3–4, 9, 45, 75–76, 167;
    ABO groups, 103–4, 188n13; antigens, 4, 13,
    46–47, 104; Factor S/s, 104; hepatitis B,
    surface antigens of, 4, 46–47; proteins, 4,
    46–47, 49, 137–38; varied Indigenous Aus-
    tralian views on, 39–40. *See also* serology
blood quantum, 12–13; "full-blood," xi, 86, 104,
    107, *113*, 192n22; "half-castes," xi, 94, 108–9,
    111–13
blood samples, 29, 37, 46; and haunting,
    58–59, 61; Indigenous-majority governance
    board, 62; lists of names, kin, and language
    groups, 61; ownership of by collecting

institution, 39; as persons, 41; repatriation
    of, 40–41, *41*, 59, 61, 64–65; stored in medi-
    cal research institutes, 57, 64; tolerated
    in biomedical contexts, 40; voluntary
    moratorium on use of, 61–62
Blumberg, Baruch, 4
Blumenbach, Johann Friedrich, 2
Board for Anthropological Research, 26, 34–35,
    123, 131; 1931 expedition, 1–2, *35*, 124–28, *125*,
    126, 183n2; 1950s expeditions, 102
Bory de Saint-Vincent, Jean-Baptiste
    Genevieve-Marcellin, 74
Bourke, Colin, 51
bracketing, 88
Brahmin caste, 103
"breeding out the colour," 50
Brennan, Gloria, 51
Bringing Them Home report, 115
Brownless, Anthony, 97
Buckley, William, 95–96
Bunce, Michael, 81
Bunga (Aboriginal man), 95, 191n11
Bunjilaka Aboriginal Cultural Centre, 152
Bunjilaka exhibit (Melbourne Museum),
    151–54, *153*; "Belonging to Country" sec-
    tion, 151, 159; decommissioning of, 154–56;
    "Dialogue" section, 196n19; goannas in,
    151, *153*, 154, 196n18; Spencer not visible
    in exhibition management systems, 154;
    "Two Laws" section, 151–52, *153*, 157. *See also*
    Spencer's double
Burnt Woman (ghost), 23–24

cadaver and embryo collections, relationship
    between, 55–56
Calloway, Ewan, 81, 82
Cambridge Anthropological Expedition
    (1898), 3, 26, 67
Cambridge Museum of Archaeology and
    Anthropology, 69; Duckworth Collection,
    77–78, 80, 182n8
Campbell, Thomas Draper, 45, 124
cancer, killer T cell research, 13
Cape York Indigenous population, 9
Capricornia (Herbert), 110, 111, 112
carbon dating, 4
Carlson, Bronwyn, 13
Carnegie Institute for Nutrition, 123

National Film and Sound Archive (NFSA), 33–35, 43
National History Museum (London), 80
National Museum of Australia, 29, 35, 58, 186n39
National Museum of the American Indian, 149
National Museum of Victoria, 146. *See also* Museums Victoria
National Science Museum of Japan, 48
Native Americans, xii, 87. *See also* Kennewick Man (the Ancient One)
Native BioData Consortium, 17
Native Title Act (1993), 51, 190n2
Native Tribes of Central Australia, The (Spencer and Gillen), 144, 148
natural selection, 103, 105, 138
Nature: Dammann's book, review of, 84; missing data/conspiracy of silence, 123, 137, 139–43, *140*, 195n15; question of permissions, 71, 80–82, 88–89
Nazi science, 45, 73, 76
"Negroid" group, 95, 99, 102, 103, 104
Nelson, Alondra, 17
Neville, A. O., 68, 107, 112, 116, 187–88n3
"newly identified" status, 116, 193n36
New South Wales, 2019 parliamentary election, 10, 11–15
Newton, Isaac, 79
New Zealand. *See* Aotearoa/New Zealand
Nielsen, Rasmus, 81
non-indigenous people: and biological difference, 9–10; decolonial deemphasis on, 150, 160, 197n36; progressive, xii, 147–48; as viewers of Spencer's double, 160, 195n5
non-indigenous researchers: biological knowledge, production of, 4–5, 8–9, 16, 26, 37, 47, 145, 170–71; historical consciousness of, 147
nutrition, studies of, 123–24
Nuu-chah-nulth (Canadian West Coast), 40
Nyangumarta people, 96, 191n10

objects: bodily substances as, 39; folded, 21–22, 89; landscape, as object of white desire, 109; social life of material substrates, 56; temporary disposal of, 65–66; tied to descendant communities, 158; two-stage burial applied to, 38, 41, 153, 161

One Nation political party, 11–15, 19, 182nn2–3
ontologies, 20; of bones and cultural objects, 39; Indigenous, 26, 39; Western, 38
Original Australians, The (Abbie), 93, 94, 100–102, *101*; frontispiece, 93, 94, 100, *101*, 105, 107, 112, 169; map, 105, *106*, 107, 112
origin theories, 167; and biological research, 3–4, 9; Out of Africa hypothesis, 181n1; polygenic Darwinism, 102; tri-hybrid hypothesis, 105, 190n5, 192n30. *See also* "archaic Caucasian" theory; evolution; racial groups
osteology, 52, 56, 185n25. *See also* archaeology
Other, 114–15, 148
Our Culture, Our Future (Janke), 59
ownership, traditional, xi, 57, 92, 190n2
oxidative stress, 129

Pääbo, Svante, 79
Pacific Islanders, expelled from Queensland, 98
paleogenomics, 57, 80
"paleolithic," as term, 124, 134, 194n4
"pan-indigeneity," 115–16
Pan-Pacific Science conference (1923), 68
Papuan statue, 163
Pazyryk horse, 79
Peile, Anthony Rex, 40
People with Albinism: Not Ghosts but Human Beings (United Nations), 100
Perry, J. M., 99
Peters-Little, Frances, 161
physical anthropology, 25, 45; anthropometry, 3, 8, 18, *35*, 70, 75–78, 79, 84, 89, *125*; decline of, 50–52, 55–56; of hair, 75
physiology, 2–3, 5, 28. *See also* basal metabolic rate (BMR), "Aboriginal"
Pitjantjatjara people, 49, 132, 135
Pitt-Rivers, George, 76
pluriversal politics, 24
polio epidemics, 42
population genetics, 8, 39, 71–72, 78–79, 136, 189n20; "Isolates of Historical Interest," 6, 59
Port Phillip colony, 95
postcolonialism, 148–50, 157–58, 196n11; time frame of in museology, 160–61. *See also* colonialism

precision medicine, 7, 8, 13, 168, 182n6
Preston, Margaret, 110
"primitive," as term for Indigenous Australians, xi, 3–4, 103, 105, 110, 119; used to justify dispossession, 92, 113, 121
provenance. *See* genetic provenancing
Pruner-Bey, Franz, 67, 74, 82
pseudoscience, 4, 9, 15
psychoanalytic theories, 146–47
Publicist, 110–11
Pulleine, Robert, 124
Purula (Parunda), 144, *144*

Queensland: Coen (northern Queensland), 24, 27–28; health disparities in, 8; Indigenous researchers in, 17, 51; Pacific Islanders expelled from, 98
Queensland Institute of Medical Research, 8

race: changing conceptions of, 8; "crisis" of, 10; ethnic group as preferred term for, 76, 77; hair-based classifications, 74, 102; "hybrid" race approach, 94, 99; individuals as "representatives" of, 85–87, 89; "mixed-race" Indigenous people, 53–54, 88, 94, 108; nineteenth-century science, 8–9; photographic portraits used to describe, 83–87. *See also* "archaic Caucasian" theory; doomed race theory; miscegenation (race mixing)
Race and Culture Committee (Royal Anthropological Institute), 76
Race Crossing in Man (Duckworth), 77–78
"race mixing," 75, 77, 93, 107, 108, 115
Races of Man and Their Distribution, The (Haddon), 74, 85, *85*, 88, 188n11
"race suicide," 98, 191n15
racial desires, 107, 109, 114–15
racial groups: "Aryan race," 76, 103, 111, 190n4; "Australoid/Archaic Caucasoid" group, 104; "Australoid" group, 102, 104; "Caucasian" group, 104; "Caucasoid" group, 104, 134; "Mongoloid" group, 102, 104, 105; "Negroid" group, 95, 99, 102, 103, 104. *See also* origin theories
racial hierarchies, 5; discredited by serology, 78; evolutional ladder, 102; mirrored in biological research, 3; skulls used to emphasize, 44, 52–53, 184nn13–14; subspecies classifications of *Homo sapiens*, 83. *See also* "primitive," as term for Indigenous Australians
racial science, post–World War II backlash against, 10, 14, 45
racial scripts, 86–87
racial types, concept of, 9, 83–87
radiocarbon dating, 87
Rank, Otto, 146–47, 195n5
Reardon, Jenny, 10, 121–22, 136
reconciliation movement, 21
reconciliation projects, 17–18, 148
Reich, David, 10
reparations for slavery, genetic findings tied to, 17
repatriation of human remains, 18; blood, 40–41, *41*, 59, 61, 64–65; to Galiwin'ku community, 64–65; Kennewick Man (the Ancient One), 18, 57, 73, 87; Mungo Lady, 61; by Museums Victoria, 145; ontologies of bones and cultural objects, 39; and restricted or secret/sacred museum rooms, 154–55; reversal of colonial flow of remains, 79; rise of movement, 51; Truganini, 37, 53–55, 186n33; unprovenanced remains, 18, 27, 35, 57–58, 187n46. *See also* human remains
repression, 183n7; Freudian concept of, 20, 147, 183n7; and museums, 160, 161; required for functioning of settler state, 20, 92–93
resource extraction, 51
respiratory research, 49, 50
response, task of, 28
Retta Dixon home (Darwin), 112
Reynolds, Henry, 97–98
right-wing politics, 11–16, 157, 182nn2–3
Road to Botany Bay, The (Carter), 109
Roberts, Dorothy, 8
Robinson, George Augustus, 53
Robinson, Michael, 114
Rockefeller Foundation, 124
Roper River community, 52
Royal Anthropological Institute (Britain), 76
Royal Commission into Aboriginal Deaths in Custody (1980s), 51, 185n20
Royal Geographical Society of Australasia, 97
Royal Society of Tasmania, 53–54

Stocking, George, 74
Stolen Generations (mass child removal), 30, 148–49, 193n31; Abbie as key architect of, 50; and black mother/pale child dyad, *101*, 112; *Bringing Them Home* report, 115; child sexual abuse in institutions, 112, 113; and imagined racial kinship, 94; samples used to locate family and provenance, 64. *See also* assimilation
strategic biological essentialism, 27
Strehlow, T. G. H. "Ted," 131
subaltern studies, 149
"survivability," 129
Systema Naturae (Linnaeus), 83

TallBear, Kim, 18, 187n47
Tanzania, albinism in, 100
Tasmanian Aboriginal Centre, 152, 186n34
Tasmanian Museum and Art Gallery, 54
Tasmanian people, 3, 185n30; "extinction" of, 37, 53, 185–86n30, 192n22; growing recognition of, 53–55; Truganini, 37, 53–54, 186nn33–34, 192n22. *See also* Indigenous Australians
Taylor, Griffith, 103, 105
temporality, 20, 24, 28, 110, 171; and folding, 21–22, 89
terra nullius, 92, 109
Thomas, David, 148
Thompson, Charis, 72, 73, 89
Thomson, Arthur, 75
"Thomson's rule," 75
Thorne, Alan, 52–53, 60–61, 185n25, 186n33
Thornton, Warwick, 28–29, 34
thyroid function, 139; misconduct of researchers, 136; thyroxine levels, 123, 124, 136, 137–38. *See also* basal metabolic rate (BMR), "Aboriginal"
Tindale, Dorothy, 108, 186n38
Tindale, Norman B. "Tinny," 26, 92, 93, 107–8, 124, 190n5, 192n30
Tobler, Ray, 189n15
topology, 21–22
torpor (temporary hibernation), 122; apoptosis, 129; basal metabolic rate (BMR), "Aboriginal," 1–2, 3–4, 30–31; definition of, 129; estivation, 128, 129; futuristic narratives, 137; hibernation induction triggers,

129–30; "insulative cooling" investigations, 132–34, *133*; potential applications of, 129; space travel studies, 122, 129–30, 134; types of, 128–30, 194n7; used by endotherms, 128–29. *See also* basal metabolic rate (BMR), "Aboriginal"
Tout, Dan, 110
Trans-Australian Railway, 67–68, *68*, 88, 187–88n3
Trevor, J. C., 77–78, 80, 88–89
Tridico, Silvana, 81
Trotter, Mildred, 75
Truganini (Tasmanian woman), 37, 53–54, 186nn33–34, 192n22
Tsosie, Krystal, 17
Tucker, Margaret, 113, 115
two-stage burial, 38–39, 170–71; applied to disciplines, 56–57; applied to objects, 38, 41, 153, 161; spacing and timing of, 65. *See also* disposal
Tylor, Edward B., 84–85

Ucko, Peter, 50, 51, 53, 54, 168, 185n19
Uighur minority research (China), 195n13
uncanny, the, 21, 146, 169, 183n10; and Spencer's double, 147, 161. *See also* double; haunting
Uncanny Australia (Gelder and Jacobs), 21
Under the Same Sun, 191n17
UNESCO statements of 1950s, 10, 14, 78
United Nations Convention on Biological Diversity (1992), 59
United Nations High Commissioner for Human Rights' albinism website, 100
United Nations Permanent Forum on Indigenous Issues, 64
United States: Alaskan Natives, experiments on, 136; embryology, 55–56; military research, 120, 129, 135–36, 194n8, 194–95n12; "one drop rule" ("hypodescent"), 107; US Air Force, 120; US Department of Defense, 129; US Navy SEALs, 2; US Office of Naval Research, 120
University of Adelaide, 1, 3, 25, 45, 123. *See also* Board for Anthropological Research
University of Copenhagen, 80–81
University of Melbourne, 51, 62, 143, 145, 146
University of New South Wales, 49

University of Sydney, 45, 183n11, 192n20
University of Western Australia, 47

"vampire project"/vampire-scientist trope, 6, 59–61, 60, 65, 186n43
Veddah people (Ceylon), 102, 104–5
visual anthropology: cartes de visite (calling cards) of "typical natives," 84; individuals as "representatives" of race, 85–87; photographic portraits used to describe race, 83–87
Vos, Gerard, 47
"vulnerable" or "high-risk" groups, and ethics, 72–73

Wadawurrung people, 95–96
Walker, Alan, 99, 100–101, 112, 192n19
Wallace, Alfred Russel, 3, 103
Walsh, R. J., 104
Wangarr (spirits of ancestral beings), 23
Warburton, Peter Egerton, 96
Warramirri clan (Yolngu people), 49
"Warrior Gene" controversy, 121
Washington University, 75
Water and Eliza Hall Institute, 13
Watson, Sam, 52
We Europeans (Huxley, Haddon, and Carr-Saunders), 73, 76–77, 104
Weiner, J. S., 46
Weinstock, Jeffrey, 171
Wells, H. G., 76–77
Wentworth, Bill, 45
"white men's countries," concept of, 98–99
white nationalism, 12, 93–94, 97–98, 110
whiteness: attributed to Indigenous Australians, 30, 93; ghost terms used for white people, 23, 100; "global," 97–98; Indigenous, failure of, 94; "lost white tribes," 95, 191n8, 193n33; Stolen Generations as making

a place for, 94. *See also* albinism; settler belonging
white tribes, white fascination with, 93, 95, 100, 103, 114, 191n8, 193n33
Whitlam, Gough, 5
Wik people (Cape York Peninsula), 24, 170
Wilde, Oscar, 147
Wilkinson, Herbert John, *125*
Willerslev, Eske, 18, 57, 69, 79–82, 190n23; desert sleeping, focus on, 139; Kennewick Man/the Ancient One returned by, 73; *Nature*'s questions about approval, 80–81, 88; *New York Times* profile of, 87; public reception of research, 87; research on Indigenous population history, 138–39. *See also* "first Aboriginal genome"
Willerslev, Rane, 80
Williams, Michael, 51
Wilson, Alan C., 79
Wittenoom, Edward, 92, 96
Wittenoom, Frank, 92, 96
Wood Jones, Frederic, 123, 124, 188n9
World War I–era research, 3
World War II: identification of US soldiers' bodies, 75; postwar backlash against racial science, 10, 14, 45
Wren, Christopher, 43
Wright, Joanne, 57
Wunungmurra, Ross Mandi, 64

Yamaguchi, Bin, 48–49, 185n16
Yanomami (Brazil and Venezuela), 27; measles accusations against vaccine researchers, 136; radiation research on, 136; repatriation of blood samples, 40–41, *41*, 59, 64–65
yogis, trope of, 127
Yolngu people (Arnhem Land), 229
Yracheta, Joseph, 17
Yuarrick (Indigenous man), 95, 191n10

www.ingramcontent.com/pod-product-compliance
Lightning Source LLC
Chambersburg PA
CBHW020846270326
41928CB00006B/573